THE 2002 REPORT OF THE NATIONAL CONFIDENTIAL ENQUIRY INTO PERIOPERATIVE DEATHS

Data collection period
1 April 2000 to 31 March 2001

Compiled by:

K G Callum MS FRCS (Surgical Clinical Co-ordinator)

N J Carr MB BS FRCPath (Chair of Pathology Advisors Group)

A J G Gray MB BChir FRCA (Anaesthetic Clinical Co-ordinator)

C M K Hargraves BSc RGN DipHSM MBA (Chief Executive)

R W Hoile MS FRCS (Principal Surgical Clinical Co-ordinator)

G S Ingram MBBS FRCA (Principal Anaesthetic Clinical Co-ordinator)

I C Martin LLM FRCS FDSRCS (Surgical Clinical Co-ordinator)

K M Sherry MBBS FRCA (Anaesthetic Clinical Co-ordinator)

Published 11 November 2002 by the National Confidential Enquiry into Perioperative Deaths

35-43 Lincoln's Inn Fields, London WC2A 3PE

Tel: (020) 7831 6430
Fax: (020) 7430 2958
Email: **info@ncepod.org.uk**
Website: **www.ncepod.org.uk**

Requests for further information should be addressed to the Chief Executive

ISBN 0-9539240-1-7

A company limited by guarantee – Company number 3019382

Registered charity number 1075588

This report is printed on paper produced from wood pulp originating from managed sustainable plantations and is chlorine-free, 100% recyclable and biodegradable.

Additional information

This report is available for downloading from the NCEPOD web-site at **www.ncepod.org.uk**
Copies can also be purchased from the NCEPOD office.

The analysis of data from anaesthetic and surgical questionnaires is not included in full in this report. A supplement containing additional data is available free of charge from the NCEPOD office, as are copies of the questionnaires.

Design and production by Interface, Bristol. Telephone 0117 923 2235

CONTENTS

ACKNOWLEDGEMENTS

This is the fourteenth report published by the National Confidential Enquiry into Perioperative Deaths and, as in previous years, could not have been achieved without the support and co-operation of a wide range of individuals and organisations. Our particular thanks go to the following:

- The Local Reporters, whose names are listed in Appendix F, and those who assist them in providing initial data on perioperative deaths.

- All those surgeons and anaesthetists, whose names are listed in Appendices G and H, who contributed to the Enquiry by completing questionnaires.

- The Advisors whose names are listed overleaf.

- Those bodies, whose names are listed in Appendix D, who provide the funding to cover the cost of the Enquiry.

The Steering Group, Clinical Co-ordinators and Chief Executive would like to record their appreciation of the hard work of the NCEPOD administrative staff: Peter Allison, Paul Coote, Sheree Cornwall, Jennifer Drummond, Dolores Jarman and Tessa Sandall.

This work was undertaken by the National Confidential Enquiry into Perioperative Deaths, which received funding from the National Institute for Clinical Excellence. The views expressed in this publication are those of the authors and not necessarily those of the Institute.

CLINICAL CONTRIBUTORS

SPECIALTY ADVISORS

Anaesthesia

P.B. Harvey — Major GU, Maxillofacial and Obstetrics
Plymouth Hospitals NHS Trust

A. Dennis — Colorectal and Emergency
Sheffield Teaching Hospitals NHS Trust

A.J Kilner — ICU and Renal
Newcastle upon Tyne Hospitals NHS Trust

D.J. Niblett — ICU, Orthopaedic, Ophthalmology and General
Bedford Hospital NHS Trust

J. Rickford — Pre-assessment, Plastic, Head and Neck and Day Surgery
East & North Hertfordshire NHS Trust

A.C. Timmins — ICU, Upper GI and Orthopaedic
Essex Rivers Healthcare NHS Trust

S. Underwood — Cardiac
United Bristol Healthcare NHS Trust

P.M. Upton — Vascular and Paediatric
Royal Cornwall Hospitals NHS Trust
Hospital SubDean
Peninsula Medical School

P. Fernando (Staff Grade) — General
King's Lynn & Wisbech Hospitals NHS Trust

M. Grocott (Specialist Registrar) — ICU and Trauma
University College London Hospitals NHS Trust

R. Yetton (Associate specialist) — General and special interest in sedation
Brighton and Sussex University Hospitals NHS Trust

NCEPOD CO-ORDINATORS

K.G. Callum — Clinical Co-ordinator, NCEPOD and Consultant General and Vascular Surgeon, *Southern Derbyshire Acute Hospitals NHS Trust*

A.J.G. Gray — Clinical Co-ordinator, NCEPOD and Consultant Anaesthetist, *Norfolk and Norwich University Hospital NHS Trust*

R.W. Hoile — Principal Clinical Co-ordinator, NCEPOD and Consultant General Surgeon, *Medway NHS Trust*

G.S. Ingram — Principal Clinical Co-ordinator, NCEPOD and Consultant Anaesthetist, *University College London Hospitals NHS Trust*

I.C. Martin — Clinical Co-ordinator, NCEPOD and Consultant Oral and Maxillofacial Surgeon, *City Hospitals Sunderland NHS Trust*

K.M. Sherry — Clinical Co-ordinator, NCEPOD and Consultant Anaesthetist, *Sheffield Teaching Hospitals NHS Trust*

SURGERY

Cardiothoracic surgery

M. Jones *South Manchester University Hospitals NHS Trust*

P. Kay *Leeds Teaching Hospitals NHS Trust*

S. Livesey *Southampton University Hospitals NHS Trust*

General surgery

N. O. Aston *Queen Elizabeth Hospital NHS Trust*

A. Ball *Surrey & Sussex Healthcare NHS Trust*

P. Edwards *Countess of Chester Hospital NHS Trust*

P. Hurst *Brighton and Sussex University Hospitals NHS Trust*

M. Lansdown *Leeds Teaching Hospitals NHS Trust*

H. Sweetland *Cardiff and Vale NHS Trust*

R.W. Talbot *Poole Hospital NHS Trust*

Gynaecology

H.J. Mellows *Doncaster and Bassetlaw Hospitals NHS Trust*

J.B. Murdoch *United Bristol Healthcare NHS Trust*

A.R.B. Smith *Central Manchester & Manchester Children's University Hospitals NHS Trust*

Neurosurgery

S. Marks *South Tees Hospitals NHS Trust*

C.G.H. West *Salford Royal Hospitals NHS Trust*

Ophthalmology

M. Wishart *North Cheshire Hospitals NHS Trust*

Oral and maxillofacial surgery

V. Ilankovan *Poole Hospital NHS Trust*

Orthopaedic surgery

D. Chan *Royal Devon & Exeter Healthcare NHS Trust*

C.M. Dent *Cardiff and Vale NHS Trust*

R.A. Hill *Great Ormond Street Hospital for Children NHS Trust*

A.C. Hui *South Tees Hospitals NHS Trust*

F. Monsell *Great Ormond Street Hospital for Children NHS Trust*

J. Murray *Pontypridd & Rhondda NHS Trust*

T.L. Thomas *Essex Rivers Healthcare NHS Trust*

Otorhinolaryngology

G. Cox *Oxford Radcliffe Hospitals NHS Trust*

Paediatric surgery

M. Jones *Royal Liverpool Children's NHS Trust*

E. Cusick *United Bristol Healthcare NHS Trust*

Plastic surgery

D.J. Ward *University Hospitals of Leicester NHS Trust*

PATHOLOGY

Urology

D.R.J. Greene *City Hospitals Sunderland NHS Trust*

H.G. Kynaston *Cardiff & Vale NHS Trust*

R. Persad *United Bristol Healthcare NHS Trust*

Vascular surgery

C.P. Gibbons *Swansea NHS Trust*

D. Hocken *Swindon & Marlborough NHS Trust*

G. Stansby *Newcastle upon Tyne Hospitals NHS Trust*

K. Varty *Addenbrooke's NHS Trust*

M. Burke *Royal Brompton & Harefield NHS Trust*

N.J. Carr *Southampton University Hospitals NHS Trust*

K.P. McCarthy *East Gloucestershire NHS Trust*

V. Suarez *Mid Staffordshire General Hospitals NHS Trust*

FOREWORD

National CEPOD has repeatedly emphasised the need for the development of multi-professional and multidisciplinary teams to provide optimum care for the most seriously ill patients. This was also one of the principal recommendations made by Professor Kennedy in his report into paediatric cardiac surgery in Bristol [1]. In this report, based on deaths within three days of an intervention, NCEPOD looks at how far team working has developed and, most particularly, at weaknesses in the systems which create barriers to change.

The issue of shared responsibilities in multi-professional teams raises the need for appropriate and effective leadership, a skill not evident in everyone and not taught as part of the undergraduate curriculum to health care workers. Yet, with older and sicker patients presenting to hospitals, frequently as emergencies, successful outcomes depend on the disciplined care provided by integrated and well functioning teams with good leadership to ensure effective communication between all parties. Regrettably, communication failures are evident throughout many cases in this report.

Examination of patients scheduled for elective admission in preoperative assessment clinics is good practice which, if properly conducted, should lead to internal referral to appropriate team members when unexpected comorbidities are detected. Unfortunately, this does not seem to happen with any regularity. If this fundamental element of team working is lacking in the most ideal of planned circumstances, it is hardly surprising to find there is greater failure when it matters most, namely with emergency admissions. Failure to recognise comorbidities and act upon them preoperatively jeopardises the postoperative outcome and no example is more pressing than those seen under critical care circumstances.

Teams involved in a patient's perioperative care must equally be involved in morbidity/mortality reviews and receive a copy of the discharge summary or autopsy result. Autopsies should be subject to formal external audit with clinicians being involved in evaluating the quality of reports and the basis for the conclusions drawn, including the cause of death.

One encouraging finding is the increasing seniority of the clinician taking the ultimate decision to operate, a consequence of which should be a decline in the number of patients who are operated upon inappropriately. However, unless patients are seen by such experienced clinicians, the report highlights that patients can still die from a missed diagnosis of common conditions, such as acute appendicitis.

Unfortunately, the lack of a HDU/ICU, so frequently a feature of NCEPOD comment, still blights postoperative care. Returning critically ill patients to general wards postoperatively produces a poorer prognosis even amongst patients who went through ICU facilities preoperatively. The 6% who died under such circumstances are a measure of the weakness. NCEPOD has commented previously on the deficiency of suitably trained ICU nurses, but a serious lack of funded sessions for consultants trained in critical care is equally apparent. Specifically funded ICU sessions to ensure the presence of appropriate consultant medical staff is fundamental to good team working in these vital clinical areas.

The report demonstrates the need for national guidelines, for example, for clinical prescribing in hospitals to reduce the risk of drug errors and for protocols to cover actions to be taken in the event of complications associated with endoscopic surgery. Whilst recommending new parameters of care, it is distressing to see already agreed national standards for anaesthetic monitoring being ignored when we would expect those responsible for clinical governance within hospitals to insist on the maintenance of such examples of good medical practice.

In this report we also highlight issues around poor medical record keeping, a further area of clinical governance which must be addressed.

This extends to fluid balance charts and other areas of routine observations. These can be seen as further indications of pressure due to lack of staff and time. The pace of change in medical practice does seem to be running ahead of the ability to recruit suitable people into health care and unless this is overcome, weaknesses in clinical teams will continue to impede improvements in the quality of clinical care.

John Ll Williams CBE

Chairman

INTRODUCTION

The patient's journey through an illness leading to surgery is perilous at the best of times, but when the presentation is urgent or an emergency, it is even more treacherous. Over 80% of patients in this year's sample, that is those dying within three days of a surgical procedure, were urgent or emergency admissions. Inevitably, in the urgent/emergency situation there has often been no formal assessment of comorbidities and many otherwise remediable medical conditions go uncorrected. Management must be pragmatic, problems are overlooked, complication rates are high and deaths occur. This is often despite the best anaesthetic and surgical expertise available.

Despite this scenario, much can be done to pre-empt problems but this requires an adequate provision of services and a team that functions in a co-ordinated manner. For example, for elective and scheduled patients there needs to be better organisation of pre-admission assessment clinics with the appropriate involvement of anaesthetists. This would help identify high-risk cases. Unfortunately, many guidelines for preoperative assessment are for fit patients who are not at risk. From the information available to NCEPOD, it appears that the pre-assessment of high-risk patients is not always done well. There also needs to be an adequate provision of supporting services, such as hospital beds, critical care beds and imaging services (amongst others). Continuity of care and an understanding of the case throughout the patient's journey through the hospital stay must be assured.

For the process that delivers patient care, particularly for the acutely ill, to function effectively there has to be close co-ordination between all those involved. Clinicians recognise the importance of the highest quality care for urgent and emergency cases but the burden of this emergency work does interfere with the planned functioning of the elective service. Will these pieces ever link together whilst current inadequate staffing levels, restraints on working hours and short-term political incentives concerned with elective throughput are allowed to predominate? Perhaps there is a need for two systems, allowing the emergency system to function without the impact on the elective system, but with shared experience influencing the quality of both.

Where does responsibility for the patient's care reside? Individual clinicians are becoming transient acquaintances during the surgical patient's passage through an illness rather than having a continuing responsibility for care. There appears to be an emerging picture of poor ward care by medical staff. This may be the impact of staffing arrangements and shift working, which disrupts the continuity of care. Currently the only constant factor is the individual consultant who is now subject to increasing and conflicting pressures. Too often he or she is left in a state of uncertainty as to their responsibility in guaranteeing continuity of patient care; this undermines his or her ability to fulfil their professional role satisfactorily.

There has to be more working as a team. This involves not only consultants working together but also trainees, nurses, managers, professions allied to medicine and sometimes patients themselves (who must recognise their responsibility to maintain general health and fitness). We need anticipation and co-ordinated thinking to smooth the patient's progress through an illness. No longer should individual surgeons make decisions in isolation.

The ability to work in teams is becoming the cornerstone of modern medical practice. Decisions to operate in difficult circumstances cannot be made by one individual alone. There should be multidisciplinary team discussions rather than a decision that is solely made by the surgeon. However, every ship needs a captain and it is for individual teams to decide who ultimately, with team support and ownership, makes the final decision. The risks associated with the specific decision should then be fully understood, documented and described to the patient. Emergency situations may militate against this way of working but, with time, specialist groups should be able to anticipate and plan for most common scenarios of presentation and the associated complications.

Even after death that continuity should continue with the direct interaction between the pathologist and the clinical teams. In the event of a patient's death there are lessons to learn. These may only point out the natural progression and lethality of a particular pathology, the impact of comorbidity or the effects of age. Conversely, there may be errors in decision-making, team working, diagnosis, technical performance etc. The autopsy is pivotal to revealing these lessons. When asked to do an autopsy on a case involving a perioperative death, the pathologist effectively becomes a member of the multidisciplinary team. At present the majority of these examinations are conducted under the auspices of the coroner, whose aim is to determine where and how – but not why – the death occurred. The result is that the autopsy has become a process that has lost its link with clinical medicine. In the context of the team approach, the role of the autopsy is not just to fulfil the coroner's requirements as to how the patient died but also to verify the patient's last illness and to study the effects of treatment. The sequence of events leading to death can be difficult to determine in complex perioperative cases; discussions with clinical colleagues before and after the autopsy are essential in ensuring that the examination and report are problem-orientated and that the cause of death accurately reflects what happened. Hopefully the examination and subsequent discussion will confirm that the management was appropriate, safe and of a high standard. If not, what lessons can be learnt? The problem is that the coronial system, which, unlike hospital autopsies, was not set up to help clinicians, is failing to provide the lessons we need to learn in order to understand a patient's death. This system, based mainly on coroner's autopsies, must adapt or be radically altered. This need to review working relations and communications between clinicians, pathologists and coroners was mentioned in the 2001 NCEPOD

Report [2] and it still remains an important concern. It is to be hoped that the Home Office review, currently ongoing, of death certification and of the coronial system will address these issues.

A key role of NCEPOD is to set agendas which other institutions or organisations can take up. This report highlights the need for the delivery of care to be a co-ordinated process, with various disciplines functioning as an effective team. But who is going to put this together? There are many different facets of care within individual hospitals and then there are regional and national requirements. There is a need for a philosophical fusion between views of care as seen at local, regional and national levels. Only then will the system function seamlessly to the benefit of patients.

Ron Hoile and Stuart Ingram

Principal Clinical Co-ordinators

PRINCIPAL RECOMMENDATIONS 2002

- Management should ensure that an appropriate number of funded sessions for consultants trained in critical care are allocated to the ICU to allow appropriately qualified medical staff to be available to the ICU at all times.

- There are national agreed standards for anaesthetic monitoring. The absence of an essential anaesthetic monitor constitutes an unacceptable clinical risk that must be the subject of audit.

- There need to be national guidelines for clinical prescribing in hospitals in order to reduce the risk of drug error.

- Failure to diagnose acute appendicitis can still cause death in fit young adults. It is essential that experienced clinicians are available to ensure that cases are not missed.

- If a medical team is involved in a patient's perioperative care it should also be involved in any morbidity/mortality review of the case and receive a copy of the discharge summary and, where available, the autopsy report.

- Complications may arise following endoscopic surgery. Protocols should be available to deal with these and remedial actions should be rehearsed and involve senior experienced clinicians.

- Autopsies should be the subject of a formal external audit process. Clinicians should be involved in evaluating the quality of reports and the basis of conclusions drawn, including the cause of death.

GENERAL DATA

Recommendations

It is the responsibility of management to ensure that all deaths are reported to NCEPOD in a timely manner.

There should be a record of the name of the supervising consultant anaesthetist.

Standard information on hospital facilities should be available and should be accurate.

The adequacy of recovery beds should be reviewed.

Management should ensure that an appropriate number of funded sessions for consultants trained in critical care are allocated to the ICU to allow appropriately qualified medical staff to be available to the ICU at all times.

INTRODUCTION

The data presented in this report relates to deaths occurring between 1 April 2000 and 31 March 2001. The period through which questionnaires were distributed ran through until 31 August 2001 with the final deadline for return being 31 December 2001. Last year, there was a reduction in the number of questionnaires that were returned too late for inclusion but it is unfortunate to note an increase in late returns for this period. The protocol for data collection is detailed in Appendix E.

As anticipated last year, it has now been made mandatory for the independent sector to participate in the Confidential Enquiries with effect from

1 April 2002. Sanctions by the National Care Standards Commission could be applied if hospitals fail to comply.

NCEPOD continues to be concerned about the accuracy of the numbers of deaths reported to it and as a result of last year's detailed comparison with Hospital Episode Statistics (HES) data, it will undertake a detailed audit in a small number of hospitals in the coming year.

Whilst NCEPOD has always requested information on deaths within 30 days of an operative procedure performed by a surgeon or gynaecologist regardless of the place of death, it has always been recognised that accurate information on deaths in the community has not been available. NCEPOD has provided evidence to both the Review of Coroner Services and the Shipman Inquiry this year in relation to death certification and it is hoped that a new method of ensuring a complete information set will be achieved in the future, although at the time of writing of this report the details have not yet been agreed.

The sample reviewed in detail during this period was of patients who died on the day of or within three days of an operation. This is a repeat of the data collected in 1994/95 [3] and, where appropriate, comparisons will be made both with that year and with last year. It should be noted however, that in order to ease the burden on clinicians, a detailed questionnaire was only sent for the first such death for each surgeon.

DATA COLLECTION

Data was requested from all hospitals in England, Wales, Northern Ireland, Guernsey, Jersey, Isle of Man and the Defence Secondary Care Agency. In addition, the majority of hospitals in the independent sector contributed data. Data was not collected from Scotland where the Scottish Audit of Surgical Mortality (SASM) performs a similar function.

GENERAL DATA ANALYSIS

Figure 1.1 shows that a total of 21 991 reports of deaths within 30 days of an operation were received. Of these, 1255 were excluded from further analysis: 865 were deemed inappropriate according to the NCEPOD protocol (Table 1.1 and Appendix E), 337 were received after the deadline and 53 remained incomplete despite efforts by NCEPOD staff to identify the missing information by close liaison with the hospital. This left 20 736 deaths to be used as the sample pool, which was a similar number to last year.

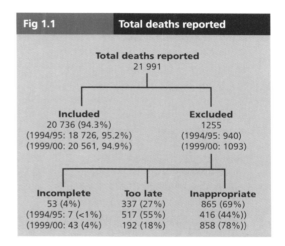

Fig 1.1 — Total deaths reported

Total deaths reported
21 991

Included
20 736 (94.3%)
(1994/95: 18 726, 95.2%)
(1999/00: 20 561, 94.9%)

Excluded
1255
(1994/95: 940)
(1999/00: 1093)

Incomplete
53 (4%)
(1994/95: 7 (<1%)
(1999/00: 43 (4%)

Too late
337 (27%)
517 (55%)
192 (18%)

Inappropriate
865 (69%)
416 (44%))
858 (78%))

The number of reports received too late for inclusion has increased since last year and this is of concern to NCEPOD. Every effort is made to keep hospitals and trusts informed of progress by way of quarterly reports to the Medical Director and Local Reporter. Despite this, there has been a marked increase in reports not received within the timeframe allowed, which is some four months after the data collection ended.

Table 1.1 shows that there has been a further increase in the number of cases reported where the procedure was not performed by a surgeon, lending support to the extended remit of NCEPOD to cover physicians' interventions which takes effect from 1 April 2002.

Table 1.1	Inappropriate reports received and excluded		
Reasons for exclusion	2000/01	1994/95	1999/00
Death occurred more than 30 days after a procedure	259	264	265
Procedure not performed by a surgeon	383	50	319
Duplicate report	175	41	161
No surgical procedure performed or procedure excluded by NCEPOD criteria	48	52	110
Other	-	9	3
Total	865	416	858

A breakdown of the remaining 20 736 deaths, by region is shown in Table 1.2. A trust or hospital (for the independent sector) breakdown is shown in Appendix A. As a result of regional boundary changes, no comparison to 1994/95 is given.

Table 1.2	Deaths reported to NCEPOD by region	
	2000/01	1999/00
Eastern	1764	1809
London	2718	2558
North Western	2866	2754
Northern & Yorkshire	3004	3183
South Eastern	2758	2531
South & West	2147	1834
Trent	2077	2104
West Midlands	1723	1895
Wales	1017	1217
Northern Ireland	399	360
Guernsey	22	14
Jersey	21	31
Isle of Man	26	22
Defence Secondary Care Agency	0	7
Independent Sector	194	242
Total	20 736	20 561

NCEPOD continues to be concerned that all relevant deaths are not reported.

As reported last year, NCEPOD has little confidence that the number of reports received is a true reflection of the actual number of deaths that take place within 30 days of a surgical procedure being performed, and a comparison with HES in last year's NCEPOD report [2] highlighted this fact. It does not surprise NCEPOD to read in the NHS's own magazine that '...*many hospitals don't even know what their body count is* '[4]. NCEPOD has raised this issue for several years now and there is other evidence to support this [5]. The Audit Commission's management paper on health data published in March of this year has also pointed out the difficulties in the coding of cases, which will lead to invalid codes in HES and therefore poor information [6].

Figure 1.2 shows the distribution of the number of calendar days between operation (day 0) and death.

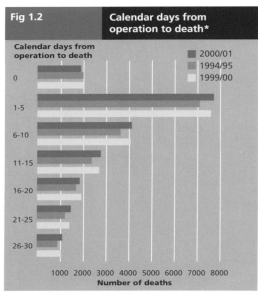

Fig 1.2 — Calendar days from operation to death*

* Throughout this report the year 1999/00 stands apart as it is not a 3 day death sample.

Patients in this sample were older compared with previous years. This is reflected in the small but evident increase in the percentage of patients that die after their operation (Figure 1.3) who are over 70 years. This now stands at 69% of the total cases compared to 68% in 1994/95 and 61% in 1999/00.

The number of days taken for Local Reporters to inform NCEPOD of deaths is shown in Table 1.3. There is a decrease from 30% of deaths being reported within 29 days in 1994/95 to just 19% in 2000/01 that is difficult to understand. Variation in the length of time between hospitals is largely due to the different data collection methods used by Local Reporters. Whilst understanding constraints on the time available, a reduction in days taken to report deaths would undoubtedly be helpful both to

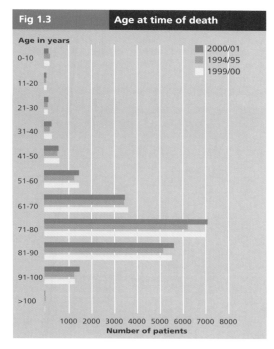

Fig 1.3 — Age at time of death

Age in years

2000/01
1994/95
1999/00

0-10
11-20
21-30
31-40
41-50
51-60
61-70
71-80
81-90
91-100
>100

1000 2000 3000 4000 5000 6000 7000 8000

Number of patients

NCEPOD and to the local audit programme. The sooner questionnaires can be dispatched to clinicians the more likely it is that the medical records will be available, the case clearly remembered and the relevant clinicians still working at the hospital. In addition it allows more time for questionnaires to be completed and returned by the annual deadline of 31 December.

Table 1.3	Calendar days between deaths and receipt of report by NCEPOD		
Calendar days (i.e. not 24 hour periods)	**Number of deaths reported**		
	2000/01	**1999/00**	**1994/95**
1-29	3872 (19%)	4330 (21%)	5547 (30%)
30-59	3975 (19%)	4213 (20%)	3915 (21%)
60-89	3495 (17%)	3277 (16%)	2733 (15%)
90-119	2188 (11%)	2089 (10%)	1800 (10%)
120-149	1586 (8%)	1581 (8%)	1146 (6%)
150-179	1391 (7%)	1179 (6%)	830 (4%)
180+	4229 (20%)	3892 (19%)	2757 (15%)
Total	**20 736**	**20 561**	**18 728**

From 1 April 2002, Local Reporters are being asked to return their details of deaths bi-monthly with the hope that this should improve the situation. It has also been suggested by NCEPOD that hospital information systems should be used to compile the death reports to ease the burden on Local Reporters.

SAMPLE DATA ANALYSIS

The detailed sample for 2000/01 was based around the first perioperative death reported for each consultant surgeon or gynaecologist, **occurring on the day of surgery itself or within the next three calendar days.** The day following the operation was counted as the first postoperative day. Using this method, each consultant surgeon or gynaecologist received a maximum of one questionnaire. From a total of 20 736 deaths reported to NCEPOD, the number of deaths falling within the first three days was 7184 (35%). (Figure 1.4).

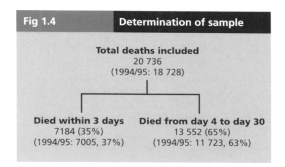

Fig 1.4 — Determination of sample

Total deaths included
20 736
(1994/95: 18 728)

Died within 3 days
7184 (35%)
(1994/95: 7005, 37%)

Died from day 4 to day 30
13 552 (65%)
(1994/95: 11 723, 63%)

Figure 1.5 shows that 4689 surgical questionnaires were not sent, as NCEPOD had already been notified that in 80 cases the consultant had left the trust/hospital and in 4609 cases the consultant had already received one questionnaire.

> **In 5% of the sampled cases it was not possible to identify the supervising anaesthetic consultant.**

In the 4974 cases where no anaesthetic questionnaire was sent, this was either because no surgical questionnaire was sent based on the one questionnaire per surgeon rule (4540, 91%), the consultant surgeon had left the hospital (94, 4%), the procedure was performed without an anaesthetist present (191, 7%), the name of the appropriate anaesthetic consultant was unobtainable (120, 5%), the name of the anaesthetist was notified too late (17, 1%), or NCEPOD had been notified that the appropriate consultant had left the trust/hospital (12, <1%).

Last year NCEPOD made special comment about the large number of cases where the name of the consultant anaesthetist supervising the trainee was not known. This should be recorded on the anaesthetic record. This is a fundamental failure by hospitals to ensure that all key personnel involved in the care of the patient are named.

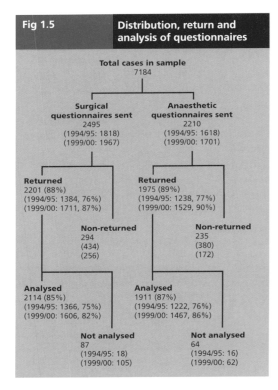

Fig 1.5 — Distribution, return and analysis of questionnaires

Total cases in sample
7184

Surgical questionnaires sent
2495
(1994/95: 1818)
(1999/00: 1967)

Anaesthetic questionnaires sent
2210
(1994/95: 1618)
(1999/00: 1701)

Returned
2201 (88%)
(1994/95: 1384, 76%)
(1999/00: 1711, 87%)

Returned
1975 (89%)
(1994/95: 1238, 77%)
(1999/00: 1529, 90%)

Non-returned
294
(434)
(256)

Non-returned
235
(380)
(172)

Analysed
2114 (85%)
(1994/95: 1366, 75%)
(1999/00: 1606, 82%)

Analysed
1911 (87%)
(1994/95: 1222, 76%)
(1999/00: 1467, 86%)

Not analysed
87
(1994/95: 18)
(1999/00: 105)

Not analysed
64
(1994/95: 16)
(1999/00: 62)

2201 surgical questionnaires were returned (88%) and 1975 anaesthetic questionnaires (89%) were returned (Figure 1.5). These return rates are very similar to 1999/00 and an improvement on 1994/95. 87 surgical questionnaires were excluded from analysis for the reasons given in Table 1.4. Similar exclusions occurred for 64 anaesthetic questionnaires (Table 1.5). It is encouraging to see a slight reduction in excluded cases from last year, although it is interesting to note that in 1994/95 the exclusion rate was also very low.

Table 1.4 — Reasons for exclusion of surgical questionnaires from analysis

Reason for exclusion	2000/01	1994/95	1999/00
Questionnaire completed for an earlier operation	24		57
Questionnaire received too late	58		40
Questionnaire incomplete	1		6
Questionnaire related to excluded procedure	3		2
Questionnaire completed for wrong patient	1		0
Total	**87**	**18***	**105**

*Only total figure for exclusions available for 1994/95.

Table 1.5 — Reasons for exclusion of anaesthetic questionnaires from analysis

Reason for exclusion	2000/01	1994/95	1999/00
Questionnaire completed for an earlier operation	13		25
Questionnaire received too late	47		34
Questionnaire incomplete	2		0
Questionnaire related to excluded procedure	1		1
Questionnaire completed for wrong patient	1		2
Total	**64**	**16***	**62**

*Only total figure for exclusions available for 1994/95.

The response rates for each trust/hospital are shown in Appendix A. Individual trusts/hospitals are kept informed of their return rate on a quarterly basis so there is an opportunity to improve return rates where there are difficulties.

Table 1.6 — Return rate of surgical questionnaire by specialty

	No of Qs sent	No of Qs returned	% of Qs returned	No of Qs analysed
Accident & Emergency	4	2	50	2
Cardiac/ cardiothoracic/ thoracic	175	143	82	133
General	1147	1032	90	999
Neurosurgery	116	94	81	89
Obstetrics & Gynaecology	58	50	86	46
Ophthalmology	18	17	94	16
Oral/ maxillofacial	9	9	100	9
Orthopaedic & Trauma	648	572	88	555
Otorhino- laryngology	60	51	85	46
Paediatric	24	23	96	23
Plastic	34	27	79	23
Spinal Injuries	1	1	100	1
Transplant	7	6	86	5
Urology	124	116	94	108
Vascular	70	59	84	59

Table 1.6 analyses the return rate of surgical questionnaires by the declared specialty of the surgeon. Some specialties are well below the average return rate of 88%.

Reasons for non-return of questionnaires

As can be seen in Table 1.7, there has been a small reduction in the number of questionnaires not returned because the patient's case notes were missing or unavailable. This is to be commended. It is NCEPOD's hope that this is due in a large part to an improvement in the storage and retrieval mechanisms for notes. However, we do in fact believe that this is because an increasing number of trusts/hospitals are utilising their Clinical Audit or Clinical Governance Departments to assist NCEPOD and more effort is being made searching for apparently missing notes. It is hoped that this trend will continue.

Despite missing notes some consultants go to great lengths to complete the questionnaires.

'I have been asked by Dr … to help with your enquiries regarding this patient as he has now left this hospital to take up a post of a consultant anaesthetist elsewhere. I do apologise for the delay in returning your questionnaire but the medical notes have gone missing. I have tried to obtain as much of the information as I could from other records and also from memory.'

This is typical of the support that NCEPOD has received over the past fifteen years and it is this type of support that has made the Enquiry so successful.

Table 1.7	Reasons for non-return of questionnaires		
	2000/01	1994/95	1999/00
Surgical questionnaires	*n=2495*	*n= 1818*	*n= 1967*
No reason given	189	323	182
Notes lost	45	78	41
Other reason	60	33	33
Anaesthetic questionnaires	*n= 2210*	*n=1618*	*n= 1701*
No reason given	148	212	101
Notes lost	63	125	50
Other reason	24	43	21

It is also to be commended that there has been a reduction in the number of questionnaires not returned without any reason since 1994/95. However, there is a minor increase in non-returned cases without a reason since 1999/00.

NCEPOD was interested in whether consultants were not returning questionnaires because they thought that the procedure was so minor that it could not possibly have played a role in the cause of death (despite this not being the purpose of the NCEPOD study), or that the patient was elderly and there would be nothing to learn. We therefore looked at the age groups involved.

Table 1.8	Non-returned questionnaires where no reason given				
	0-20 years	21-40 years	41-70 years	71-80 years	80+ years
Surgical	5	7	54	55	68
Anaesthetic	5	5	48	37	53

NCEPOD is particularly concerned about the five surgical and five anaesthetic questionnaires not returned for patients under the age of 21 who died. This represented nine cases in total as there was just one case – that of an 18-year-old undergoing cardiac surgery – where neither the surgical nor the anaesthetic questionnaires were returned.

FACILITIES

> **The quality of data regarding facilities within hospitals is questionable.**

In April 2001, NCEPOD sent a separate questionnaire to chief executives at all hospitals (NHS and independent) asking about their facilities. This was in response to a suggestion that we should not be asking these questions of clinicians within the individual questionnaire. Although a return was requested for each hospital, 19 trusts could not provide the answers by hospital and therefore provided a combined return. As only 487 questionnaires were physically returned, this is the denominator used. 81% were returned (487/603). Two reminders were sent over a three month period. Questions were asked about a variety of facilities including beds, inpatient and accident and emergency activity, radiological, theatre and critical care resources. This information was used in two ways. Firstly, to assist Advisors in understanding the facilities available within each hospital when reviewing particular cases, and secondly, to allow NCEPOD to review the availability of facilities across hospitals. It is disappointing that the quality of some of this data is questionable and it is of great concern that some hospitals cannot readily provide accurate information.

Operating facilities

Operating theatres

NCEPOD asked how many operating theatres there were in the hospital. 99% (480/487) of respondents answered this question. Of those respondents 4% (21/480) had no operating theatres. 96% (459/480) had one or more operating theatres but 28% (132/480) had only one or two operating theatres. Figure 1.6 depicts the range of number of operating theatres. Reviewing hospitals with one or two operating theatres, 77 of them were private hospitals, but six of the 37 with only one theatre had more than 100 beds and five had an accident and emergency department. NCEPOD is concerned about the logistical difficulties of these hospitals providing out-of-hours medical cover, particularly for postoperative complications or emergencies.

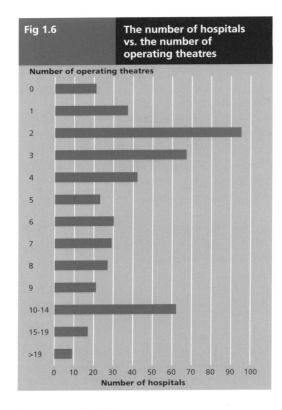

Fig 1.6 The number of hospitals vs. the number of operating theatres

Recovery facilities

> **Lack of recovery beds in some hospitals may hinder theatre throughput.**

NCEPOD asked hospitals with an operating theatre whether they had a recovery room and how many recovery beds/trolleys there were in the hospital. For 424 hospitals, NCEPOD could cross-reference the number of recovery beds to the number of operating theatres and so derive the number of recovery beds per theatre. This is shown in Table 1.9.

Table 1.9	Number of recovery beds per operating theatre
Number of recovery beds/theatre	**No of hospitals in sample**
<0.5	4
0.5-<1.00	56
1.0-<1.50	177
1.5-<2.00	87
>2.00	100
Total	**424**

Hospitals tell us that they have problems with turning over operating lists because recovery is full and so patients have to be recovered in theatres. The current Modernisation Agency work on improving operating theatre performance [7] does not acknowledge this issue, yet it is a very real one. As part of the Who Operates When II study to be published in 2003, NCEPOD has sought to determine the extent of this problem. Certainly there is a guideline for new buildings that recommends that the number of recovery spaces should be calculated from the number of cases and the average time spent in recovery. It proffers a rule of thumb of two recovery beds per operating theatre [8]. It must be recognised that if there are insufficient recovery spaces for the number of operating theatres working, patients cannot be transferred out of the theatre at the end of the procedure and operating lists will be delayed, possibly resulting in cancellation of patients on the day of operation. One of the factors included in the performance rating for hospitals is the number of patients cancelled on the day of operation.

Only 46% (196/424) of recovery units were staffed 24 hours, 7 days/week. For the remainder, hospitals were invited to explain their out-of-hours recovery arrangements. In some hospitals, arrangements were not indicated as no out-of-hours emergencies were undertaken although NCEPOD is aware that there will be some patients who are not recovered in normal working hours even though their operation will have been performed within core time. Many hospitals did not specify their arrangements. Most of those that did specify their arrangement had an on-call theatre team, the training of which was not specified. One hospital stated that their team may not include a dedicated recovery nurse. Three hospitals stated that recovery was by the anaesthetist.

NCEPOD has previously expressed concern about the arrangements for the recovery of patients out-of-hours when the recovery facility is not formally staffed [2]. Hospitals should note the recommendations of the Royal College of Anaesthetists [9] and ensure appropriate arrangements for the recovery of patients at all times.

Critical care facilities

High Dependency Units (HDU)

61% (297/487) of hospitals had an HDU, 38% (185/487) had no HDU and five hospitals did not answer the question. Over the years, NCEPOD has been reporting an increase in the number of HDU beds. However, the increase has been slow and in 1999/00 [2] 31% of patients reviewed were treated in a hospital that had no HDU facility. The 7% discrepancy between this year's findings and

last year is due to the fact that the data presented is on facilities in all hospitals, not those available to patients who died. Included in these are some hospitals where a HDU may not be indicated e.g. those without operating theatres or undertaking only minor surgery. NCEPOD recognises that a HDU is not indicated in all hospitals but it certainly is for those hospitals admitting patients for intermediate or major surgery. For those hospitals with a HDU, the range of size is indicated in Figure 1.7.

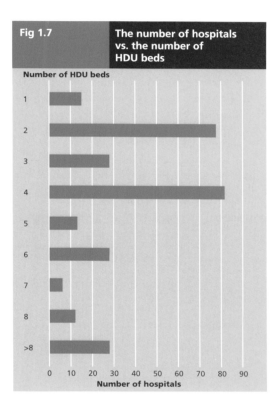

Fig 1.7 **The number of hospitals vs. the number of HDU beds**

93 hospitals had small units comprising one or two HDU beds. Seven of these hospitals had between 400 and 499 beds and nine were hospitals of over 500 beds.

Where a HDU existed, it was part time, i.e., not available 24 hours a day, 7 days a week, in 13% of hospitals (40/297). In 32 of these it was open either for booked admissions only or as required. In one it was only open Monday to Friday 07.30 to 16.00. One can only imagine the difficulties of relocating patients at the end of each day. Is it hoped that they recover sufficiently to go to a ward by 16.00? This must create difficulties of relocating patients at the end of each day and significantly interfere with the smooth running of the hospital and its delivery of health care.

Intensive Care Units (ICU)

> **There were 59 ICUs with one or less funded consultant sessions per day.**

53% (258/487) of hospitals had an ICU, 46% (225/487) had no ICU and four hospitals did not answer this question. The high number of hospitals without an ICU was not anticipated, as almost uniformly there is an ICU in the hospital of the final operation of patients reviewed by NCEPOD. 117 (117/225) of these were private hospitals, 51/225 had over 100 beds and of these 7/225 had over 300 beds. The 46% of hospitals that have no ICU accords numerically with the 45% of hospitals with three or fewer operating theatres. For those hospitals with an ICU, the range of ICU size is indicated in Figure 1.8.

It is a recommendation of a recent working party of the Royal College of Physicians that units without critical care services should not admit acutely ill medical patients[10].

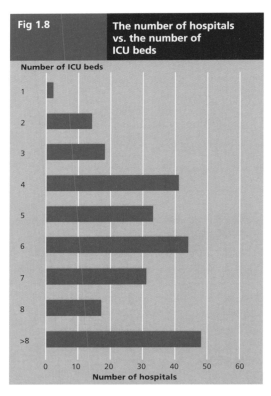

Fig 1.8 — The number of hospitals vs. the number of ICU beds

Number of ICU beds (vertical axis: 1, 2, 3, 4, 5, 6, 7, 8, >8)
Number of hospitals (horizontal axis: 0, 10, 20, 30, 40, 50, 60)

Of the hospitals with an ICU, 86% (223/258) had funded consultant sessions, 12% (30/258) had no consultant sessions and five hospitals did not answer this question. ICUs with no funded consultant sessions are of concern. It is difficult to see how a satisfactory standard of care can be provided in an ICU without supervision from a consultant trained in intensive care medicine and this may result in

medico-legal consequences. Indeed, the Intensive Care Society [11] states that there should be a minimum of ten fixed consultant sessions a week and a minimum of five flexible sessions for out-of-hours emergency and on-call commitments.

71% (185/258) of hospitals with an ICU supplied information on the number of funded consultant sessions each week and these are presented in Table 1.10. 32% (59/185) of these ICUs had less than seven funded consultant sessions per week, i.e. less than one per day. Who is supervising the patients on a day to day basis? No matter how this data is interpreted, it is an inescapable fact that at least a third of hospitals have inadequate funded consultant sessions for ICU.

It should be noted that 21 of these are in the independent sector. As more NHS patients are being treated in the private sector the same standards of care must apply. The National Minimum Standards Regulations [12] say that whilst a patient is in a level 2 or 3 critical care facility (i.e. ICU/HDU) then the consultant responsible for their care should visit the patient a minimum of twice daily. However, the experience required of this responsible consultant is not specified. The same guidelines also say that a designated resident medical practitioner, who has the adult advanced life support certification, should be on duty at all times. Is this level of care sufficient?

Table 1.10	The number of funded consultant ICU sessions vs. the number of hospitals
No. of funded sessions per week	**No of hospitals**
0	30
1	2
2	2
3	1
4	6
5	11
6	7
7	9
8	9
9	8
10-14	96
>14	34

There is a need to monitor the type of operations undertaken in hospitals with limited or no critical care facilities. In hospitals with a small or part time HDU as their only critical care facility, there is a need to ensure the maintenance of critical care skills of the nursing and medical staff.

CLINICAL DATA

Recommendations

There are national agreed standards for anaesthetic monitoring. The absence of an essential anaesthetic monitor constitutes an unacceptable clinical risk that must be the subject of audit [13].

It is inappropriate for an SHO to anaesthetise an ASA 5 patient.

When operations are performed by the surgeon without the presence of an anaesthetist, the existing guidelines on patient monitoring, observation and record keeping should be followed.

Postoperative deaths should be the subject of anaesthetic and surgical review.

INTRODUCTION

This section of the report reviews selected data from the anaesthetic and combined surgical specialties. The full data from the anaesthetic and surgical questionnaires can be obtained from the NCEPOD website **www.ncepod.org.uk** or as a separate document on application to NCEPOD. The sample was from patients who died between 1 April 2000 and 31 March 2001 and comprised the first postoperative death reported for each consultant surgeon or gynaecologist, on the day of operation or within the next three calendar days. The report analysing the data of 1999/00 [2] sampled 10% of deaths within 30 days of an operation and the report for 1994/95 [3] reviewed deaths on or before the third postoperative day; comparisons will be made with those reports where appropriate.

COMPLETION OF QUESTIONNAIRES

A total of 2114 surgical questionnaires and 1911 anaesthetic questionnaires were analysed. NCEPOD is grateful to all clinicians that support this Enquiry. The consultant surgeon in charge of the case completed 1633/2114 (77%) of questionnaires and a member of the surgical team completed 400/2114 questionnaires, of which 344/2114 (16%) were reviewed by the consultant before their return to NCEPOD. Therefore, there was consultant surgical involvement with 94% of questionnaires.

An anaesthetist involved with the case completed the questionnaire in 1321/1911 (69%) of cases. The proxy anaesthetists who completed the questionnaire, but were not directly involved with the case, are presented in Table 2.1. A duty consultant completed the majority of these, usually because he/she was the supervisor when a trainee was the senior anaesthetist present during the operation. Anaesthetists without any involvement in the case, and hence with no personal knowledge of it, completed a further 13%. NCEPOD is indebted to all proxy anaesthetists for their contribution. A consultant anaesthetist either completed or reviewed the questionnaire in 94% of cases.

Table 2.1	Anaesthetists who completed the questionnaire but were not directly involved with the case
Chairman of division	22
College tutor	73
Duty consultant	341
Other consultant	141
Trainee	10
NCCG	3
Total	**590**

When non-consultant anaesthetists or surgeons complete a NCEPOD questionnaire, the supervising consultant should review the case notes and questionnaire.

PATIENT PROFILE

Age and sex

The age profile of patients in this sample is similar to that of the 1994/95 sample (3 day deaths) and 1999/00 sample (10% of 30 day deaths). Figure 2.1 shows the age profile of the patient at the time of the operation. 71% of the patients were 70 years of age or older. 51% of patients were male.

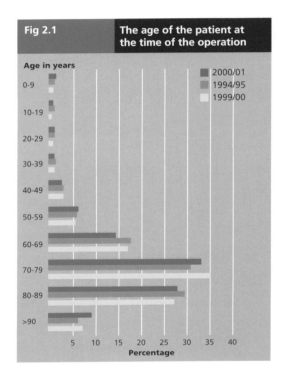

Fig 2.1	The age of the patient at the time of the operation

Age in years

■ 2000/01
■ 1994/95
□ 1999/00

0-9, 10-19, 20-29, 30-39, 40-49, 50-59, 60-69, 70-79, 80-89, >90

Percentage: 5 10 15 20 25 30 35 40

Preoperative status

> **Disorders of the cardiovascular system were the most common comorbidities in the sample.**

The physical status of patients, as reported in the anaesthetic questionnaire, is presented in Figure 2.2. Compared with the sample of 1999/00 (10% of 30 day deaths) there is a trend for patients who die on or before postoperative day 3 (samples of 2000/01 and 1994/95) to be of a poorer physical status. There was a smaller percentage of ASA 2 and 3 (40% vs. 51%), and a larger percentage of ASA 5 (20% vs. 12%) patients.

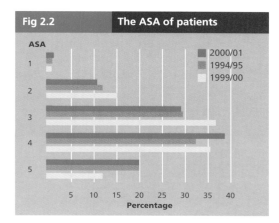

Fig 2.2   The ASA of patients

ASA

2000/01
1994/95
1999/00

Percentage

From the anaesthetic questionnaires, 96% of patients had one or more co-existing medical problems at the time of their operation. The systems involved are presented in Table 2.2.

Table 2.2	Co-existing medical problems at the time of the final operation (answers may be multiple n=1911)
None	3%
Cardiovascular	76%
Respiratory	56%
Neurological	37%
Alimentary	25%
Renal	21%
Sepsis	20%
Endocrine	17%
Musculoskeletal	13%
Haematological	11%
Hepatic	6%
Other	11%
Not answered	1%

The reporting of renal disorders, which NCEPOD had thought previously to be under recognised [2], has increased; 21% compared with 16% in 1999/00.

A table of common diseases is presented in Table 2.3.

Table 2.3	Common co-existing diseases (answers may be multiple n=1911)
Ischaemic heart disease	37%
Hypertension	31%
Chronic cardiac failure	20%
Atrial fibrillation	18%
COPD	15%
CVA or TIAs	13%
Diabetes mellitus	12%
Peripheral vascular disease	12%
Active chest infection	10%

There was a lower incidence of myocardial ischaemia in this sample of deaths on or before postoperative day 3, compared to deaths within 30 days of operation.

In this sample (3 day deaths) 37% of patients had ischaemic heart disease at the time of their operation, compared with 60% in 1999/00 (10% of 30 day deaths). One reason for the lower incidence of myocardial ischaemia may be the different sampling technique. It may be that this sample contained a greater number of patients whose death was related primarily to their surgical condition or some unanticipated cause (e.g. ruptured abdominal aortic aneurysm, acute abdominal catastrophe or PE). However, in a sample of deaths within 30 days of an operation, later postoperative deaths are more likely to be associated with the patient's underlying medical condition, and that includes myocardial ischaemia.

There was a high incidence of atrial fibrillation when compared to that expected in the general population.

There is a 10% incidence of atrial fibrillation in the non-surgical population over the age of 70 [14]. However, the incidence of atrial fibrillation and of other types of arrhythmia in this sample was higher. Often the arrhythmia was of recent onset and precipitated by an acute medical disorder such as myocardial ischaemia, chest infection or sepsis. In these conditions arrhythmia may be a marker of the severity of the systemic illness.

ADMISSION AND OPERATION

Admission

The admission categories of the patients are presented in Figure 2.3. The pattern of admissions is similar for patients who died on or before postoperative day 3 (sample 2000/01 and 1994/95) and the sample of 10% of deaths (1999/00).

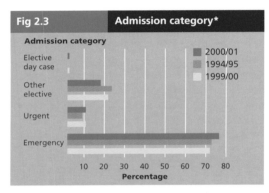

Fig 2.3	Admission category*

*In 1994/95 the elective category comprised both elective day case and inpatients.

In this sample, 36% of patients were admitted via an A&E department, 26% were referred by their general medical or dental practitioner, 14% were transferred as an inpatient from another hospital and 13% were admitted following a previous outpatient consultation.

For the patients transferred as inpatients from other hospitals, the types of referring hospitals are presented in Table 2.4.

Table 2.4	Patients transferred from another hospital
District general hospital	200
University teaching hospital	35
Limited surgical specialties	14
Community	32
Independent	5
Psychiatric	2
Overseas	4
Not answered	3
Total	**295**

Most patients in this sample were admitted directly to the surgical specialty that undertook the operation but 31% were referred from another specialty. The source of intra-hospital referral to the final surgical team is presented in Table 2.5.

Table 2.5	The source of intra-hospital referral to the surgical team
Medical specialty	402
Same surgical specialty	123
Another surgical specialty	118
ICU	10
Not answered	6
Psychiatry	1
Total	**660**

Of note, almost one-fifth of all patients (19%) were admitted to a medical specialty within the admitting hospital before referral to a surgeon.

Operation

The surgical specialties of the operation are presented in Table 2.6.

Table 2.6	Surgical specialty of the operation	
	2000/01	**1994/95**
General surgery	808 (38%)	35%
Orthopaedic	562 (27%)	23%
Vascular	236 (11%)	17%
Cardiothoracic	123 (6%)	6%
Urology	12 (6%)	6%
Neurosurgery	83 (4%)	4%
Paediatric*	48 (2%)	
Gynaecology	45 (2%)	5%
Otorhinolaryngology	44 (2%)	1%
Plastic surgery	19 (<1%)	1%
Ophthalmology	16 (<1%)	1%
Oral/maxillofacial	9 (<1%)	<1%
Total	**2144**	

*Paediatric surgery was not analysed as a separate specialty in 1994/95, 1.7% of patients in 1994/95 were aged 0 to 10 years and 1% were aged 11 to 20 years.

As this sample is made up of the first death on or before postoperative day 3 reported by each surgeon or gynaecologist, the proportion of deaths in each specialty will to some extent reflect the number of consultants in that specialty. The distribution of cases between the specialties in the two samples 1994/95 and 2000/01 is the same.

The urgency of the final operation according to the surgical questionnaires is presented in Figure 2.4 and the anticipated risk in relation to the operation is presented in Table 2.7.

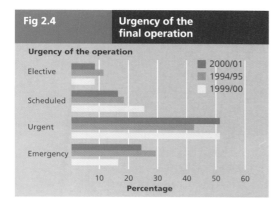

Fig 2.4 — Urgency of the final operation

Urgency of the operation

Legend: 2000/01, 1994/95, 1999/00

(Categories: Elective, Scheduled, Urgent, Emergency; Percentage axis 10–60)

A greater percentage of patients who died on or before postoperative day 3 (2000/01 and 1994/95) underwent an emergency operation compared with 10% of 30 day deaths (1999/00) (26.5% vs. 16%). In contrast, fewer underwent a scheduled operation in 2000/01 and 1994/95 compared with the sample of 1999/00 (17% vs. 25%). In this sample, when compared with 1994/95, the percentage where death was expected was greater (15% vs. 9%) (Table 2.7).

Table 2.7	The anticipated risk of death related to the proposed operation		
	2000/01	**1994/95**	**1999/00**
Not expected	12%	13%	15%
Small but significant risk	17%	18%	22%
Definite risk	53%	60%	54%
Expected	15%	9%	8%

Delays to operation

8% of operations were delayed for non-clinical reasons.

From the anaesthetic questionnaires, 28% (527/1911) of patients had their operation delayed in order to improve their physical state, compared with 22% of the sample of 1999/00 (10% of 30 day deaths). The systems that needed attention are presented in Table 2.8.

Table 2.8	System(s) needing attention before operation as a percentage of those delayed for medical reasons (answers may be multiple n=1911)
Cardiac	56%
Metabolic	41%
Respiratory	31%
Haematological	26%
Other	4%

From the surgical questionnaire, 8% of patients had their operation delayed for reasons other than clinical, mostly due to limited operating theatre availability.

STAFFING

The grade of the most senior operating surgeon is presented in Figure 2.5 and the grade of the most senior anaesthetist is presented in Figure 2.6.

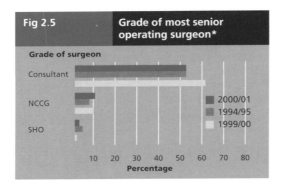

Fig 2.5 — Grade of most senior operating surgeon*

* Analysis in 1994/95 excluded 27/1366 operations that were undertaken in independent hospitals. Comparisons of the registrar grades cannot be made with the sample of 1994/95 because of the changes following the introduction of Calman training. In this sample a SpR was the most senior operating surgeon in 27% of cases.

Despite the patients who died on or before postoperative day 3 being of poor physical status, the most senior operating surgeon was a consultant in only 54% of cases and has not changed since 1994/95. The percentage where the most senior operating surgeon was an SHO was 2% in 2000/01 and 4% in 1994/95. A consultant surgeon was involved in the decision to operate in 87% of cases.

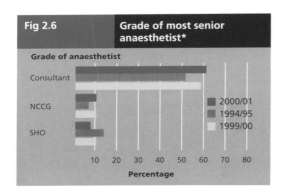

Fig 2.6 — Grade of most senior anaesthetist*

* Comparisons of the registrar grades cannot be made with the sample of 1994/95 because of the changes following the introduction of Calman training. In this sample a SpR was the most senior anaesthetist in 20% of cases.

In this sample the most senior anaesthetist was a consultant for 61% of cases, compared with 52% in 1994/95 (3 day deaths), and the most senior anaesthetist was an SHO for 7% compared with 13% in 1994/95.

The halving of the proportion of cases in which the senior operating surgeon was an SHO, and in which the anaesthetist was a SHO, between 1994/95 and 2000/01, indicates that now, care of the sickest

patients is more likely to be by more experienced medical personnel.

The qualifications of the most senior operating surgeon and anaesthetist were analysed. 1% (25/2114) of operating surgeons held no higher diploma in surgery and 6% (110/1911) of anaesthetists held no higher diploma in anaesthesia. The fellowship of their college was held by 76% (1597/2114) of operating surgeons and 78% (1488/1911) of anaesthetists.

14% (301/2114) of patients were graded ASA 5 on the surgical questionnaire and 20% (383/1911) of patients were graded ASA 5 on the anaesthetic questionnaire. The grade of the senior operating surgeon and anaesthetist in theatre for these patients is presented in Table 2.9; mainly they were of appropriate experience.

Table 2.9	The grade of the most senior operating surgeon and anaesthetist for ASA 5 patients	
	Surgeon	**Anaesthetist**
Consultant	230 (76%)	272 (71%)
NCCG	9	10
SpR>year3	50	81
SpR1/2	6	11
SHO	0	7
LAT/LAS	3	0
Not answered	3	2
Total	**301**	**383**

The operations of the seven ASA 5 patients that were managed by an SHO anaesthetist were: laparotomy (4), insertion of a Sengstaken tube for bleeding oesophageal varicies (1), salvage thoracotomy following trauma (a consultant then joined the anaesthetist in theatre) (1) and a femoral embolectomy (1). Except in exceptional circumstances, it is inappropriate for a SHO to anaesthetise an ASA 5 patient.

ANAESTHESIA AND OPERATIVE MONITORING

Anaesthesia

> **There was a trend towards increasing use of regional techniques, and towards use of higher epidural analgesia.**

The type of anaesthesia used is presented in Table 2.10 and compared with those in 1994/95 (deaths on or before postoperative day 3). There appears a trend for an increase in anaesthetics where a regional technique is used.

Table 2.10	The type of anaesthesia used	
	2000/01	**1994/95**
General alone	1260 (66%)	77%
General and regional	351 (18%)	11%
Regional alone	89 (5%)	5%
Regional and sedation	120 (6%)	4%
General and local infiltration	56 (3%)	3%
Sedation and local infiltration	13 (1%)	<1%
Sedation alone	7 (<1%)	<1%
Local infiltration alone	8 (<1%)	0%
Not answered/not known	7 (<1%)	<1%
Total	**1911**	

The types of regional techniques used are presented in Table 2.11 and are compared with those in 1994/95.

Table 2.11	If anaesthesia included a regional technique, which method was used *(answers may be multiple n=560)*	
	2000/01	**1994/95**
Epidural - thoracic	130 (23%)	14%
- lumbar	67 (12%)	22%
- caudal	3 (<1%)	2%
Spinal (subarachnoid)	213 (38%)	42%
Combined spinal/epidural	11 (2%)	0%
Plexus block (e.g. 3 in 1 block)	108 (19%)	12%
Cranial or peripheral nerve block	34 (6%)	7%
Intravenous regional	2 (<1%)	0%
Surface (e.g. for bronchoscopy)	1 (<1%)	0%

There is a trend towards an increase in the use of thoracic epidural analgesia, and a corresponding decrease in the use of lumbar epidural analgesia. For 2000/01, 126 of the thoracic epidurals were performed for abdominal operations and four for thoracic operations. Of the lumbar epidural procedures, 41 were for abdominal operations and 26 for lower limb operations. Similar data for 1994/95 is not available. NCEPOD again cautions that heavy-handed use of epidural local anaesthetic, particularly for patients with sepsis, can cause operative hypotension [2]. It is likely that the trend towards using a higher spinal block will predispose also to greater sympathetic block and haemodynamic compromise.

Operative monitoring

> **The patient's temperature was not always monitored when active warming devices were being used.**

The monitoring devices used during the management of the anaesthetic are presented in Table 2.12 and the measures taken to maintain body temperature are presented in Table 2.13.

Table 2.12	Monitoring devices used during the management of the anaesthetic	
ECG	1894	(99%)
Pulse oximeter	1897	(99%)
Indirect BP	1468	(77%)
Direct BP	929	(49%)
Expired CO_2 analyser	1702	(89%)
O_2 analyser	1714	(90%)
Peripheral nerve stimulator	324	(17%)
Temperature	653	(34%)
Urine output	1135	(59%)
CVP	922	(48%)
Pulmonary artery pressure	97	(5%)
Cardiac output	56	(3%)

Many of these patients were very sick and this is shown by the high usage of invasive monitoring. Should the pulmonary artery pressure and cardiac output have been measured more often?

Table 2.13	The measures taken to maintain body temperature
None	331 (17%)
IV fluid warmer	1022 (53%)
Warm air system	930 (49%)
Heated blanket under the patient	582 (30%)
Blankets/foil wraps	313 (16%)

It is evident that the patient's temperature was not monitored in all cases where active warming systems were used. It cannot be assumed that the use of active warming devices will fully compensate for temperature loss (hypothermia) during an operation, and their use does not obviate the need for temperature monitoring. Conversely, temperature monitoring is necessary to detect hyperthermia.

There was a lack of monitoring equipment in 18 cases and these included: anaesthetic agent monitor (9), inspired oxygen analyser (3), end tidal CO_2 monitor (2), ventilation volume and ventilation disconnect device (1) and an appropriate transport monitor for transfer between theatre and ICU (only NIBP and pulse oximetry available) (1). That these devices were not available contravenes the Association of Anaesthetists of Great Britain and Ireland recommendations for monitoring during anaesthesia [13]. They advise that *"If a monitoring device deemed essential is not available and anaesthesia continues without it, the anaesthetist must clearly state in the notes the reasons for proceeding without the device."* The absence of any essential monitor should be brought to the attention of the clinical director of anaesthesia and recorded via the clinical risk management system.

Operations under local anaesthesia or sedation provided by the surgeon

There were cases where operations were performed without the presence of an anaesthetist and monitoring devices were not used when indicated.

6% (123/2114) of operations were performed under local anaesthesia and/or sedation administered by the surgeon without an anaesthetist being present. The surgical specialty of the surgeon for these operations is presented in Table 2.14 and the monitoring devices used during these procedures is presented in Table 2.15.

Table 2.14	Surgical specialty for cases under local anaesthesia and/or sedation without an anaesthetist present
General	49
Urology	20
Vascular	13
Ophthalmology	9
Orthopaedic	9
Neurosurgery	5
Otorhinolaryngology	5
Gynaecology	4
Cardiothoracic	3
Plastic	3
Oral/maxillofacial	2
A&E	1
Total	**123**

Table 2.15	Monitoring devices used during operations solely under local anaesthesia or sedation administered by the surgeon (*answers may be multiple n=123*)
Pulse oximeter	77 (63%)
Blood pressure	60 (49%)
Pulse	73 (59%)
ECG	49 (40%)
None	26 (21%)

The use of sedation during an operation mandates an appropriate level of monitoring and in 2001 the Academy of Medical Royal Colleges reviewed the evidence on safe provision of sedation services [15]. They recommended *"Clinical and instrumental monitoring, to a degree relevant to the patient's medical status and the sedation method, should be used. In addition, one member of the care team must have a defined responsibility for patient observation and record keeping."* Existing guidelines have identified that pulse oximetry is a minimum monitoring requirement when a patient receives sedation, and that blood pressure and ECG may be essential in older patients, especially if there are any cardiovascular problems. There is a paucity of guidelines for monitoring patients whose operation is under local anaesthetic without sedation, but the patient's physical status is a consideration. There are guidelines for eye surgery that stipulate *"All patients having cataract surgery under local anaesthesia should be monitored with ECG and pulse oximetry by a member of the theatre staff dedicated to this task, who should be in constant contact with the patient throughout the procedure."*[16] and *"From prior to the administration of the LA to the end of the operation, continuous monitoring of ventilation and circulation by clinical observation and pulse oximetry is essential."*[17].

21% (26/123) of cases that had local anaesthesia and/or sedation administered by the operating surgeon had no monitoring devices attached. Unfortunately, NCEPOD cannot identify how many of these cases involved sedation, so should at least have had pulse oximetry, and how many were performed under local anaesthesia alone. The operations are presented in Table 2.16.

17 patients were ASA 4, so for those some form of monitoring device, pulse oximetry or ECG, was likely to have been indicated.

Three questionnaires stated that no resuscitation facilities, including airway management, were immediately available. These cases were: a Denham pin for an ASA 5 patient in ICU (resuscitation facilities were likely to have been available) and pleural aspiration for two ASA 4 patients. A patient may experience an adverse reaction or require sedation during any surgical procedure under local anaesthesia, and resuscitation equipment should always be immediately available, no matter where the procedure is undertaken.

Table 2.16	Cases where no anaesthetist was involved and no monitoring used	
Specialty (total no.)	No.	Operation
General (6)	4	Paracentesis
	1	Dilatation of PEG track, insertion of tube
	1	Percutaneous drainage of abdominal abscess
Maxillofacial (2)	1	Excision and graft of cheek lesion
	1	Suture of forehead laceration
Ophthalmology (2)	1	Laser photocoagulation of the retina
	1	Weiss procedure of the lower eyelid
Orthopaedic (3)	1	Debridement of wounds and closure
	1	Excision of a sebaceous cyst
	1	Denham pin
Otorhinolaryngology(2)	1	Nasal packing
	1	Tracheostomy
Thoracic (3)	3	Pleural aspiration
Urology (8)	4	Flexible cystoscopy
	2	Suprapubic catheter
	1	Nephrostomy
	1	Prostate biopsy
Total	26	

POSTOPERATIVE CARE AND CAUSE OF DEATH

6% of cases could not be transferred to a critical care facility when clinically indicated.

The destination of the patient after the operation, as recorded in the anaesthetic questionnaires, is presented in Table 2.17, and compared with the sample of 1994/95.

Table 2.17	The destination of the patient after the operation	
	2000/01	**1994/95**
ICU	679 (36%)	33%
HDU	131 (7%)	3%
Ward	795 (42%)	46%
Died in theatre	208 (11%)	12%
Died in recovery	74 (4%)	4%
CCU*	5 (<1%)	
Another hospital	2 (<1%)	1%
Other/not answered	17 (1%)	1%
Total	**1911**	

*Not recorded in 1994/95 .

Table 2.18	Systems implicated in the cause of death *(answers may be multiple n=1911)*	
Cardiac	1133	(59%)
Respiratory	664	(35%)
Renal	418	(22%)
Septicaemia	403	(21%)
Haematological (including coagulopathy/ blood loss)	226	(12%)
Gastrointestinal tract	212	(11%)
Metabolic	189	(10%)
Progress of surgical condition	173	(9%)
Central nervous system	158	(8%)
Hepatic	63	(6%)

This sample shows a trend towards increasing use of critical care facilities compared with 1994/95, nevertheless 42% of patients who died within three days of their operation returned directly to the general ward. 6% of cases could not be transferred to an ICU, HDU or other specialised nursing area when clinically indicated, mainly because there were no beds available. The systems implicated in the cause of death are presented in Table 2.18 and illustrate a prevalence of cardiac, respiratory, renal and septic disorders.

AUDIT

57% of deaths were not reviewed by anaesthetists and 19% not reviewed by surgeons.

6% of patients died in hospitals where no anaesthetic morbidity/mortality review meetings take place and 2% died in hospitals without surgical audit meetings. Morbidity/mortality review meetings should be conducted in all hospitals and by both surgeons and anaesthetists. There should be multidisciplinary review meetings whenever appropriate.

The percentage of all cases that were discussed in surgical and anaesthetic morbidity/mortality review meetings is presented in Figure 2.7.

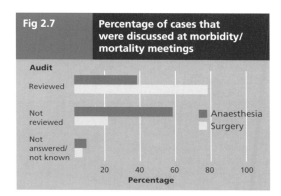

Fig 2.7 — **Percentage of cases that were discussed at morbidity/ mortality meetings**

It is unacceptable that anaesthetists did not review 57% of deaths and the surgeons did not review 19% of deaths. Problems in the delivery of patient care locally are difficult to detect without formal review of the care of critically ill patients.

PREOPERATIVE CARE

Recommendations

The anaesthetist, or the anaesthetic department, should be notified of elective patients who have significant operative risks, preferably in advance of their admission.

National protocols should be formulated to identify which inpatients would benefit from a more detailed preoperative cardiovascular assessment, including echocardiography.

When a formal preoperative medical assessment is indicated, an experienced physician, preferably a consultant, must make it. It is the responsibility of that physician to fully understand the operative risks of the patient's medical condition.

There need to be national guidelines for clinical prescribing in hospitals in order to reduce the risk of drug error.

INTRODUCTION

This section of the report will concentrate on the preoperative assessment of patients for their final operation. It must be remembered that the patients reviewed by NCEPOD were mostly those that were of poor physical status and undergoing high-risk surgery, all of whom died within three days of their operation. Most patients reviewed were likely to die irrespective of excellent care. Nevertheless there were remedial factors that may have contributed to an adverse outcome in some patients and lessons to be learned that can improve future patient care.

PRE-ADMISSION PROCEDURES

Pre-admission assessment clinics

> **88% of hospitals now run pre-admission assessment clinics for one or more surgical specialties.**

Pre-admission assessment clinics allow the clinical history and examination of patients to be documented before their admission, enable appropriate routine investigations to be arranged and identify those patients that may need further investigations or treatment before an elective or scheduled operation. They can reduce the period of hospital inpatient stay and reduce the number of operations cancelled at short notice, therefore improving the hospital throughput of surgical patients and helping to reduce the waiting times for operations. A questionnaire on hospital facilities that was circulated to all trusts/hospitals enquired whether the hospital ran pre-admission assessment clinics. 88% (430/487) of hospitals reported that preoperative assessment clinics were being run in their hospital and 10% (51/487) had no pre-admission assessment clinics. It is desirable that all patients for whom it would be appropriate are seen in a pre-admission assessment clinic. A breakdown of the health professionals who run these clinics is presented in Table 3.1 and, if the assessor is a nurse, the health professional that examines those patients who need a more detailed clinical assessment is presented in Table 3.2.

Table 3.1	The health professionals that run the pre-admission assessment clinics
Nurses	266 (62%)
Nurses & doctors	121 (28%)
Doctors	36 (8%)
Not answered	7 (2%)
Total	**430**

Table 3.2	When a nurse makes the assessment, the health professional who makes a more detailed assessment of the cardiac or respiratory system, when indicated
Doctors	106
Nurses	85
Nurses & doctors	59
Not answered	16
Total	**266**

In most cases, when nursing staff undertake the initial assessment and problems are detected, the patient is referred for a second opinion. It is of concern that in 85 hospitals where nurses ran the clinics there appeared little recourse to a medical opinion. However, it is possible that those who were completing the questionnaire may not have fully understood the protocols of their clinics.

Pre-admission assessment of patients

> **34% of elective admissions did not attend a pre-admission assessment clinic.**

From the surgical questionnaires, 17% (356/2114) of patients were admitted either as a day case or an elective admission. The rest were either urgent or emergency admissions and were therefore unlikely to have had a pre-admission assessment. 234 patients (i.e. 66% of the elective admissions) were assessed in a pre-admission assessment clinic. The health professionals that ran those clinics are presented in Table 3.3.

Table 3.3	Health professional who assessed patients before admission (answers may be multiple n=234)
Nurse/nurse practitioner	129 (55%)
Preregistration HO	77 (33%)
Surgical SHO	72 (31%)
Anaesthetic consultant	31 (13%)
Surgical consultant	9 (4%)
Anaesthetic SHO	6 (3%)
Surgical NCCG	5 (2%)
Anaesthetic NCCG	5 (2%)
Medical SHO	4 (2%)
Medical NCCG	3 (1%)
Medical consultant	1 (<1%)

There should be comprehensive training of pre-admission assessment staff in preoperative clinical assessment skills.

A nurse or preregistration house officer performed the majority of pre-admission assessments for these patients. It is appropriate for nurses and junior doctors to assess patients before admission providing they are fully trained in clinical assessment skills to identify those patients at risk, and are properly supported. Although some of the pre-admission assessment staff may lack experience they are not the sole preoperative assessor but are part of a chain of operative care. Only 15% (34/234) of patients were reported to have had preoperative therapeutic manoeuvres initiated as a result of their pre-admission assessment; at least seven of these interventions could be considered routine (Table 3.4).

Table 3.4	Therapeutic manoeuvres initiated from pre-admission assessment clinic
Cardiology review/ echocardiogram	10
Routine screening tests*	4
Anticoagulation arranged**	4
Preoperative blood transfusion	2
Correction of low serum K+	2
Hypertension control	1
ICU bed booked	1
Radiological malignancy staging	1
Haemodialysis	1
Postoperative epidural	1
Sliding scale insulin regimen arranged	1
Carotid endarterectomy before TKR	1
Visit by stoma nurse	1
Stabilise blood sugar and thyroid function	1
Skin swab MRSA treated	1
Not specified	2
Total	**34**

*These included clinical history, haematology and biochemistry investigations, ECG and CXR.

**These included routine perioperative thromboprophylaxis in three patients.

The most common single intervention was referral to a cardiologist for investigation and review of treatment. This included echocardiography in at least four cases and coronary angiography in one.

The following case studies of patients that were assessed at a pre-admission assessment clinic are presented, not to criticise the assessment but to illustrate the place of the pre-admission assessment in the chain of patient care. NCEPOD has tried to illustrate both good and poor practice, and show that assumptions made at the pre-admission assessment may influence subsequent management.

Case Study 1

A 73-year-old, ASA 4 male was admitted for a scheduled transverse colectomy. He had previously undergone repair of an abdominal aortic aneurysm and his medical history included ischaemic heart disease, angina, CCF and TIAs. He was assessed in a pre-admission clinic that was run by nurses and preregistration house officers, and was referred from there for an echocardiogram and review by a cardiologist. A consultant anaesthetist provided general anaesthesia supplemented by epidural analgesia. Postoperatively he was nursed on a HDU, where he developed CCF and died there on the second postoperative day. An autopsy revealed a myocardial infarction.

Case Study 2

An 83-year-old, ASA 2 male was admitted for an elective completion colectomy two years after a left hemicolectomy. A preregistration house officer assessed him at a pre-admission clinic and noted an ejection systolic murmur that had not previously been detected; no action was taken. On admission one week later, a consultant anaesthetist again noted the systolic murmur, but as the patient had no cardiac history or symptoms, no further investigations were deemed necessary. (Results of his CXR and ECG were not forwarded to NCEPOD.) General anaesthesia was supplemented by epidural analgesia using 30 ml of 0.25% bupivacaine. No invasive monitoring was used. The patient's preoperative blood pressure was 150/80 mmHg and for three hours during the operation his systolic blood pressure was between 90-110 mmHg. He had persistent hypotension postoperatively, BP <90/60 mmHg, and his urine output was low. He had received 4940 ml of fluid intravenously (about 500 ml/hour) and had produced 176 ml of urine by the time of his fatal cardiac arrest 10 hours postoperatively. An autopsy revealed severe aortic stenosis, mitral stenosis, severe cardiomegaly, left ventricular hypertrophy and subendocardial ischaemia.

Case Study 3

A 73-year-old female, ASA 2 patient weighing 45 kg was admitted for a total hip replacement. A nurse and preregistration house officer assessed her at a pre-admission clinic. At that clinic an asymptomatic ejection systolic murmur radiating to the neck, which was thought to be aortic stenosis, was noted for the first time. The ECG was reported as showing LVH and anterolateral ischaemia. No action was taken. A consultant anaesthetist provided a general anaesthetic, supplemented by spinal analgesia. The patient's preoperative blood pressure was 125/70 mmHg and during the operation 2500 ml of fluid (56 ml.kg^{-1}) and ephedrine 18 mg IV were used to attain a target systolic blood pressure of 80-90 mmHg. The operation finished at midday. Postoperatively the patient remained hypotensive until 04.30 the following morning, at which time she was reviewed. From an ECG taken at that time (and despite the changes on the preoperative ECG) a medical SHO diagnosed an acute anterior MI. Two hours later she suffered a fatal VF arrest. The cause of death was assumed MI, so no autopsy was performed.

Case Study 4

An 82-year-old, ASA 2 female was admitted to a limited surgical specialty hospital without critical care facilities for wide local excision of breast carcinoma and axillary node sampling. She had a history of IHD and was on diuretics; her exercise tolerance was limited by arthritis but she denied shortness of breath. Preoperative assessment was in a pre-admission clinic that was run by nurses and NCCG surgeons. She was admitted at 13.00 on the day before her operation, but was in the anaesthetic room when first seen by an SHO anaesthetist, who had been in that grade for more than two years but had no anaesthetic qualifications. Postoperatively, whilst in recovery, she developed fulminating pulmonary oedema and required tracheal intubation and ventilation to the lungs. She was transferred to another hospital for ICU care.

Case Study 5

A 62-year-old, ASA 3 female patient was admitted for a scheduled diagnostic removal of a submandibular gland. She had undergone CABG seven years earlier, had paroxysmal SVT and NIDDM. She was assessed at a pre-admission clinic by a SHO surgeon. Routine haematology and serum biochemistry investigations were normal. The ECG (that was sent to NCEPOD) suggested acute ischaemia in addition to a previous Q wave infarction. There were Q waves in leads III,

AVF and V1-V4, a raised ST segment in lead III and flattened or inverted T waves in lead III, AVF and all chest leads. She did not have an echocardiogram or medical referral. The SpR anaesthetist (year 3/4) who assessed her on admission commented that the ECG was unchanged since 1990, three years before her CABG. After induction of general anaesthesia she developed severe hypotension and her blood pressure was not recordable for 20 min. Postoperatively whilst in the recovery area she developed VT with LVF and died. An autopsy revealed severe coronary artery disease and cardiac sarcoid, which may have precipitated the arrhythmia; there was no evidence of myocardial infarction.

Would appropriate investigation instigated from the preadmission clinic have alerted the anaesthetist to these patients poor cardiac status and have modified the anaesthetic care that they received?

> **Protocols for preoperative assessment and referral of patients by the pre-admission assessment clinic need to be explicit.**

> **Anaesthetists should be involved in the development of pre-admission assessment guidelines.**

Many patients reviewed at a pre-admission assessment clinic are well and require no or only basic investigation. It cannot be assumed their well-being is indefinite. There needs to be an accepted limit on the time between the pre-admission assessment and the date for operation.

One of the roles of staff in a pre-admission assessment clinic is to detect patients who are at an increased operative risk and, if necessary, refer them for further assessment or investigation. In the main, the staff that run the clinics are doctors in the early stages of their training, or nurses. These staff should have a written protocol for pre-admission assessment and training in its application. Guidelines as to which patients have operative risks and which need to be referred should be explicit. Referral must be to clinicians of appropriate experience. Anaesthetists should be involved in the development of pre-admission assessment clinic protocols and guidelines.

In this sample, few patients were referred for a further medical opinion, and it was usually a referral to a cardiologist or their general practitioner. None was reported as being referred to an anaesthetist. Policies setting out which patients should be referred, and to whom, vary greatly between hospitals. It is essential that pre-admission assessment personnel have access to an anaesthetist [18].

The involvement of consultant anaesthetists in pre-assessment admission clinics has implications for consultant workload, which must be recognised in anaesthetic staffing reviews and job plans.

General practitioners and experienced surgeons review patients before they attend pre-admission assessment clinics. It should be possible to identify patients with operative risks in advance of these clinics. Perhaps the primary care physician, or consulting surgeon, could identify those patients with operative risk at the time of surgical referral, or when the decision to operate is made. The organisation of the preoperative assessment process should ensure that physicians and/or anaesthetists review those patients who require it, preferably before admission. The anaesthetist, or the anaesthetic department, should be notified of all patients who have severe operative risks in advance of their admission in order for an appropriate care plan to be formulated.

The pre-admission assessment should not be the final preoperative assessment; it does not obviate an anaesthetic assessment. An anaesthetist should see all patients before they undergo an operation that requires the services of an anaesthetist [18] and the anaesthetic room is not the appropriate place for this. Is there an assumption that once the patient is admitted for surgery the anaesthetist should accept the findings of the pre-admission assessment? The findings of the pre-admission assessment need to be reviewed by an anaesthetist preoperatively, and any further investigations deemed necessary instigated before the patient's operation. Ultimately, the anaesthetist is responsible for deciding whether a patient is fit for anaesthesia [18].

> **The findings of morbidity/mortality reviews should be considered when the pre-admission assessment clinic protocols are being evaluated and modified.**

The cases in this sample illustrate that unanticipated adverse outcomes can occur during elective surgery. Hospitals should conduct morbidity/mortality review of patients that are assessed at the pre-admission clinics. Findings of such reviews should be considered when the pre-admission assessment

clinic protocols are being re-evaluated and modified, which should be on a regular basis.

There is a much ongoing investigation into preoperative assessment. The Association of Anaesthetists of Great Britain and Ireland has produced guidelines [18]. Guidelines by NICE and the Modernisation Agency are in preparation at the time of writing.

ADMISSION

> **Some patients are admitted into an inappropriate area of the hospital because of the pressure on beds.**

The area to which the patient was admitted for their final operation is presented in Table 3.5.

Table 3.5	The area to which the patient was admitted for their final operation	
Surgical specialty ward	722	(34%)
General surgical ward	491	(23%)
A&E ward	223	(11%)
Medical ward	218	(10%)
Admission ward	99	(5%)
ICU	88	(4%)
Direct to theatre	85	(4%)
Elderly medicine ward	43	(2%)
Coronary care unit	33	(2%)
HDU	32	(2%)
Gynaecology/Obstetric ward	25	(1%)
Not answered	25	(1%)
Day unit	20	(<1%)
Private bed	8	(<1%)
Recovery	2	(<1%)
Total	**2114**	

In 4% (91/2114) of cases this area was considered by the surgeon to be inappropriate. 43 patients were admitted to a medical ward, mostly because a diagnosis of acute abdomen was missed and so these could be considered inappropriate only with the benefit of hindsight. 42 patients were admitted to a surgical ward that the surgeon considered inappropriate for a variety of reasons, but often due to lack of beds on the appropriate ward or a missed diagnosis. Patients who are admitted into an inappropriate area of the hospital because of the pressure on beds are likely to suffer from delays in their diagnosis or treatment. In 10 cases the surgeon thought that the patient should have been admitted to a critical care facility and of these two were not because the unit was full, and two because there was no HDU in their hospital.

Preoperative transfer of care

> **It is essential that when the care of a patient is transferred, those referring the patient give the receiving team all the necessary relevant clinical information.**

14% (295/2114) of patients were transferred from another hospital to that of their final operation, mainly either for specialised surgical care or a critical care facility, and 31% (660/2114) were referred to the final surgical team from another specialty/team within the hospital.

Case Study 6

A 65-year-old male was admitted to a district general hospital with a history of collapse, onset of slurred speech and ataxia. The GCS on admission was 14, but overnight deteriorated to 6. A CT scan demonstrated a cerebellar haemorrhage and hydrocephalus. Mannitol and dexamethasone were administered, the lungs ventilated and the patient was transferred to a neurosurgery unit. On arrival at the neurosurgical unit, the patient had decreased movement of the right hemithorax and a blood pressure of 80/40 mmHg. There was no mention of any attempt to insert a subclavian CVP line in the transfer note, however, there were signs of recent attempted venepuncture in the right subclavian region. The patient went to the operating theatre for insertion of a ventricular drain where a tension pneumothorax was diagnosed by an "on the table CXR" and a chest drain was inserted.

A tension pneumothorax that develops while a patient is receiving intermittent positive pressure ventilation can be difficult to diagnose. This case illustrates that it is vitally important that all interventions should be recorded in the medical notes and, when a patient is transferred, they should be communicated to the receiving medical team.

Delays after admission

NCEPOD is concerned by delays in assessment, diagnosis and referral of patients following their admission into secondary or tertiary care.

Case Study 7

A 24-year-old, ASA 4 female was admitted to a cardiology ward as an emergency with a two-day history of nausea and vomiting. She was known to have severe aortic stenosis and mixed mitral valve disease and her operation to replace these valves had already been delayed for several months (from "Spring" to December) following a pregnancy that resulted in a miscarriage. On admission she complained of shortness of breath and palpitations, and was noted to have right heart failure with an enlarged pulsatile liver. A diagnosis of helicobacter pylori was considered, but apparently was not excluded until 13 days later. Her nausea and vomiting persisted and she was scheduled for aortic and mitral valve replacement three weeks after her admission. She started menstruating three days before the planned operation. The consultant surgeon was unaware of this and because of it cancelled the case in the anaesthetic room. The operation was booked again for two weeks later. The following day she went into fast AF and circulatory collapse followed by cardiac arrest. Salvage surgery was attempted but she died in the operating theatre.

Case Study 8

A 78-year-old, ASA4 male was admitted with a fractured hip. He suffered from recurrent chest infections, had suffered a previous CVA and was in AF and on warfarin therapy. He was referred to a haematologist who advised that he should be given two units of fresh frozen plasma to reduce his INR, and his operation was scheduled for two days after admission. Despite treatment, at this time his INR was still too high so the operation was postponed for another three days. Again his INR was high and he finally underwent his operation eight days after admission. After the initial two units of FFP he received no treatment to correct his INR. Possibly as a result of his prolonged bed rest, by the time of his operation he had developed another of his recurrent chest infections. He died of bronchopneumonia on the second postoperative day.

Case Study 9

A 71-year-old female with no previous medical problems was admitted at 03.00 with an acute abdomen. At this time a HO assessed her and noted that she was shocked. The results of her serum biochemistry investigation were urea 24.4 m mol/l, creatinine 471 micromol/l and metabolic acidosis with a base excess of -11.8 m mol/l. At 07.40, over four hours after admission, she was reviewed by a surgical SHO who confirmed the admission findings. At 09.30 she was referred to a surgical registrar and consultant.

At 11.30 she was reviewed by a consultant anaesthetist who agreed to take her to the ICU for resuscitation and a bed was available there at 14.00 (11 hours after admission). A three-hour laparotomy with limited right hemicolectomy, small bowel resection and Hartmann's procedure was started at 16.50. After her operation she returned to the ICU where she died of multiple organ failure on the second postoperative day.

Case Study 10

A seven-year-old fit child fell from a bicycle at 11.30. The child was admitted to a DGH at 12.15 with vomiting, headache and a GCS 15/15. X-ray showed a temporal skull fracture. At 16.00 the GCS had decreased to 13/15. No further neurological observations were done until 19.00, by which time the level of consciousness had deteriorated and the left pupil was dilated. A CT scan at that time showed an extradural haematoma. The child was then referred to the regional neurosurgical centre and arrived there at 22.00 six hours after the first signs of deterioration, with bilateral fixed dilated pupils. The child was taken to theatre immediately and the extradural haematoma was removed at 22.35. Although there was some immediate improvement in the neurological signs, tragically neurogenic pulmonary oedema developed, which was followed by multiple organ failure, and the child died on the second postoperative day.

These case studies illustrate that delays can and do occur after admission to secondary or tertiary care, and they may adversely affect outcome. Mainly the impression conveyed by the sequence of events was that after admission hospital staff assumed that patients were in a safe environment and the necessity for urgency had passed. This was not so. It is difficult for NCEPOD to assess delays because it has no in-depth knowledge of the individual circumstances; particularly it does not currently enquire into events on the medical wards. Nevertheless, these and other cases cause disquiet. Moreover, the prevalence of delays is difficult to quantify as NCEPOD reviews only those patients who suffer adverse outcome, which is more likely following delays in treatment. The case of the patient with a head injury is more clear-cut. There are guidelines for the management of patients with a head injury and these were not followed [19,20].

Only 5% of all head injuries are managed in neurosurgical units; medical and nursing staff without specialised neurosurgical experience manage the rest [21] and only 48% of consultant general surgeons and 40% of consultant orthopaedic surgeons have been trained in the management of head injury patients [20].

All wards admitting head injury patients need a clear management protocol to identify which patients require neurosurgical referral, and to ensure any referral is timely.

An assessment of the process of patient care and delays preoperatively should be part of mortality/morbidity review, and organisational changes should ensure that any such delays are eliminated.

PREOPERATIVE INVESTIGATIONS

Preoperative investigations of the patients in this sample are presented in Table 3.6. These are compared with the report of 1994/95 which also reviewed deaths on or before the third postoperative day.

Table 3.6	Preoperative investigations (answers may be multiple n=1911)	
	2000/01	1994/95
None	23 (1%)	1%
Haemoglobin	1835 (96%)	96%
White cell count	1782 (93%)	90%
Platelets*	1753 (92%)	
Coagulation screen	997 (52%)	31%
Serum electrolytes	1779 (93%)	93%
Serum urea	1703 (89%)	88%
Creatinine	1731 (91%)	81%
Bilirubin (total)	885 (46%)	35%
Glucose	982 (51%)	51%
Serum albumin	927 (49%)	40%
Amylase	370 (19%)	16%
Blood gas analysis	591 (31%)	24%
Chest X-ray	1183 (62%)	70%
ECG	1540 (81%)	84%
Respiratory function tests	69 (4%)	5%
Special cardiac investigations (e.g. ECHO, angiography)	273 (14%)	8%
CT scan/ultrasound/MRI/NMR*	310 (16%)	
Others relevant to anaesthesia**	52 (3%)	7%

* Not collected in 1994/95.

**Others included thyroid function tests, 5; calcium, 4; cardiac enzymes, 2; cardiac output studies, 2; phosphate, 1 and magnesium, 1. Most others were not specified.

A high percentage of patients had haemoglobin, blood count, urea and electrolytes measured preoperatively, and this was expected in this sample as many patients were of a poor physiological status. There was evidence of increased preoperative investigation of coagulation, renal (creatinine), hepatic (bilirubin) and respiratory (blood gas) disorders in this sample, when compared with 1994/95. It was a concern that in 12% (70/591) of the analyses of blood gases there was no record of the inspired oxygen concentration, limiting the value of the investigation. The proportion of patients who had a preoperative chest X-ray examination has decreased, and this is probably due to the guidelines of the Royal College of Radiologists [22]. These state that chest X-ray is not indicated routinely except before cardiopulmonary surgery, likely admission to ITU, suspected malignancy or possible TB. It may also be indicated in dyspnoeic patients, those with known cardiac disease and the very elderly. A Health Technology Assessment report that investigated the value of routine preoperative chest X-rays concluded that they are of value in less than 9% of patients but that a chest X-ray is more likely to be abnormal in those patients who are elderly and of poor physical status [23].

When analysed further, only 70% of urgent, scheduled or elective operations on patients of ASA 3, 4 and 5 had a chest X-ray. It was surprising that only 51% of patients had their blood glucose measured in the sample where 87% of patients were ASA 3 or poorer.

Preoperative investigations are important. They may influence the patient's management or allow fuller information to be provided on the risks and benefits of the proposed operation.

The operations of patients that had no preoperative investigations are presented in Table 3.7.

Table 3.7	Number of patients who had no preoperative investigations
Leaking abdominal aneurysm repair	9
Thoracotomy for thoracic trauma	4
Cataract operation	3
Internal fixation of fracture	2
Others*	5
Total	**23**

*The others were reduction of a dislocated prosthetic hip, removal of an external fixator, oesophagoscopy with oesophageal stenting, biopsy of a brain tumour and insertion of a ventricular drain.

Most patients that had no preoperative investigations were admitted as an emergency and were undergoing resuscitation at the time of their operation. Of note are the three patients who had cataract operations. Eye surgery is recognised as being low risk. However, no operation is free of stress, and stress may have an impact on patients with cardiovascular disease. There are guidelines on local anaesthesia for intraocular surgery[17] which state that for the patient with no history of significant systemic disease and no abnormal findings on examination at the nurse-led assessment, no special investigations are indicated. The three

patients that underwent cataract operations were all female. These were a 91-year-old, ASA 2 patient who suffered from dizzy spells and who died from a CVA, an 87-year-old, ASA 2 patient with COPD who died from an AAA and a 62-year-old, ASA 3 patient with a history of MI and CVA, who had angina and who died from a myocardial infarction. According to these guidelines, all three patients should have had some preoperative investigations.

Further investigation of cardiovascular disease

Specific cardiac investigations, echocardiography and/or angiography were performed in 14% of patients, but this included those undergoing heart operations. Only 9% of patients undergoing non-cardiac operations had any specific cardiac investigations other than an ECG, and this despite 76% of the sample having some cardiovascular disorder.

Case Study 11

A 71-year-old, ASA 2 male was admitted for a left-sided petrosectomy, parotidectomy, neck dissection and reconstruction with latissimus dorsi flap and skin graft from the thigh. He had asbestosis and IHD with stable angina. He was not assessed in a pre-admission assessment clinic. However, preoperative echocardiography was performed in order to assess his left ventricular function, which was described as mildly impaired. Operative monitoring included CVP and direct arterial pressure. His operation lasted for 9 hours 30 minutes after which he went to the HDU. He died of a myocardial infarction on the second postoperative day.

Case Study 12

An 82-year-old female was admitted to a medical ward for investigation of nausea, vomiting, weight loss and renal impairment. She had undergone a nephrectomy in 1963 and suffered a MI with LVF in 1987. The day after admission her heart rate was 120-130 beats/min, her blood pressure was 105/40 mmHg, and she had pain in her right shoulder and a reversible ST elevation. A diagnosis of MI was considered but not confirmed. She remained in hospital and four weeks later she underwent an EUA cystoscopy, at which time her preoperative anaesthetic assessment recorded mild CCF. Operative findings were of a lengthy ureteric stricture that could not be crossed or stented. On the first postoperative night she developed acute LVF. Ten days later she underwent an unsuccessful attempt at nephrostomy insertion and a CT scan demonstrated a large stone in the renal pelvis. The next day she was admitted to HDU for CVP line insertion before an operation to explore her right kidney, at which time she was noted to be breathless and in "gross pulmonary oedema" with a CVP of 4 mmHg. Later that day she underwent an exploration of the right kidney, biopsy of the renal pelvis and pyelolithotomy. She was nursed on an ICU postoperatively, where she died two days later.

Case Study 13

An 87-year-old, 60 kg, ASA4 male was admitted with a fractured neck of femur. He had COPD and was on domiciliary oxygen. On admission an apical systolic murmur was detected and a presumed diagnosis of mitral regurgitation, pulmonary regurgitation and tricuspid regurgitation was noted (presumably, as regurgitation of the right heart valves was thought likely, pulmonary hypertension of cardiac or respiratory origin was considered). An ECG showed changes consistent with right axis deviation and anterolateral ischaemia. His serum creatinine was 239 micromol/l. No medical referral or echocardiogram was obtained. His preoperative blood pressure was 120/60 mmHg. Spinal anaesthesia resulted in a blood pressure between 80/50 mmHg and 90/50 mmHg during the operation that lasted for 1 hour 20 minutes. Postoperatively he returned to the ward where despite intravenous inotropic drugs his systolic arterial pressure was between 110-65 mmHg for three days until his death.

Case Study 14

An 82-year-old, 55 kg, ASA 3 man was admitted with a fractured neck of femur. He had COPD with an acute chest infection, severe IHD with angina and CCF, hypertension, PVD, NIDDM and had suffered a previous CVA. Chest X-ray revealed cardiomegaly and upper lobe blood diversion. The ECG showed AF (that was misdiagnosed as sinus rhythm by the ECG machine) and bifascicular block. The patient was reviewed by one of the specialist orthopaedic medical team (grade unknown), and deemed fit for surgery. No echocardiogram was obtained. During a hemiarthroplasty the patient suffered a cement reaction at which time his systolic blood pressure decreased to 60 mmHg and heart rate decreased to 60 beats/min, which responded to intravenous atropine and vasoconstrictors. He returned to the ward and suffered a fatal cardiac arrest the following day.

Case Study 15

A 63-year-old male was known to have type II diabetes mellitus and hypertension. One week before the final operation he was admitted with right-sided abdominal pain, vomiting and abdominal distension. The clinical diagnosis was biliary colic. Initial investigations were unremarkable with a raised WCC 17.9 x 10^9/l and creatinine 160 micromol/l as the only abnormalities; serum amylase was normal at 20 iu/l. Four hours after admission he developed "heartburn", tightness in his chest and shortness of breath. He was found to be clammy with a pulse rate of 116 beats/min. At this time a history of chest pain on walking 20 yards was elicited. ECG showed atrial premature beats, left axis deviation, poor R wave progression and an inverted T wave in AVL. The findings were discussed with the medical registrar, who did not see the patient but advised that troponin I should be checked in eight hours time. The following day a CT scan revealed cardiomegaly and an inflammatory mass in the RIF. The medical registrar, who was again asked to review the patient, commented that structural heart disease was likely and that a laparotomy should await the results of troponin I measurement and the heart should be further investigated. The surgeons continued to plan for surgery. At preoperative assessment the SHO anaesthetist noted angina, CCF, SOB on walking and bending, orthopnoea, bilateral basal crepitations and rapid respiratory rate and commented that ICU would be required postoperatively. Following a normal troponin I level a laparotomy was undertaken. No abnormality was found. The patient was critically ill postoperatively with low cardiac output and despite full cardiovascular and respiratory support he died two days later. An autopsy revealed that he had been in congestive cardiac failure for some time and had a cardiomyopathy of unknown aetiology.

The patients in these case studies all had known severe cardiac disease, some with decompensation, as well as other serious comorbidity. The first patient was a scheduled admission who received a well-considered preoperative workup. Although the other five patients were urgent admissions, there was time for a consultant cardiological opinion and further investigation before their operation. Such action may have affected their preoperative preparation or anaesthetic management and in the last case the diagnostic confusion, between acute abdominal pathology and liver engorgement from cardiac failure, may not have occurred.

There is plenty of interest in developing pre-admission and preoperative assessment protocols. However, most of the patients reviewed by NCEPOD are urgent or emergency admissions so they bypass the established pre-admission protocols, even though often they are sicker than most elective admissions. Inpatient preoperative assessment guidelines should be established. Following an urgent admission there is heterogeneity of urgency for the operation, and that makes guidelines more difficult; nevertheless it is possible. Multidisciplinary teams manage some patients, particularly those admitted following trauma and it would be appropriate to establish guidelines for their preoperative investigation. The American College of Cardiology/American Heart Association have reviewed the evidence and produced updated guidelines on cardiovascular evaluation for non-cardiac surgery [24]. This is valuable reading for anaesthetists, as well as those cardiologists or physicians involved in preoperative assessment of patients. The guidelines are mainly applicable to non-emergency surgery, and there is a useful algorithm for assessment before urgent or elective operations. However, a high proportion of cases that NCEPOD reviews are of an urgency that precludes following this pathway and it must be recognised that some patients need to be investigated and managed in a more pragmatic way.

Lee and co-workers [25] identified predictors of cardiac risk of major non-emergency, non-cardiac surgery (see Table 3.8).

Table 3.8	Revised cardiac risk index
Risk factor	**Definition**
High risk type of surgery	Intraperitoneal, intrathoracic, suprainguinal vascular
Ischaemic heart disease	History of MI, positive exercise test, angina, use of nitrates, evidence of Q wave infarct
History of congestive heart failure	History of CHF, pulmonary oedema, PND, bilateral rales or S3 gallop, upper lobe blood diversion
History of cerebrovascular disease	History of transient ischaemic attack(s) or stroke
Insulin therapy for diabetes	
Preoperative serum creatinine >177 micromol/l	

Other recognised risk factors include severe valvular heart disease, unstable angina, high-grade atrioventricular block, symptomatic ventricular arrhythmias in the presence of underlying heart disease, supraventricular arrhythmia with uncontrolled ventricular rate, emergency or urgent

major operations particularly in the elderly, and prolonged surgical procedures associated with large fluid shifts and/or blood loss [24].

Echocardiography is a simple, rapid and useful assessment that can be made at the bedside, and it is being used increasingly as part of patient preoperative assessment. Trained non-medical staff now perform echocardiography examinations, and the cost of transthoracic echocardiography equipment is decreasing. The results of echocardiography can influence the choice of the anaesthetic, operative monitoring and the requirement for postoperative critical care. Currently there is little evidence, and few guidelines, as to which patients should have an echocardiogram as part of their preoperative assessment. An asymptomatic cardiac murmur, particularly in the aortic area, may indicate significant cardiac disease and should be investigated appropriately [2]. Patients with heart failure or previous Q wave myocardial infarction also have an indication for some assessment of left ventricular function, especially before intermediate or major surgery, and that may include echocardiography [24]. Agreed national and local protocols as to which patients would benefit from a more detailed preoperative cardiovascular assessment, including echocardiography, should be formulated jointly by anaesthetists and cardiologists.

There is no benefit to be gained by performing any preoperative investigation if an abnormal result is disregarded.

Case Study 16

A 76-year-old, 68 kg female was admitted following a fractured neck of femur. Ten years previously she had episodes of sinus tachycardia, accompanied by angina, and a diagnosis of aortic stenosis was made. She was started on atenolol, which controlled her symptoms and underwent yearly cardiology review. An echocardiogram one month before admission showed severe aortic stenosis with an estimated aortic valve gradient of 95 mmHg and a LV ejection fraction of 71%. She was assessed preoperatively by a trust anaesthetist who discussed the case with an associate specialist before providing anaesthesia for her operation one day after admission. There was no cardiology referral. Her preoperative haemoglobin was 10.8 gm/dl. She received a general anaesthetic without invasive monitoring. During the operation, that lasted for one hour, her systolic arterial pressure was recorded as between 90-110 mmHg and she received 3000 ml of fluid intravenously (44 ml/kg); the blood loss was not recorded. Postoperatively, whilst in the recovery area, her haemoglobin was 4.6 gm/dl (was that due to excess clear fluid or blood loss?). No ICU or HDU bed was available, so she returned to the ward where she received a blood transfusion. Whilst on the ward she developed LVF, tachycardia and hypotension that did not respond to epinephrine. Twelve hours later she was admitted to the HDU, where she died after two hours.

Preoperative investigations are usually organised by the surgical team. However, the decision on whether the patient has been investigated adequately rests with the anaesthetist.

PREOPERATIVE MEDICAL REFERRAL

Care was undertaken on a formal shared basis in 21% (449/2114) of cases. NCEPOD did not ask whether care was shared before, or not until after the operation. The specialties involved in shared care are presented in Table 3.9.

Table 3.9	Specialties involved in formal shared care (answers may be multiple n=449)
General medicine	146
Other medical specialty	107
Other surgical specialty	102
Care of the elderly	84
Paediatric	21
Other	21

Care was shared with a medical specialty in 17% (358/2114) of cases. This was a surprisingly low percentage of shared medical care for a sample with such a high incidence of serious medical disorders. In the case of some medical referrals the physicians involved were of an inappropriate grade and many did not appear to fully understand the operative risks associated with the patient's medical condition.

Case Study 17

A 71-year-old, ASA 4 female was admitted following a fractured neck of femur. She was recognised as having a high operative risk. She had severe IHD and had suffered two myocardial infarctions, eight and ten years previously. Three weeks before admission she had suffered a third myocardial infarction complicated by a VF cardiac arrest. She had a history of multiple pulmonary emboli and had suffered an episode of LVF after a previous anaesthetic. She was a non-insulin dependent diabetic. The consultant anaesthetist who assessed her noted that she had a two-day history of shortness of breath at rest, orthopnoea and PND. Her chest X-ray revealed bilateral pleural effusions that were thought to be secondary to cardiac failure. Her ECG showed evidence of old inferior and anterolateral infarction, there was first degree heart block and low voltage complexes throughout all leads. The anaesthetist requested that she had an echocardiogram and a medical review. The echocardiogram showed that there was moderate mitral regurgitation, mild tricuspid regurgitation, poor LV function (ejection fraction of <30%), poor RV function and dilatation of both ventricles. The opinion of the medical SHO who reviewed her two days after referral was that she was now in optimal condition. Nine days after her admission she underwent an operation for insertion of a DHS. She had central venous and arterial cannulae inserted before receiving a cautious incremental epidural anaesthesia. The first recorded CVP measurement was 19 mmHg. She was nursed on the ICU postoperatively, before discharge to the ward on the following morning. There was no further entry in the notes until her death 48 hours later.

Case Study 18

A 73-year-old, ASA 4 female was admitted with abdominal pain and peritonism. She had ischaemic heart disease with atrial fibrillation and peripheral vascular disease. Regular drug treatment included digoxin, warfarin and large doses of diuretics. On admission she had an acute chest infection and her heart rate was poorly controlled at a rate of 130 beats/min. A medical SHO reviewed her antiarrhythmia treatment on the day of admission, a medical registrar provided telephone advice one day after admission and a consultant cardiologist reviewed her three days after admission; she had a heart rate of between 130-150 beats/min throughout. She was ASA 5 and her heart rate was still 150 beats/min when she went for a laparotomy at 03.00, four days after admission.

Medical SHOs, who apparently failed to recognise the risk or improve the patient's medical condition, reviewed both these patients at some time.
If a preoperative medical assessment is indicated an experienced physician should make it, preferably a consultant. It is inappropriate for a preoperative medical assessment to be made by a medical SHO or inexperienced SpR (year 1/2). If necessity dictates the initial medical assessment is by an experienced trainee (SpR ≥ year 3) or NCCG doctor, the medical consultant should review the patient at the earliest opportunity. It is the responsibility of the physician to fully understand the operative risks of the patient's medical condition. Referral is a process of consultation and there must be clear communication between the surgeon anaesthetist and physician on the aims of the referral to enable them to better understand each other's concerns [26].

PREOPERATIVE DRUG TREATMENT

Many patients do not receive essential regular medication preoperatively.

In this sample NCEPOD asked about maintenance drug treatment for medical conditions, and whether they were given on the day of operation. Table 3.10 shows how many patients were on specified treatments and the percentage of cases where the drugs were not given on the day of operation. The fourth column indicates the percentage of cases where drugs were not given on the day of operation for urgent, scheduled and elective operations. This assumes that for emergency cases, an omission of maintenance drugs may be unavoidable, however most of the urgent, and all scheduled and elective patients should be able to take their maintenance drugs on the morning of operation.

Table 3.10	The number of patients on specified drug groups and percentage not given on the day of operation		
Drug class	No. of patients	Not given - all patients	Not given-urgent/ scheduled/ elective operations
Anti-anginal	393	27%	22%
Anti-arrhythmics	326	25%	20%
Anti-hypertensive	660	34%	23%
Thyroid/anti-thyroid	121	43%	31%
Bronchodilators	261	16%	15%
Steroids	180	19%	17%

It is interesting that giving thyroid-related medication on the day of operation appears to be a low priority. Of concern is the information on antianginal, bronchodilator and steroid treatment. These drugs should be given throughout the operative period and when the patient cannot take their oral drugs, there are simple topical, inhaled or parenteral replacement formulations readily available. Some of the drug charts returned to the NCEPOD office show clearly that the reason given for the patient not receiving the drug is because they were classified as "nil by mouth" for the preoperative period. Doctors and nurses need to understand the difference between preoperative oral medication and the full English breakfast.

Drug prescribing errors

> **Legal responsibility for prescribing rests with the doctor who writes or alters the prescription.**

NCEPOD did not request the prescription charts for this sample. Nevertheless, from the ones that were sent, NCEPOD could see that dose alteration was not uncommon, and often it was impossible to know the date or time the alteration was made, or by whom.

Case Study 19

A 78-year-old, 82 kg, male was admitted for a total hip replacement. He had undergone CABG two years earlier specifically to enable this operation. He had angina, AF, NIDDM, hypertension and bilateral 80% carotid artery stenosis. He was on maintenance doses of warfarin 3.5 mg od, digoxin 125 micrograms bd, ramipril 10 mg od, glipizide 5 mg tds and metformin 850 mg bd. He was assessed by a surgical SHO two days before admission, who liaised with a haematologist about the anticoagulation control and documented clear advice, but did not notify the anaesthetic department of his high-risk patient. The patient's drugs and their doses were recorded in the pre-admission notes. The patient was admitted three days before his operation. At this time his drugs were initially prescribed as follows; warfarin was discontinued, digoxin, ramipril and metformin were prescribed as above and the glipizide dose was increased to 10 mg bd. For some reason the digoxin 125 micrograms was crossed through and 250 micrograms written above it, although the instruction for it to be given twice a day was left unchanged. The patient received digoxin 500 micrograms per day, given according to an altered prescription, for the three days until his operation. A staff grade anaesthetist who assessed him at 08.00, half an hour before induction of anaesthesia commented that he was "very unfit" and ASA 3, but failed to notice the drug error. Systolic blood pressures, which had been recorded between 160-180 mmHg before, were between 70-80 mmHg for one hour during the operation. One day after his operation the patient was noted to be drowsy and a medical registrar reviewed him. The patient had a bradycardia (heart rate 35 beats/min), metabolic acidosis, hyperkalaemia (7.7 mmol/l), creatinine of 266 micromol/l (136 micromol/l previously), glucose 21 mmol/l, and a digoxin level 5 nmol/l (therapeutic limits 1-2.6 nmol/l). He was treated with digoxin-specific antibody fragment (Fab) and his blood sugar was controlled. Nevertheless he became increasingly drowsy

and acidotic, and died on the second postoperative day. The coroner's autopsy reported non-haemorrhagic brain infarct and ischaemic heart disease. In the report there was no mention of an examination of the stenosed carotid arteries, or of his diabetes or digoxin toxicity.

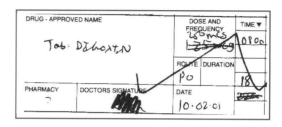

This case illustrates a drug error as a consequence of poor practice. If a completely new dated and signed prescription is required when a change in drug dose is made, the sequence of prescribing events can be clarified and errors reduced. At present there are no national guidelines for prescription writing in hospitals. The guidelines in the British National Formulary relate more to prescribing by general practitioners. The amount of training in writing clinical prescriptions given to medical students varies between medical schools. The amount of training in writing clinical prescriptions given to postgraduate doctors during their induction to a new appointment varies between hospitals, and hospitals have different local practices. Increasingly, hospital pharmacists are monitoring drug prescriptions and they are qualified to determine the clinical suitability of a prescribed medicine [27]. Experienced nursing staff should be encouraged to, and often do, question prescriptions if they have concerns. Ultimately, the legal responsibility for prescribing lies with the doctor who writes, or alters the prescription.

DECISION-MAKING & SURGERY

Recommendations

The decision to operate in complex cases can benefit from the formal involvement of others apart from the surgeon. Critical care specialists should be more directly involved.

Failure to diagnose acute appendicitis can still cause death in fit young adults. It is essential that experienced clinicians are available to ensure that cases are not missed.

Non-availability of a patient's previous notes at the time of an acute admission is a major administrative failure and should be exposed as such.

INTRODUCTION

This section focuses on the decision-making concerning the need for surgery and the timing of the operation. Clinical practice can vary considerably between individual anaesthetists and surgeons and many decisions about disease management cannot be made with mathematical precision. There are many factors that influence a clinician's judgement including knowledge, advice and support from colleagues and previous experience. The challenge of older, sicker patients undergoing increasingly complex surgery requires continuous review of routine practice in anaesthesia and surgery. Examining the management of cases such as those described here helps to identify where there is potential for improving current practice.

INVOLVEMENT OF THE CONSULTANT SURGEON

When deaths within the first three days of a surgical operation were last examined by NCEPOD in 1994/95 [3] it was reported that the consultant surgeon was involved in the decision-making prior to surgery in 88% (1201/1366) of cases. In this report, the figure has increased to 93% (1958 of the total operations of 2114). The working diagnosis was made by the consultant surgeon in 85% (1805/2114) of patients.

> **The number of cases in which the consultant surgeon is involved in the decision-making continues to increase and this involvement is now very high.**

For three out of four patients, their operation was either urgent or an emergency (1582/2114). This is a reflection of the fact that deaths within the first three days of their operation will be more frequent in patients admitted in these categories. Clearly, it is essential that consultants are involved in decision-making in these patients. It is therefore reassuring that, over the years, successive NCEPOD reports have shown a steady increase in consultant involvement in decision-making.

INVOLVEMENT OF OTHERS INCLUDING CRITICAL CARE PHYSICIANS IN THE DECISION TO OPERATE

Traditionally, the consultant surgeon has been solely responsible for taking decisions concerning the management of their patients. Whilst discussion may take place with the anaesthetist, whose views can influence the course of action, ultimately the surgeon decides, obtains the patient's consent and then the operation takes place. When, in the past, a successful outcome was primarily dependent on the quality of the surgery, the dedication of the nursing staff and the patient's own willpower, this approach was not questioned. However, as surgery has become more complex and the patients accepted for surgery are increasingly less fit, it is evident that the surgeon alone does not always have the ability to weigh up all the risks and benefits in the decision to operate. Critical care has become an essential adjunct to major surgery, both in the preparation of the patient and the immediate postoperative care. In many cases, it is now the quality of the critical care that determines the surgical outcome.

Modern critical care is highly interventional and is very often stressful for the patient. Decisions as to the appropriateness of its use for any individual require a high level of judgement. The required resource, ethical and other aspects of its use, place the clinician concerned in a vulnerable position. In many ways, it is easier for the surgeon to ignore these difficulties and to go ahead and operate, sending the patient to the intensive care unit after the operation and leaving the intensive care team to continue the management. If the consequence is a series of patients with a hopeless prognosis receiving major surgery with no prospect of a successful outcome, then it is clear that, as NCEPOD has recommended in the past, surgery is inappropriate. Optimism cannot be a substitute for realism.

Because NCEPOD only examines cases where the patient has died following surgery, it is not possible to cite examples of successful outcomes which were primarily the result of excellent critical care. However, within the cases examined there are examples where a more inclusive approach to decision-making would have been of value.

Case Study 20

An 80-year-old female was admitted directly from the surgical outpatients' clinic with a history of chronic constipation and lower abdominal pain. She was recorded as being extremely thin (38 kg) and cachectic in appearance; she was also anaemic (Hb 8.7 gm/dl). In the past, she had had two myocardial infarcts and continued to have unstable angina. A CT scan soon after admission showed features of extensive intra-peritoneal malignancy and dilated large bowel. After just over three weeks in hospital a decision was made to operate. The surgeon states that "although she was frail, she was otherwise reasonably well". Despite the apparent risks the family, "together with the patient, decided on the surgical option".

At operation, there was ascites and widespread metastases. A palliative transverse loop colostomy was performed. The anaesthetist notes "it was felt that once paralysed and ventilated it would be virtually impossible to get this patient off the ventilator, therefore a laryngeal mask was used and spontaneous ventilation". However following what was described as a gentle gas induction and 25 mcg of fentanyl, the blood pressure fell to 50/40 mm Hg. Towards the end of the operation the patient again became hypotensive and required inotropic support, which continued postoperatively. The patient continued to deteriorate and died 24 hours later in the HDU.

The surgeon's comment that the patient was frail but otherwise reasonably well would seem to indicate a limited understanding as to the significance of comorbidity on surgical outcome. Is not justifying of the decision to operate on the wish of the patient and family alone, an abrogation of professional responsibility? The undoubtedly difficult decision might have been better managed by wider professional involvement. If there was to have been even the remotest prospect of a successful outcome for the patient, then high quality critical care was going to be needed. A more formal part in the decision to operate should surely have come from critical care doctors together with the anaesthetist who might well have been able to have provided an objectivity that the surgeon and relatives clearly lacked. It is not enough to dismiss a case such as this as an inevitable death from inoperable carcinoma. If resources are to be used effectively and patients such as this are to die with dignity, then the decision to operate requires the most careful consideration and should include critical care doctors. In the three weeks between admission and operation there was plenty of time for this to have occurred.

> **In taking the decision to operate in complex cases, which will almost certainly require critical care and where there is a high probability of death, surgeons should directly involve critical care specialists in the decision to proceed. Their views may well assist in achieving a greater objectivity in these difficult circumstances. Local arrangements may need to be in place out of hours to achieve this.**

Case Study 21

At 07.00, an 88-year-old female was admitted to the A&E Department with a ruptured abdominal aortic aneurysm. She was in hypovolaemic shock with a blood pressure of 55/35 mm Hg and a heart rate of 110. A massive transfusion was started as she was prepared for theatre but the blood pressure remained low and she became increasingly acidotic (pH 7.26). In theatre there was little improvement on the application of the aortic clamp. A Dacron graft was sutured in place but the patient developed a coagulopathy with widespread bleeding. Eventually the abdomen was packed and the patient was transferred to the ICU at 13.15 where she died just over two hours later.

It is inevitable that in emergencies of this type events take on a momentum of their own; the patient had a good past medical history and age alone cannot of itself be a contradiction to surgery. But, it is not difficult with hindsight to see that the outcome was inevitable. On the decision to operate the surgeon states "I spoke to the son pre-op, who clearly indicated that he would wish his mother to have an operation, fully aware of the possible outcome". For assent to be of value, it needs to be informed. On what basis could the son have been able to make a decision in such exceptional circumstances? Involving relatives in discussion and keeping them informed is essential, but it must be very difficult to find oneself part of a real life drama and required to make decisions when one's only previous experience of such events may have been in fiction. However in criticising the surgeon, it must be recognised that there was probably weakness by the anaesthetists in not taking a more active part in these decisions.

A short pause before proceeding and an opinion from critical care doctors with their broader experience might, one would suggest, have been of more value than giving unrealistic deference to the assent of the son.

Case Study 22

A 77-year-old woman was admitted under the care of a consultant physician with nausea, vomiting and constipation. She was noted to have hepatomegaly. Four days later, her general condition deteriorated and a perforated viscus was suspected when air was seen under the diaphragm on the chest X-ray. A consultant general surgeon advised urgent laparotomy and the patient was taken immediately to theatre. She was assessed by an anaesthetic SHO who thought her to be in septic shock on the basis of tachycardia, hypotension and a low oxygen saturation. The consultant anaesthetist was called but by the time he/she arrived the patient was already in the operating theatre. The anaesthetist considered that death was inevitable but, when challenged, the surgeon declared that he was only the technician required to open the abdomen and that he would leave the decision-making to the anaesthetic team. The patient was so sick that the consultant anaesthetist asked another senior colleague for an opinion. Eventually the abdomen was opened and a perforated tumour of the sigmoid colon was found. There was faecal peritonitis and hepatic metastases. A Hartmann's procedure was carried out. At the end of the operation, the patient was transferred to ICU but died after a short time.

Communication between the surgeon and anaesthetist appears to have totally failed. Surgeons should not abdicate from decision-making and should not coerce colleagues into anaesthetising unfit patients. In addition, the operation note received by NCEPOD for this case was extremely poor, being both incomplete and illegible.

This case is a further example of the abrogation of responsibility and an ineffectual team approach in a patient where the outcome of surgery and consequent death was never in doubt. The practice adopted in some hospital of utilising a multidisciplinary team approach with a formal meeting and discussion of complex cases prior to operation in those patients where there is time for such consideration, may well be beneficial when decisions have to be taken in an acute situation. A greater understanding of what others can provide and achieve is an essential aspect of working as a team.

The ability to work in teams is becoming a cornerstone of modern medical practice. The decision to operate in these difficult circumstances therefore needs to be a team decision rather than that solely of the surgeon.

PROBLEMS WITH DIAGNOSIS

Patients admitted under the care of physicians

Physicians need to raise their awareness of surgical conditions existing or developing in patients under their care.

Initial admission into a medical bed under the care of physicians of patients who were subsequently shown to have a surgical problem did, on occasion, result in unreasonable delay in making a diagnosis of the surgical condition.

Case Study 23

An 81-year-old patient was admitted under the care of the physicians having, as is recorded in the admission note, "gone off legs". During three weeks on the medical ward the patient who was passing faeculent urine, gradually became septic. There was a mass in the left iliac fossa, which was thought to be due to diverticulitis. A CT scan was carried out but was not able to differentiate whether the mass was indeed due to diverticulitis or carcinoma. The patient subsequently had a perforation of the colon secondary to a carcinoma of the sigmoid.

Case Study 24

A 75-year-old was admitted under the care of the physicians with general deterioration. The next day an X-ray of the abdomen showed free gas under the diaphragm and the patient was taken to the theatre. The creatinine was raised prior to the operation and the patient was considered to be ASA 5. At operation, purulent peritonitis was found which was due to a perforated diverticular abscess. A Hartmann's operation was performed and the patient transferred to the ICU postoperatively, but died the following day.

These two cases show both a delay in diagnosing the surgical condition and a general absence of urgency in the management of the patient.

Case Study 25

A 79-year-old lady was admitted under the care of the physicians with abdominal pain and vomiting. Four days later an abdominal X-ray showed small bowel obstruction. At operation, a strangulated left femoral hernia was found and a small bowel resection performed. The patient was transferred to the HDU but subsequently died.

It is not uncommon for a patient to be unaware of the presence of a femoral hernia and if strangulation occurs, it may be misdiagnosed as gastroenteritis. However, the hernia is usually detectable on clinical examination by careful inspection and palpation. Clearly physicians, as well as surgeons, need to be aware of this so that this condition, which is eminently correctable, can be diagnosed and treated.

Case Study 26

A 75-year-old male was admitted under the care of the physicians with epigastric pain and uncontrolled atrial fibrillation. The blood tests for Wegener's granulomatosis were strongly positive and the patient was started on a high dose of steroids and cyclophosphamide. Eight days later the patient complained of increasing abdominal pain and distension. At subsequent laparotomy there was widespread peritonitis due to gangrenous small bowel caused by a volvulus.

The scenario of a patient in hospital labelled with a firm diagnosis, who then develops a second condition, is well recognised. This case emphasises the importance of acting appropriately and promptly, in this case seeking the opinion of the general surgeons, when clinical features develop which are at variance with the established diagnosis.

Case Study 27

A 70-year-old female with diabetes and Addison's disease was admitted to a medical ward with a history of falls and fatigue. She was treated for a chest infection. Attempts at mobilisation proved difficult as she complained of pain in the hip, but it was not until nine days later that a diagnosis of fractured neck of femur was made. A hemiarthroplasty was performed. There was a failure in the management of her diabetes, possibly because the drug chart was not sent when the patient was transferred. and it was recorded that shortly before death the blood glucose had decreased to 1.3 mmol/l.

The care of this patient both in the medical and surgical ward was unsatisfactory. Only by recognising inadequacies in cases such as these through open discussion at multidisciplinary audit will those involved understand their responsibility for what occurred. In all probability only the clinicians at NCEPOD are aware of the level of clinical inadequacy in this case.

Appendicectomy

Appendicitis can still result in death in otherwise fit young patients. Its diagnosis requires skill and experience. Hospitals should ensure that those seeing potential cases either have the requisite skills and experience or are adequately supported by those who do.

There were twelve deaths in patients with appendicitis, but what is perhaps more alarming is that two of these were in previously fit young men, and another was a child aged three.

Case study 28

A previously fit 21-year-old male was seen in the A&E Department by an SHO five days before his ultimate admission. He had peri-umbilical pain and vomiting. It is not clear exactly why, but he was thought to have a urinary tract infection and was catheterised. At that time his pulse was 90 per minute, WBC 12.6, temperature 38.6ºC and preliminary urine examination was normal. He was allowed home, but was re-admitted five days later moribund. He collapsed in the A&E Department, following vomiting, and had an asystolic cardiac arrest from which he was resuscitated and transferred to ICU. After ICU resuscitation he was taken to theatre where a gangrenous appendix and widespread peritonitis was found. An appendicectomy and lavage were performed but he died 24 hours later of ARDS.

Case study 29

A previously fit 22-year-old male was admitted with a seven-day history of abdominal pain associated with vomiting and diarrhoea. He had previously been thought to be suffering from gastroenteritis. His white count was 22,000. A working diagnosis of appendicitis with peritonitis was made. The patient was taken to theatre where a gangrenous appendix and pelvic abscess, with free pus throughout the abdomen, was found. Postoperatively he was sent back to the general ward and the next day had a sudden collapse and was transferred to the ICU where a diagnosis of septic shock was made. Despite full intensive care, on the following day he suffered a fatal cardiac arrest and died.

There is perhaps a tendency to look on appendicitis as a trivial condition, but these two cases show that it can cause death, even in previously fit young men. For these patients, it was the failure to make the diagnosis that resulted in delay. A patient presenting with abdominal pain, vomiting and pyrexia should not be sent home on the decision of an inexperienced SHO. In the second patient, the diagnosis was missed in primary care. Patients with appendicitis who develop a pelvic abscess can get symptoms very similar to a severe case of gastroenteritis and this needs to be more widely known both in general practice and among junior hospital staff.

In young children diagnosis can be even more difficult.

Case study 30

A previously fit three-year-old child was seen in the A&E Department of a district general hospital with a 24 hour history of pyrexia, vomiting and diarrhoea. The patient was obviously very unwell, being drowsy, floppy and breathless with a rapid pulse and a rigid abdomen. Transfer was arranged to a tertiary specialist paediatric unit. There was some delay in transfer and then there was no PICU bed immediately available. The patient was now dehydrated, in shock and acidotic. On arrival in the PICU, the patient was treated very actively with antibiotics, correction of the dehydration and acidosis. Increasing abdominal distension prompted drainage of the abdomen. When a peritoneal dialysis catheter was inserted, purulent fluid was washed out, but the patient was never made fit enough to have an operation. Despite inotropic support and antibiotics she became anuric and hyperkalaemic with increasing acidosis. Death followed asystolic arrest. At autopsy there was faecal peritonitis resulting from a perforated gangrenous appendix.

Other than the slight delay in transfer and in obtaining a PICU bed, it is difficult to know what more could have been done in this tragic case. Surgical trainees rarely see such severe cases but this acts as a reminder that small children can rapidly become desperately ill and indeed die as a result of appendicitis.

Vascular surgery

A leaking abdominal aortic aneurysm is a condition that may well be misdiagnosed. The consequences for the patient can be disastrous.

Case Study 31

A 78-year-old male was admitted with pain in the region of the left kidney but an intravenous pyelogram was normal. Three days later the patient collapsed and a diagnosis of ruptured AAA was made. The patient was taken to theatre but soon after clamping of the aorta, he suffered a cardiac arrest and died.

Attributing pain caused by a 'contained' leaking aneurysm to renal pathology is a common misdiagnosis. However, if the haemoglobin is low or an IVU has been performed and is normal, an aneurysm should be considered.

Case Study 32

An 85-year-old female was admitted as an emergency and was initially thought to have diverticular disease. In fact, the diagnosis of a leaking AAA was considered but no investigations were carried out. When the patient collapsed about twelve hours after admission she was immediately taken to theatre, but at operation a high neck was found and the aneurysm was considered to be inoperable.

An ultrasound scan is a simple way of aiding diagnosis, although a CT scan is to be preferred in showing whether or not there has actually been a leak. It also gives greater detail of the anatomy of the aneurysm.

Case Study 33

A 77-year-old male was admitted with pain in the right iliac fossa. The abdomen was slightly tender and rectal examination showed faecal loading. The House Officer diagnosed faecal impaction. Three hours later the patient collapsed and the true diagnosis of ruptured abdominal aneurysm was apparent.

Having the advantage of hindsight, it is important to recognise that such situations will always occur. However, early review of acute admissions by a more senior surgeon who might well be more suspicious and arrange for further investigation would undoubtedly be beneficial.

Investigations

The appropriate investigation can save a patient an unnecessary operation by enabling the correct diagnosis to be made.

Case Study 34

A patient who was on low molecular weight heparin (Clexane 80 mg) and aspirin 75 mg, was admitted with pain in the left iliac fossa and collapse. The patient was thought to have a left iliac aneurysm. A laparotomy was performed when, in fact, a spontaneous retroperitoneal haematoma was found but no evidence of an aneurysm.

Spontaneous retroperitoneal haematoma should be suspected in a patient receiving anticoagulants. More investigation, in conjunction with the resuscitation, might have avoided an operation and thereby could have given the patient a better chance of survival.

Case Study 35

A 62-year-old male had an ultrasound scan which showed a mass in the left kidney. An abdominal CT scan was subsequently performed and neither scan showed signs of spread so a nephrectomy was performed. The patient subsequently died and an autopsy showed multiple pulmonary metastases.

Careful examination of a chest X-ray might have prevented a fruitless operation.

Medical records

The failure to have available medical notes at a subsequent admission can compromise care and be directly detrimental to patient management. It is indicative of sub-standard care and should be audited as such.

NCEPOD has over many years criticised various failures in relation to the availability and maintaining of patients' medical records. This is not just an administrative problem. The following cases demonstrate that the lack of medical records or X-rays compromises the patient's management.

Case Study 36

This patient was admitted with a ruptured abdominal aortic aneurysm. In the absence of the medical records, which were missing, the clinicians involved were unaware that the patient had a carcinoma of the lung and a poor prognosis.

Had the notes been available the patient would not, in all probability, have been subjected to such an extensive operation as the repair of an aortic aneurysm.

Case Study 37

Following investigation with a barium enema and flexible sigmoidoscopy, a carcinoma of the sigmoid colon with complete obstruction was diagnosed. Two weeks later the patient was admitted with lower abdominal pain and constipation. The previous notes and X-rays were not available nor was the patient clear about his condition. The surgical team caring for the patient on this occasion was therefore unaware of the diagnosis and no operation was performed. A few days later when the patient perforated a viscus he was taken to the operating theatre but the clinicians had still not seen the original notes or X-rays.

An earlier operation would almost certainly have been performed if the notes and X-rays had been available and the outcome for the patient might have been very different.

Case Study 38

A 73-year-old lady underwent a mastectomy. 16 months prior to her admission she had had a myocardial infarction. She had also had two other admissions to the ICU with pulmonary oedema. In the absence of the medical notes the surgeons and anaesthetists were unaware of the severity of her condition. She died postoperatively as a result of left ventricular failure.

Pressures not to delay operations or extend the patient's stay in hospital can all too easily result in a decision to proceed even when there are fundamental failures in the organisation of patient care. The availability of a patient's medical records is essential.

TIMING OF OPERATION AND PREOPERATIVE PREPARATION

It is essential that all involved in the care of acutely sick patients who require urgent or emergency surgery should understand the appropriate balance between the need to get the patient to the operating theatre and the need to ensure proper resuscitation and investigation. Unnecessary delay is not acceptable. Good teamwork and mutual understanding is required between all those involved.

Case Study 39

A 78-year-old female was admitted to hospital at 02.00 with pain in the lower abdomen and signs of generalised peritonitis. She was cold, clammy and in shock. A diagnosis of a perforated viscus and peritonitis with septic shock was made. Intravenous fluids and antibiotics were given and the patient was taken to theatre at 04.00. Here, generalised peritonitis was found to be the result of a perforated appendix. Appendicectomy and peritoneal washout were performed. Postoperatively the patient was transferred to ICU, but despite all supportive care died of septic shock 48 hours later. During the operation the patient passed only 34 mls of urine.

The low urine output suggests that what preoperative resuscitation was given, was inadequate. Would it have been preferable if this patient had been admitted to ICU or HDU prior to the operation for rapid resuscitation and establishing adequate urine flow, prior to being taken to theatre?

> **A balance is required between the need to get an acutely sick surgical patient to the operating theatre and the need to ensure proper resuscitation and investigation. For this to be achieved, planning, co-operation and teamwork between all those involved are essential.**

Case Study 40

A 49-year-old male was admitted to a DGH under the care of the general physicians. He had a four-day history of a flu-like illness and increasing difficulty breathing. On admission there was neck swelling and trismus, he had bad teeth and a pyrexia. Intravenous antibiotics were administered, together with nebulised adrenaline. A decision was made to transfer him to the specialist maxillofacial hospital, but transfer did not occur for almost six hours. A staff grade surgeon was called in to see him at the maxillofacial hospital and diagnosed Ludwig's angina. The patient was transferred immediately to theatre for a tracheostomy. Fibreoptic intubation failed, as did an attempt at jet insufflation through a cricothyrotomy. An emergency tracheostomy was performed under local anaesthesia but the patient suffered a respiratory arrest and died.

Ludwig's angina is a surgical emergency requiring rapid surgical decompression and establishment of a definitive airway. One can only sympathise with the clinicians that had ultimately to manage this most difficult case. The six hour delay in transfer can only have added to their difficulties.

POSTOPERATIVE CARE

Recommendations

Postoperative problems are common. It is essential that doctors who care for surgical patients should be trained in the management of these problems.

If a medical team is involved in a patient's perioperative care it should also be involved in any morbidity/mortality review of the case and receive a copy of the discharge summary and, where applicable, the autopsy report.

The maintenance of accurate fluid balance charts by nursing staff is vital; medical staff should review these daily.

INTRODUCTION

This section of the report will examine postoperative ward care. Most patients can anticipate an uncomplicated recovery after their operation. The patients in this sample are amongst the most seriously ill and are vulnerable to complications, so they require meticulous medical and nursing care. Data returned to NCEPOD shows that some patients do suffer from oversight, errors of diagnosis and poor clinical judgement during their ward care. Throughout this section there are examples where there was evidence of a lack of teamwork between nursing, surgical, medical and critical care staff. NCEPOD does not undertake in-depth case review, so cannot determine whether sub-standard ward care arises from failures by individuals or systems, e.g. too few staff, staff who are poorly trained or inadequate supervision of inexperienced staff. Whatever the

cause, it cannot be assumed that the types of errors

described here are confined to those patients who

die. Mistakes in care lead to increased morbidity,

distress for patients and their relatives, longer

hospital stay and increased health

economy costs.

RECORD KEEPING

> **Medical record keeping is sometimes of a poor standard and needs to be improved. Poor medical records compromise clinical care.**

The documents submitted to NCEPOD for this report show that, whilst some record keeping is exemplary, poor medical notes are not uncommon.

Case Study 41

A 76-year-old, ASA 3 female without recognised co-existing medical disorders had a mastectomy and axillary clearance. Three days later she collapsed with diarrhoea, hypotension and hypoxia. There were no entries in the medical notes between her clerking on admission and this collapse, at which time the entry was "low BP all the time after mastectomy". By this time the patient was in fast atrial fibrillation, dehydrated and in renal failure. Despite aggressive resuscitation she died later that day. The autopsy reported cardiac failure due to left ventricular hypertrophy and atrial fibrillation.

Case Study 42

An 83-year-old, ASA 2 female with pre-existing renal impairment fractured her hip and underwent a hemiarthroplasty. Her blood pressure was low, both in theatre and in recovery, and transfer to a HDU might have been advisable. But after 1 hour 40 minutes in recovery she was returned to the ward at 18.25. There were no entries in the medical notes until 03.50, three days later. At this time she was found unresponsive, cold and clammy and the duty house officer was called. Blood tests showed her creatinine had risen from a preoperative value of 242 micromol/l to 457 micromol/l and her serum potassium was 6.8 mmol/l. She died two hours later.

Why were there no records of these patients' postoperative progress before their death? Had there really been no review of their condition for three days? Had no one noticed that they had been deteriorating?

Poor medical records are not acceptable. The General Medical Council states [28] *"…you must: keep clear, accurate, legible and contemporaneous patient records which report the relevant clinical findings, the decisions made, the information given to patients and any drugs or other treatment prescribed"*. The Clinical Negligence Scheme for Trusts [29] devotes one of its ten general standards, Standard 6, to Health Records. In the 2001 NCEPOD report [2] the result of a small survey of notes using the CRABEL scoring system [30], a tool for auditing medical records, was presented and this highlighted a wide variability in their quality. These findings were similar to those of the Audit Commission [31].

Poor medical records can compromise medical care, especially now that there is less continuity of care with the introduction of trainee doctors working partial and full shifts. They also expose the hospital to an increased risk if there is litigation. There is an implication that when there is no entry in the notes no one has actually seen the patient, and for almost all the patients in this sample their medical condition was such that a formal daily review was indicated. From the evidence of notes submitted to NCEPOD it is also likely that some consultants do not review what their trainees write, and therefore the extent of their involvement in the supervision of trainees, and in the care of sick patients, must be questioned. Regular departmental audit of medical notes, perhaps using a scoring system such as CRABEL, is required by CNST; this ought to result in improved record keeping.

NURSING CARE

NCEPOD has commented before about failures in nursing observations, in particular the low priority given to accurate recording of fluid balance [26]. Inadequate charting of observations was also noted in this sample.

Case Study 43

A 76-year-old, ASA 3 female with COPD was admitted with a fractured neck of the femur. The following day she had a hemiarthroplasty and at 13.20, one hour after returning to the ward, she was noted to have a blood pressure of 90/50 mmHg and a pulse of 120 beats/min. There was no medical intervention and all observations were discontinued at 23.00. At 06.00 the following morning the patient herself told the staff that she had not passed urine since admission. At 07.30 she complained of feeling faint and her blood pressure was 55/45 mmHg. An echocardiogram revealed right ventricular dilatation with poor contractility. CT scanning excluded pulmonary embolus. She died later that day.

Case Study 44

An 86-year-old, ASA 3 female with COPD, IHD, CCF and renal impairment was admitted with a fractured neck of femur. Her preoperative serum creatinine was 422 micromol/l. She had a dynamic hip screw inserted under spinal anaesthesia at 17.00 on the day of admission. No fluid balance charts were kept before or after the operation. At 07.30 on the second postoperative day (36 hours after surgery) it was noticed that the patient had been anuric since her operation. She died the following day in acute on chronic renal failure with pulmonary oedema.

Case Study 45

An 84-year-old, ASA 3 female with long-standing bronchiectasis and hypertension was admitted with a fractured neck of femur. On arrival in the anaesthetic room, whilst breathing air, her oxygen saturation was 70% and she was returned to the ward for treatment of a chest infection. She had her operation, a dynamic hip screw, four days later. Throughout this prolonged preoperative period there were repeated entries on her fluid charts of "wet bed +++" and no estimation of fluid balance. A urinary catheter was finally inserted in the operating theatre.

From the information available NCEPOD cannot identify the cause of such failures and so it can only raise questions:

- Is there always sufficient nursing staff on the ward to care for the number of patients and their level of nursing dependency?

- Is there sometimes too much reliance placed on support workers to record and communicate observations?

- From the evidence of the first case, is there a particular problem during the night?

- It may be that there has been a medical instruction to discontinue observations. If so, should this be recorded in the nursing notes? Nursing notes are not currently requested by NCEPOD.

From records submitted to NCEPOD it is clear that the nursing staff need to audit their observations and fluid balance charts on a regular basis to confirm the monitoring is appropriate to the clinical condition of the patient. Nurses must also alert medical staff when observations indicate impending or actual problems.

SURGICAL CARE

Bleeding, hypotension and oliguria, either together or separately are common postoperative problems. The causes of hypotension and oliguria may be complex and include fluid loss, cardiac failure, renal failure and the effect of epidural or spinal analgesia.

Bleeding

Case Study 46

A 44-year-old female was admitted with ascites and subacute small bowel obstruction. She had a complicated medical history that included myelofibrosis and essential thrombocytopenia, a CVA, several TIAs, portal vein thrombosis, liver and renal impairment and colitis. Her tests of clotting function were normal preoperatively. The obstruction failed to resolve and she underwent a laparotomy, at which a section of fibrotic distal small bowel was resected and an ileo-transverse anastomosis performed. General anaesthesia included CVP and arterial pressure monitoring. The patient returned to, what was described as, a HDU on a surgical ward at 15.00. At 21.00 the surgical SHO on-call was asked to review her because her pulse rate had increased to 120 beats/min and she had had minimal urine output for three hours. The SHO noted a positive fluid balance of 1500 ml, but made no comment on the CVP, and further IV fluids were prescribed. By 22.30 the patient's pulse rate had increased to 140 beats/min, her blood pressure was 100/60 mmHg and it was apparent that she had suffered a further CVA. It is not clear when a blood test was taken, but it was only at 01.30 that night, when the haemoglobin was found to be 3.1 gm/dl, that a diagnosis of bleeding was considered. A second laparotomy at 03.00 confirmed blood loss into the abdomen. The patient died later that day.

Case Study 47

An 87-year-old female had a cholecystojejunostomy to relieve jaundice caused by a carcinoma of the head of the pancreas. She was otherwise fit. At 04.00 on the second postoperative night the urine output decreased, but this was not reported to the on-call doctor until 07.00, by which time it had been 4 ml/hour for two hours. No action was taken. The SpR ward round took place at 09.00, at which time the patient showed clear signs of hypovolaemic shock. Blood results showed a haemoglobin level of 3.7 gm/dl; there was evidence of a coagulopathy and the patient died that evening.

In these cases, there was a failure to interpret the observations and clinical findings compounded by a lack of action to correct the situation.

Hypotension

Case Study 48

An 86-year-old male required a proximal femoral nail for a complex intertrochanteric fracture of the femoral neck. He was known to have angina and treated hypertension. In the recovery ward at 16.00 he had a pulse of 120 beats/min and 500 ml of Gelofusine was administered and he was returned to the general ward. At 23.00 the pulse was still raised at 125 beats/mim and the blood pressure was 88/60 mmHg. The surgical SHO on-call noted these findings, and the history of hypertension, but only advised to continue the IV infusion and "…call if required". The patient suffered a fatal cardiac arrest at 04.00 the following morning.

Case Study 49

A 79-year-old female with a fractured neck of femur had a cemented Thompson's hemiarthroplasty. She had a history of ischaemic heart disease and angina. The preoperative haemoglobin was 10.7 gm/dl. The operation took two hours, blood loss was not recorded and no blood was given. A blood test was ordered on the first postoperative day but not reviewed until the morning of the second day, at which time the haemoglobin was found to have been 6.5 gm/dl. By this time, the blood pressure was 75/45 mmHg (her normal BP was 140/70 mmHg). She was prescribed two units of blood that day and a further two units to be given the following day, but she suffered a fatal cardiac arrest at 15.00.

The risks of hypotension and anaemia in these patients with cardiac disease appeared to be poorly recognised.

Oliguria

Case Study 50

A 91-year-old, ASA 3 female underwent open reduction and internal fixation of a fractured ankle on the day of her admission. Her preoperative serum creatinine was 178 micromol/l and urea 16.4 mmol/l. Postoperatively she was oliguric and on the second postoperative day her IV fluid input was 4125 ml and urine output 538 ml. In the early hours of the morning on the third postoperative day she became acutely *distressed and wheezy, by which time she had amassed a cumulative positive fluid balance of 9.5 litres. She was started on a frusemide infusion at that time, but died one hour later.*

Case Study 51

An 89-year-old, 50 kg, generally fit female underwent a transabdominal nephrectomy for carcinoma. The operation was under combined general and epidural anaesthesia and was uneventful. The fluid charts were well completed clearly showing intravenous fluids of 3000 ml to 4000 ml per day and urine outputs between 1000 ml and 1200 ml per day so that by 02.00 on the third postoperative day she was in a total postoperative positive fluid balance of 8.5 litres. At that time she became agitated, wheezy and short of breath, and she suffered a fatal cardiac arrest one hour later. An autopsy confirmed severe pulmonary oedema. The surgical questionnaire was not returned.

The risk of pulmonary oedema developing in these patients was predictable. How closely were the nursing and medical staff monitoring the fluid balance?

The maintenance of accurate fluid balance charts by nursing staff is vital; medical staff should review these daily.

In all these cases, there was evidence that complications were developing well in advance of the ultimate critical event. There were failures by the doctors in training to anticipate complications and monitor the patient's progress, and delays in treatment. When a doctor is called to assess a postoperative complication, the management of it involves a full review of the patient, a presumptive diagnosis, preliminary treatment, subsequent re-appraisal for the effect of treatment and modification of therapy if necessary. This process may also involve consulting with a more senior, experienced doctor. It is clear from the questionnaires and photocopies of medical notes submitted to NCEPOD that such a basic model of medical care is not being followed in all cases. The Royal College of Surgeons stipulates that surgical training posts should provide training in postoperative care [32]. Postoperative complications and their management should be part of the core teaching programme.

Commonly, problems arose from a failure by the doctor in training to appreciate the patient's individual risk factors. Sometimes there was apparently poor recognition that different types of operations require different postoperative fluid strategies. Often there was a failure to recognise that those with certain comorbidities, for example cardiac, vascular or renal disease, are intolerant of even moderate hypovolaemia, anaemia or fluid overload.

Of note, most of these patients were deteriorating overnight and were being assessed by SHO surgeons. The decision-making in these cases is questioned. All doctors in training are supervised by their consultants and, in particular, SHOs have access to more senior advice - their SpR or consultant - regardless of the time of day. Doctors in training have a duty to recognise the limits of their experience and, in the interests of their patients, must not hesitate to seek advice from a more experienced colleague when it is indicated, regardless of the time of day [33]. The consultant is responsible for supervising doctors in training and must make himself/herself aware of their actions.

OUTREACH CARE

> **The benefits of critical care outreach teams still appear to be poorly recognised.**

> **Guidelines to determine which patients should be referred to a critical care team should be developed locally and subsequently validated.**

Many hospitals now have critical care outreach teams. The data received by NCEPOD suggests that the benefits of these teams is not universally recognised and often, when they are involved, it is not at an appropriately early time.

Case Study 52

A 76-year-old female underwent a laparotomy to drain 300 ml of pus from around the gall bladder. She was recognised as "sick" but no ICU or HDU bed was available, so she returned to the ward postoperatively. The clinical notes and observations showed obvious signs of further deterioration, but no assistance was sought from more senior staff or from the critical care physicians until she suffered a cardiac arrest 36 hours after the operation.

Case Study 53

A 61-year-old male was admitted with abdominal pain and rectal bleeding. He had a history of hypertension and his blood pressure was 170/100 mmHg. An intravenous infusion was started. The preregistration HO on call reviewed him during the night and noted a respiratory rate of 40 breaths/min, blood pressure 100/50 mmHg and pulse rate 150 beats/min. Blood gas analysis revealed a $PaCO_2$ of 2.94 kPa and base excess of -9 mmol/l. The HO did not appreciate the significance of these findings, nor did he/she discuss them with someone more senior, so appropriate treatment was not instituted. When the patient was reviewed next morning the gravity of the situation was obvious. The patient was referred to the critical care team and, after resuscitation, he underwent a laparotomy for resection of ischaemic bowel.

Case Study 54

An 87-year-old female presented with a carcinoma of the rectum. She was in atrial fibrillation, her chest X-ray showed cardiomegaly and her preoperative BP was 140/80 mmHg. She underwent an anterior resection under combined general and epidural anaesthesia; no invasive monitoring was used. After two hours in the recovery area she returned to the general ward with an epidural infusion running and instructions on the action to be taken if the urine output decreased. At 01.00 a surgical SHO reviewed her when her blood pressure was 53/37 mmHg and pulse was 112 beats/ min. The SHO gave a fluid challenge, after which the BP increased to 80/60 mmHg, and then prescribed two units of blood to be given over four hours. The systolic pressure remained between 55 and 75 mmHg throughout the remainder of the night, but the SHO was not called until 06.00 when the urine output had ceased. A further fluid challenge was given but the patient was not referred to the critical care outreach team until 10.00, when blood gas analysis revealed a base excess of -13.0 mmol/l. She was transferred to the HDU and died two days later.

These cases illustrate the need for timely review by a critical care outreach team. The report of 2001 [2] recommended that guidelines to determine which patients should be referred to a critical care team should be developed locally and subsequently validated. Such guidelines need to be explicit and understood by both the medical and nursing staff on the ward.

MEDICAL CARE

> **Medical staffing should be organised so that staff of appropriate seniority are available when a medical opinion is requested.**

Postoperative surgical patients with acute or complex medical problems often benefit from shared care between surgeons and physicians. In some cases an appropriate medical review can be invaluable, but the following are examples of how problems can arise.

Case Study 55

An 80-year-old male with COPD underwent sigmoid colectomy. Six days after the operation he became acutely unwell with shortness of breath and tachycardia, and was referred by the surgical team for a medical opinion. At 18.00 he was reviewed by a medical SHO who diagnosed a pulmonary embolus and prescribed enoxaparin and frusemide. By 19.30 the patient's condition had worsened and he was transferred to the ICU. A medical SpR reviewed him at 22.30 and suggested myocardial infarction as an alternative diagnosis to pulmonary embolism. However by 02.00 that night, the patient's condition deteriorated such that he required intermittent positive pressure ventilation to the lungs. Data acquired from a pulmonary artery catheter strongly suggested systemic sepsis. A laparotomy later that day revealed an anastamotic leak and widespread peritonitis.

Case Study 56

An 88-year-old, 40 kg female was admitted with a fractured neck of femur. She had a history of cardiac failure and atrial fibrillation. On admission she had hypokalaemia that was corrected with intravenous potassium in six litres of 0.9% sodium chloride over two days. On the third day after admission she received an Austin Moore femoral prosthesis under spinal anaesthesia and returned to the ward at 17.30. At 23.00 she developed hypoxia, tachycardia and hypotension. A medical SpR reviewed her, mistakenly made a diagnosis of pneumonia and started antibiotics. 36 hours later the medical team reviewed her again when she became extremely short of breath with a pulse rate of 140 beats/min, but she suffered a cardiac arrest shortly after. An autopsy found no signs of pneumonia but did show signs of cardiac failure.

Case Study 57

A 76-year-old male had a femoro-popliteal arterial bypass graft under combined spinal and general anaesthesia. He had a history of type 2 diabetes mellitus, hypertension and hypercholesterolaemia. On the second postoperative night, 36 hours after the operation, he complained of chest pain of two hours duration. The surgical HO reviewed him at 01.45. The patient was sweaty, tachycardic, hypotensive and had signs of left ventricular failure. The ECG showed changes of myocardial ischaemia. The surgical HO organised some blood tests that showed a haemoglobin of 9.0 gm/dl and at 02.20 discussed the case on the telephone with a medical SHO. The medical SHO thought the patient might be in supraventricular tachycardia and advised adenosine. At 03.40 the adenosine had been tried without effect. At 04.30 there was further discussion with the medical SHO who suggested amiodarone, and it was agreed to transfuse two units of blood, but not until daylight. At 05.35 the patient developed frank heart failure that was rapidly followed by cardiogenic shock and despite treatment he died at 12.55.

Case Study 58

An 85-year-old, 50 kg male had a gastroenterostomy to relieve gastric obstruction caused by a malignant ulcer. He suffered from type 2 diabetes mellitus, hypertension and mild angina. He was reviewed on the second postoperative day because of a poor urine output, moderate hypotension and arterial blood gas analysis revealed a PaO_2 of 5.2 kPa and base excess of -7.6 mmol/l. He had a cumulative positive fluid balance of six litres since the operation. A medical SpR reviewed him and noted that his JVP was raised to the earlobes and he had a right basal pleural effusion. The ECG showed that his heart rhythm had changed from sinus to atrial fibrillation, and there was ST segment depression in leads V5 and V6. The medical SpR was of the opinion that a cardiorespiratory cause for the patient's deterioration was unlikely, but that he might have suffered an intra-abdominal event. A laparotomy was performed later that day at which no new intra-abdominal pathology was found. The patient died the following day. An autopsy showed extensive ischaemic heart disease and signs of a recent myocardial infarct.

These case studies illustrate the difficulties of making a diagnosis in complex postoperative surgical cases, and it must be accepted that the correct one is often more obvious with the benefit of hindsight. However, they also illustrate the need for a clear process for referral of patients from the surgical to the medical team. It is inappropriate for the referral and review of a critically ill patient to be at SHO level or lower, and in such a situation, telephone advice without examining the patient is unacceptable. Ideally an experienced surgical SpR or consultant should review the patient before referral in order to exclude surgical problems; the case certainly should be discussed with one of them. Once referred, a medical consultant or SpR ≥year 3, preferably with experience in postoperative complications, should review the patient. Whenever possible the review should be made jointly by the specialties so that the case can be fully discussed. The medical team should receive feedback on the outcome of those patients whom they have reviewed, notification of any autopsy date, an autopsy report or discharge summary and be involved in the mortality/morbidity review process.

Recommendations

Where perioperative complications contribute to the cause of death, these should be recorded on the death certificate.

Complications may arise following endoscopic surgery. Protocols should be available to deal with these and remedial actions should be rehearsed and involve senior experienced clinicians.

COMPLICATIONS

INTRODUCTION

The incidence and nature of perioperative complications are directly related to the preoperative condition of the patient and the magnitude of the surgery. Careful preoperative preparation can help to reduce these complications. Surgical judgement, operative expertise and intra-operative decision-making, the nature of the disease and the site of surgery will all influence the complications that are specific to a procedure. In addition, many complications are the result of comorbidities and can be anticipated and thus treated early should they occur.

It could be expected that the incidence of postoperative complications would be highest for emergency procedures. Whatever the type of surgery, the incidence of all complications can be minimised with good perioperative care; it is often worthwhile spending some time to stabilise and improve the patient's condition if time allows. It is a matter of judgement as to how long should be spent optimising a patient's physiology (see chapter 3). Complications specific to a particular operation are reduced as a result of careful surgical technique, experience and awareness of the possible problems. However, when reviewing the deaths occurring after anaesthesia and surgery, there are frequent examples of complications that might have been prevented or detected and treated earlier, possibly with a different outcome. So, why do complications get overlooked?

One of the more frequent unforeseen complications was intra-operative haemorrhage, which occurred in 4% of this sample. We demonstrate examples across the surgical specialties, where better preoperative assessment and treatment planning, more experienced operators and better inter-disciplinary team working might have prevented problems. When operations go wrong, they are seldom cited as contributory factors on the death certificate (see chapter 7).

SURGICAL JUDGEMENT

Decision-making in surgery is not an exact science and is influenced by training, previous experience, knowledge, the individual patient's circumstances and the physical and psychological health of the surgeon [34]. On occasions, the decisions will be questionable but difficult to analyse. Some such decisions are illustrated by the case histories given below.

> **Careful patient selection (where possible), preoperative preparation and anticipation can avoid or diminish postoperative complications.**

Case Study 59

A 67-year-old female suffered a ruptured abdominal aortic aneurysm. The surgeon was not aware of the fact that there was known, marked renal impairment. A long and complex emergency operation involved a repair of the aneurysm plus repair of a renal artery aneurysm. Twelve hours after surgery there was evidence of intra-abdominal bleeding and a decision was made to re-operate. At this point, the family informed the surgeon that the patient's quality of life had been extremely poor and that she was housebound. After further discussion, and with the family's agreement, the second operation was cancelled. Resuscitative measures including correction of clotting defects continued but the patient died approximately 24 hours after the initial surgery.

Would the initial operation have taken place if the surgeon had been aware of the patient's past medical and social history? In the event, surgery did proceed but was it wise to prolong emergency surgery with the additional procedure to repair a renal artery aneurysm?

Case Study 60

A 75-year-old male presented with a ruptured abdominal aortic aneurysm. He was a heavy smoker with a known history of ischaemic heart disease. Two irreducible inguinal hernias were also noted. An emergency repair of the abdominal aortic aneurysm was done. Bilateral inguinal hernia repairs were also done. The patient suffered a massive myocardial infarction and died the same day. No autopsy was done. Neither the surgeon nor the anaesthetist returned the requested operation notes and charts.

The decision to repair the hernias in this emergency situation seems questionable but the clinicians involved have not provided the requisite information to allow in-depth analysis of their management of this case.

INTRA-OPERATIVE COMPLICATIONS

There were a total of 411/2114 (19%) cases in which unanticipated intra-operative complications occurred. This is an improvement on the 25% reported by NCEPOD in 1994/95.

Haemorrhage

> **Intra-operative haemorrhage was an unforeseen complication in 4% of operations.**

There were 83 cases in which unanticipated problems arose due to intra-operative haemorrhage (Table 6.1). In 42 cases operative haemorrhage was cited as contributing to death. However, in only 17 cases could operative haemorrhage be identified as a contributory factor from the transcript of the death certificate.

Table 6.1	Intra-operative haemorrhage by specialty
General	16
General (Vascular)	4
General (GI)	13
General (Colorectal)	6
General (Other)	2
Cardiothoracic	11
Vascular	11
Neurosurgery	5
Orthopaedic	5
Otolaryngology	3
Gynaecology	3
Urology	2
Oral & Maxillofacial	1
Paediatric	1

Consultants performed 73 of these cases and in only six cases was a consultant not present in theatre.

Case Study 61

A SpR1 with only 10 month's experience took an 88-year-old male, with a bleeding nasal melanoma, to theatre. A general anaesthetic was administered by a consultant anaesthetist, who stated "I did not think the surgeon had sufficient experience to achieve anything worthwhile with regard to haemorrhage control".

Haemorrhage could not be controlled and the patient succumbed to airway obstruction. The death certificate recorded I (a) Upper airway obstruction, I (b) Melanoma of nose (operated), II IHD. No mention was made of massive operative haemorrhage causing the acute airway obstruction.

An experienced surgeon should have been able to firstly control the haemorrhage and secondly to prevent airway obstruction, if necessary by utilising a definitive surgical airway.

Case Study 62

A 77-year-old male underwent a neck dissection and partial glossectomy, despite having neither a preoperative MRI nor CT scan. The patient was not discussed in a multidisciplinary team. At surgery the tumour was found to have invaded the carotid artery, and bleeding could not be controlled. The patient died of hypovolaemic shock. The death certificate recorded I (a) DIC, I (b) Malignancy; it failed to mention the operation, despite an autopsy which confirmed extensive haemorrhage in the neck.

Proper preoperative assessment might have indicated other methods of palliation as being preferable to a fatal operation. Experienced head and neck or vascular surgeons can usually control intra-operative carotid bleeding.

Case Study 63

An 81-year-old female with multiple trauma was admitted to a general surgery ward in a hospital with no ICU beds. The patient was taken to theatre for closed reduction of fractures of radius, ulna and humerus together with debridement and suturing of leg lacerations under general anaesthesia. No preoperative chest radiograph was taken. The patient was initially returned to a general surgery ward, but subsequently transferred to ICU in another hospital where she died of respiratory failure the same day. Fractured ribs and a haemopneumothorax were eventually diagnosed.

Should patients with multiple trauma be admitted and operated upon in hospitals that do not have sufficient orthopaedic beds or any ICU beds? Basic "ABC" principles of assessing and managing trauma should be adhered to, in hospitals that have adequate multidisciplinary facilities and expertise.

A 63-year-old male presented with massive recurrence of a previously operated and irradiated oral squamous cell carcinoma. The patient had not been considered by a multidisciplinary team. A palliative resection was undertaken and massive intra-operative haemorrhage encountered. A free latissimus dorsi flap was used to reconstruct the defect, but postoperatively the flap failed. The patient was returned to theatre and attempts to achieve flap revascularisation included infusion of streptokinase. The attempted salvage procedure took 11 hours and the patient died 12 hours later. Cause of death was recorded as a CVA. No mention of surgery was made on the death certificate.

Careful multidisciplinary planning is required for this type of patient. Heroic surgery is not always in the best interests of the patient, and skilful judgement is required in deciding when to stop operating particularly if unforeseen complications arise. Was the use of streptokinase advisable in a patient who had recently had massive haemorrhage, coagulopathy and transfusion?

A 70-year-old male underwent anterior decompression and posterior spinal fusion for an infected lumbar discitis. The patient was ASA 4 and had recently suffered from hepatic encephalopathy and bleeding peptic ulceration. The consultant had only performed one similar procedure in the previous 12 months. Despite blood loss of over 4 L during the posterior approach, the procedure was continued and bleeding from damage to the iliac vein could not be controlled. The procedure lasted over 6 1/2 hours and the patient died of uncontrollable hypovolaemia later that evening. The death certificate in this case accurately recorded blood loss following surgery.

Only surgeons who are able to maintain sufficient levels of expertise should perform this type of surgery. Where damage to major vessels might be anticipated, surgery should be planned with the co-operation of a vascular surgeon.

A 67-year-old female underwent bilateral oophorectomy, total abdominal hysterectomy, sigmoid colectomy and omentectomy for ovarian malignancy. Surgery was performed by a consultant gynaecologist.

During surgery the bowel was perforated and the splenic capsule torn. The patient died of multi-organ failure secondary to haemorrhage. The death certificate recorded the cause of death as I (a) Multi-organ failure and I (b) Ovarian cancer. Neither surgery nor haemorrhage were mentioned as causes of death.

The cases above are drawn from most of the surgical specialties. Intra-operative bleeding can be a frightening complication. The causes are multifactorial, and often start with poor decision-making or treatment planning. Lack of experience also appears to be a common theme coupled with a reluctance to involve more experienced colleagues.

The failure to mention the complication of haemorrhage as a contributory cause of death on death certificates is of concern. Does this reflect a culture of denial, or a feeling of guilt or failure on the part of the clinician? Surely we must recognise that openness is a vital element in the learning process, and we must acknowledge that intra-operative bleeding is often only the final chapter in a flawed system of care.

DELAY DUE TO LACK OF EQUIPMENT

The commonest causes of delays to operation remain lack of theatre space, theatre personnel or critical care facilities. However, we noted a new trend in reporting delay due to lack of equipment in this year's sample.

There were six orthopaedic cases where delays occurred because of lack of appropriate equipment. In four cases, appropriate prostheses were unavailable because of poor stock control and, in two cases, no sterile instruments were available. Two cases were elective joint replacements where a lack of preoperative co-ordination appeared to have occurred, and the remaining four cases were trauma patients.

Case Study 67

An 80-year-old female with a comminuted supracondylar fracture of the femur, waited seven days before surgery because the equipment to perform a closed retrograde intramedullary nail was not available and had to be obtained from the manufacturer. The patient suffered a cardiac arrest on the table and a coroner's autopsy determined the cause of death as pulmonary embolus, despite appropriate anti-thromboembolic prophylaxis having been undertaken.

Hospitals that accept trauma patients must have sufficient stocks of equipment available on-site to prevent unnecessary delays occurring. There should be standardisation of theatre equipment and in particular, prostheses, based upon clear evidence.

ENDOSCOPY AND LAPAROSCOPY

Endoscopic and laparoscopic surgery has many advantages for patients and clinicians. There has been an enormous increase in the numbers of such procedures, most of which are highly successful, so it is not surprising that minimally invasive surgery is now featuring amongst the 30 day postoperative deaths reported to NCEPOD. Some of these deaths are in the current sample, as the death occurred within 3 days of a procedure.

There is no fundamental difference in the requirements to deliver safe care to patients undergoing endoscopic techniques compared to those undergoing open surgery. Patients undergoing endoscopic procedures and laparoscopic operations (either diagnostic or therapeutic) may not be high-risk patients and may come from any age group. Unfortunately these procedures are often regarded as routine, straightforward and safe. Indeed these 'minimally invasive' interventional and corrective procedures are often thought to be of particular benefit and safer in high-risk patients; as a result there may be less vigilance and a failure to detect problems. However, there are risks to these less invasive techniques and sensible, careful patient selection should form part of their judicious application [35].

Whatever the risk involved and whatever the patient's age group, the surgery and supervision of the aftercare should only be undertaken by those who have undergone specific periods of training in the procedures, so that they are adequately skilled. These skills must then be enhanced by clinical experience. The postoperative care, in particular, needs close supervision as many complications have an insidious onset and presentation. It is an old adage in surgical teaching that 'common things are common'. Therefore, when a common complication may be present, clinicians must guard against the 'anything but that' syndrome which will lead them into a false sense of security and cause them to overlook the obvious. This can be particularly true with biliary leakage after laparoscopic cholecystectomy and ureteric damage during laparoscopic pelvic surgery.

The prudent surgical team will have a plan for the management of well-recognised complications that might occur during or after surgery. These will have been developed on the basis of evidence and experience, discussed amongst the members of the team and rehearsed (either practically on patients/simulators, or theoretically).

The cases described below illustrate some of the problems seen during the review of deaths occurring after endoscopic or laparoscopic procedures.

Case Study 68

A 60-year-old male was having a staging procedure for a malignant mesothelioma. This involved a bronchoscopy and then a mediastinoscopy. A staff grade thoracic surgeon, assisted by a locum SpR (year 1) performed the procedure. There was a consultant observing the procedure. An attempted paratracheal lymph node biopsy during mediastinoscopy resulted in massive haemorrhage, which could not be controlled by tamponade. A median sternotomy revealed a tear in the right main pulmonary artery. Despite attempts to control the bleeding, the patient died on the table.

This case was well managed despite a catastrophic complication of an endoscopy. There was an experienced surgeon immediately available and supervising the operator. This complication was obvious and immediate and appropriate steps were taken to deal with it.

> **Some patients are too ill for anaesthesia and surgery.**

Case Study 69

An 89-year-old female was admitted for an elective laparoscopic cholecystectomy following one prior admission with upper abdominal pain. There was a solitary gallstone. The patient was known to have periods of confusion and a brain scan had shown cerebral atrophy. She was falling at home, walked with a Zimmer frame and was doubly incontinent. The hospital notes were so chaotic that the 18-year history of ischaemic heart disease, hypertension and heart failure was unknown to the surgeon and the anaesthetist. The laparoscopic cholecystectomy was uneventful but postoperatively, during the first 24 hours, the patient became hypotensive, confused and developed a chest infection. By the third day after surgery the patient was admitted to a HDU but refused supportive therapy. There was a cardiac arrest and treatment was withdrawn. It was only after death that the long history of cardiovascular problems came to light. An autopsy found no problems at the operation site.

The initial indication for surgery in this patient seems questionable and injudicious. In addition, it could have been predicted that any surgery on this patient would have been associated with considerable morbidity. Careful, appropriate assessment was hampered by a 'chaotic' set of hospital notes.

> **Anticipation and early recognition of complications might have improved the outcome.**

Case Study 70

A 66-year-old female was admitted for an elective laparoscopic cholecystectomy. Seven months before this she had presented with obstructive jaundice, which had settled after an ERCP. The laparoscopic procedure was difficult due to adhesions and lasted one hour and forty-five minutes. The following day the patient suffered a fatal pulmonary embolism. No pharmacological thromboembolic prophylaxis was given during the perioperative period and no mechanical measures, such as intermittent calf compression, were used. This was in breach of the unit's prophylaxis protocol.

Did the surgical team adopt a rather *laissez-faire* approach to this case, as it was a 'routine' minimally invasive procedure? Venous thromboses are well known to occur after laparoscopic surgery.

Case Study 71

A 62-year-old female had a laparoscopically assisted vaginal hysterectomy, sacral colpopexy and a laparoscopic colposuspension for urinary incontinence and vaginal prolapse. Surgeons of varying experience did the operation; the laparoscopic part appears to have been done by a consultant. Following this procedure she never recovered fully although she was discharged from hospital. Two weeks after the surgery she was readmitted for three days and treated with antibiotics (the indication for this is unclear but may have been a presumed pelvic infection). No investigations were done because the consultant radiologist said that he did not think it was an urgent problem. The patient was discharged.

She continued to be unwell with abdominal distension, diarrhoea, lethargy and pyrexia. She was readmitted under a medical team and a pleural effusion was drained. 'Ascites' was noted. A further course of antibiotics was administered. A gynaecological opinion was sought. The gynaecological registrar who saw her wrote, "...overall picture is puzzling. While her symptoms date from the time of surgery, it is not immediately clear how this could be secondary to a gynae complication. If any of the investigations show a non-medical problem, we would be delighted to accept her back".

Eventually, two months after the initial surgery, an IVU was done. This demonstrated a unilateral hydronephrosis with a leak from the ipsilateral ureter. The following day a consultant urologist operated. A SHO (year one but with considerable experience abroad) gave the anaesthesia. The surgeon did a retrograde pyelogram and demonstrated a large leak from a ureter. The plan was to reimplant the ureter using a Boari flap. There was a large urinoma with dense fibrosis. Considerable bleeding from the pelvic and internal iliac veins occurred during the dissection. This was controlled and the surgery continued. However by this time eight units of blood, 2500 ml of colloid and 2000 ml of crystalloid fluids had been given together with fresh frozen plasma. A consultant anaesthetist was summoned. There was a cardiac arrest and the patient died on the table.

This case illustrates several points:
- The initial operation was appropriate and the laparoscopic element done by a consultant (whom we assume was experienced). However the patient was not well afterwards. Ureteric injury is not uncommon after hysterectomy, by whatever route, yet no one appears to have considered this possibility. This is the type of complication where a well-rehearsed sequence of investigations should be in place in order to help confirm or exclude the problem. Did the consultant gynaecologist know about the problems?
- No investigations were done because a radiologist decided the problem was not urgent.
- Even when the patient was clearly quite ill and required re-admission, the specialty registrar did not consider the possibility of ureteric injury, does not appear to have consulted the consultant and left the care of the patient to physicians.
- Once the penny had dropped, an appropriate referral to an urologist was made.
- The proposed surgery was clearly going to be difficult, yet a single-handed anaesthetic SHO, with no higher qualifications, was deputed to manage the case.

Readers with experience in this field may like to consider how they would have managed this case in their practice.

Case Study 72

An 83-year-old female was admitted for endoscopic biopsy of a tumour of the sphenoid sinus. Unfortunately the carotid artery was breached and catastrophic haemorrhage ensued which could not be controlled by packing.

This is a recognised complication. Could the occurrence of such events be reduced by radiological or other spatial guidance? Maintaining accurate orientation during endoscopic procedures requires good training and sufficient ongoing experience to maintain clinical skills.

Case Study 73

An 86-year-old female was referred from a district hospital to a cardiothoracic centre, following a flexible bronchoscopy which had demonstrated what was believed to be a foreign body in the left upper lobe bronchus. Three rigid bronchoscopies and biopsies were undertaken under GA at the centre over the following two weeks. On the third occasion, a massive blood loss of 2.5 L occurred following the sixth biopsy. An autopsy revealed pulmonary TB. Histology from the three biopsy procedures was unavailable. Death certificate recorded I (a) Haemoptysis and I (b) Pulmonary tuberculosis. There was no mention of operation or haemorrhage.

Why were a total of four bronchospies undertaken? Why was no histology available? Was a Heaf test performed? We do not know the answers and no histology was submitted to NCEPOD, but it seems strange that this patient underwent so many bronchoscopies in such a short period of time, and that so many biopsies were taken for what was believed to be a foreign body.

Case Study 74

A 77-year-old male was admitted with stridor due to an advanced stenosing carcinoma of the larynx. Endoscopic biopsy and debulking of the tumour was undertaken and the patient returned, with an endotracheal tube, to the ICU after surgery. Following extubation on ICU the patient suffered a respiratory arrest and died.

Debulking of tumours can cause significant postoperative oedema. Should a tracheostomy have been performed?

OPERATIVE COMPETENCE

This is clearly an area where the individual surgeon and the surgical team can influence the outcome. The manner in which this competence manifests itself will vary between specialties. In the specialty of General Surgery, there were several examples where a patient died following surgery that involved an incidental injury to the spleen. This mainly followed colonic surgery.

Case Study 75

A 77-year-old male presented with a perforated colonic tumour (rectosigmoid). A registrar operated (with the knowledge and agreement of the consultant surgeon). A subtotal colectomy, small bowel resection and ileostomy was done. During this procedure there was splenic bleeding (approximately 4 L) due to surgical trauma and a splenectomy was required. Postoperative care was delivered in ICU but the patient died from sepsis and heart failure.

It is impossible to guarantee avoidance of splenic damage, especially when mobilising the splenic flexure. However, experienced surgeons use several techniques to protect the spleen. Firstly, a moist pack can be placed behind the spleen to lift it forward, having first ascertained that there are no adhesions between the spleen and diaphragm. This helps to reduce tension on the splenic pedicle during mobilisation of the colonic splenic flexure. The tissues should always be handled with the utmost gentleness. The next technical point is to mobilise the colon, both from below and across from the transverse colon, rather than from one direction only, and to approach the spleen in this manner. Finally, and most importantly, an inspection of the splenic area should always be made at the end of the operation. By doing this, inadvertent splenic damage will be detected and corrected at the time of the initial operation.

Some intra-operative complications are due to inept surgery.

Case Study 76

A right hemicolectomy was planned for an 85-year-old male with a caecal carcinoma. During surgery on the right colon the inferior mesenteric and splenic veins were torn. The surgeon suggested that the veins were congested due to hepatic cirrhosis. All attempts to stop the bleeding failed and the patient died on the table. There had been a blood transfusion of 50 units. An unhelpful autopsy gave the cause of death as carcinoma of the caecum. The liver was said to be normal.

It is difficult to conclude anything other than the fact that surgical trauma caused the haemorrhage.

INTRA-OPERATIVE DECISION-MAKING

The planned operative procedure may need to be varied due to changing circumstances such as pathological anatomy, reassessment of the pathological process, deterioration in the patient's condition, intra-operative mishaps etc. What is required is the ability to change direction and technical versatility. Blinkered adherence to the proposed surgical treatment, albeit based on sound principles, may lead to disaster.

Case Study 77

A 58-year-old male was listed for an elective coronary artery bypass. His surgery was expedited due to unstable angina. The triple bypass went well but there was a tear in a mammary artery that was repaired before use. The patient developed ventricular fibrillation as the chest was being closed; cardiopulmonary bypass was re-established and the heart examined. There was a significant myocardial infarct and bleeding from the repaired internal mammary artery. The artery was repaired and re-implanted. The patient was returned to ICU but continued to show evidence of myocardial ischaemia. He was returned to theatre and the heart was re-explored. There was evidence of further myocardial damage and an additional vein graft was inserted. The patient returned to ICU but developed fatal biventricular failure.

The surgeon wished to use the internal mammary arteries because of the better long-term outcome. However once the artery was damaged an alternative might have been sought.

Case Study 78

A 46-year-old male was referred for cardiac surgery because of unstable angina and a possible myocardial infarct. He was an insulin-dependent diabetic. Surgery consisted of seven coronary artery bypass grafts using either reversed vein, mammary artery or radial artery. The surgery went well but there was spasm of the radial artery graft leading to myocardial ischaemia and haemodynamic collapse. Despite maximal inotropic and intra-aortic balloon pump support, the patient did not survive.

This was a high-risk case with extensive coronary artery disease. Here too, the surgeon was using an arterial graft for better long-term patency but once the spasm was appreciated, an alternative strategy might have been considered.

POSTOPERATIVE COMPLICATIONS

The postoperative complications reported to NCEPOD are listed in Table 6.2. These relate to the sample of 2114 patients who died within three days.

Table 6.2	Common postoperative complications (n=2114 cases)
Cardiac failure (IHD/ arrhythmia)	29
Respiratory	27
Cardiac arrest	26
Renal failure	19
Generalised sepsis	17
Postoperative haemorrhage requiring transfusion	8
Stroke or other neurological problems	5
Thromboembolic	4
Persistent coma	3
Hepatic failure	3
Other organ failure	3
Bleeding at another site (e.g. GI)	2

In 12% (255/2114 cases) nothing was done (apart from anaesthetic room management) to improve the patient's condition. In only 4% of deaths (90/2114 cases) did surgeons think that preoperative manoeuvres might have prevented these complications.

The majority of surgery is safely concluded with satisfactory outcomes. Many procedures are associated with recognised complications and these can be dealt with in an appropriate manner should they occur. Occasionally, common, well-recognised complications occur yet the surgeon appears to deny the possibility. Perhaps this is an example of surgical optimism?

Case Study 79

A 74-year-old male who was a diabetic had an anterior resection of the rectum for a carcinoma of the rectum (Dukes A). The following day he required a further laparotomy for intra-abdominal bleeding from a mesenteric artery. All was well until the seventh postoperative day when his diabetes became unstable and he developed fast atrial fibrillation. The patient was transferred to HDU. An anastomotic leak was suspected but a contrast study did not show a leak. He remained unwell but it was a further 13 days before a laparotomy was done because of his deteriorating

*condition and overwhelming sepsis. There was an
anastomotic leak and a Hartmann's procedure was
done. He was nursed in ICU where he developed a
bleeding diathesis, respiratory failure and a wound
dehiscence. He died three days after the laparotomy.
An autopsy confirmed peritonitis. The autopsy
report contains contradictory statements. Firstly that
the leaking anastomosis cannot be attributed to the
original surgery and then that a late breakdown of an
anastomosis is a recognised complication of surgery.*

A leaking anastomosis following an anterior
resection is a well-recognised complication and,
despite a negative contrast enema, the surgeon
should have entertained a high index of suspicion in
the face of a deteriorating patient. This is a classic
example of the 'anything but that' syndrome.

Case Study 80

*A 25-year-old female was re-admitted in hypovolaemic
shock as an emergency with secondary haemorrhage
following an elective tonsillectomy. A SpR 1 in ENT
took the patient to theatre. Two and a half hours
later the bleeding had apparently been controlled,
and the patient was returned to the recovery area.
On extubation by the SHO anaesthetist, massive
haemorrhage was encountered and further intubation
proved impossible. The patient died of respiratory
arrest and an autopsy confirmed the cause of death as
asphyxia due to inhaled blood.*

This tragic case illustrates the difficulty in dealing
with secondary haemorrhage. Clearly the SpR had
difficulty arresting the haemorrhage and it would
have been prudent to seek help from an experienced
colleague. The importance of airway management
cannot be stressed enough where upper aero-
digestive tract bleeding is concerned, and the airway
must be protected until the patient is adequately
recovered.

It is not known what type of diathermy equipment
was used in this case.

Recommendation

Autopsies should be the subject of a formal external audit process. Clinicians should be involved in evaluating the quality of reports and the basis of conclusions drawn, including the cause of death.

THE AUTOPSY

INTRODUCTION

This section of the report presents an analysis of the available pathological information about the patients in this year's sample. The analyses are made from the perspective of both pathologists and clinicians. There is much common ground and recognition that there is a need to revise parts of the current process for evaluating the delivery of care to our patients.

An autopsy should improve the understanding of the pathological events involved in a patient's death and also enable surgeons to assess the technical performance of surgery, where this has been done. The lessons learnt from autopsies should lead to improvements in health care. In order to do this, there is a perceived need to improve communication between clinicians and pathologists and adopt the modern thinking of multidisciplinary team working within the context of clinical governance requirements. In the sample of deaths used to compile this report, 11% (91/857) of the autopsies took place under the auspices of the hospital pathologist (consent autopsies). The remaining 89%

(766/857) were coroner's autopsies. Clinicians are

feeling more and more disillusioned and frustrated

with the information obtained from coroner's

autopsies, which may not help in the understanding

of a patient's death. The problem appears to lie with

the basic reasons for the existence of the coronial

system, the purpose of which is quite different from

that required by clinicians. In addition, coroners may

prohibit the pathologist from sharing information

until after an inquest, and even so, mechanisms

for dissemination of the pathologists' reports are

far from standard. Previous NCEPOD reports have

highlighted this issue and have quoted the limited

financial resources made available to coroners as an

explanation. The current coronial system, which

is now the main route for clinicians to obtain an

autopsy of a patient, puts limits on the quality of

information which a pathologist can contribute

and the ability to function within a team. Under

such conditions, how can a coroner's pathologist

contribute to knowledge and audit?

THE PATHOLOGISTS' PERSPECTIVE

As in previous years, the review of autopsy reports was performed by the Pathology Advisors, a panel of consultant histopathologists. The results were compared with the report for 1994/95 [3] since this was based on a similar sample of deaths occurring within three days of operation, as well as the last report, which covered data for 1999/00 [2]. The advisors used the Royal College of Pathologists' 'Guidelines for Postmortem Reports' as the exemplar for autopsies [36], although useful information on standards of examination can also be found in 'Best Practice' guidelines produced under the auspices of the Association of Clinical Pathologists [37].

The problems in standards of autopsy and communication with clinicians that are highlighted in this report are not new. They have been raised before by NCEPOD and it is disheartening to encounter the same problems again.

AUTOPSY RATE

> **Most autopsies were performed for HM Coroner.**

Of the 2114 cases included this year, an autopsy was performed in 857, representing an overall rate of 41%. There were 1724 cases referred to the coroner, who ordered an autopsy in 44% (766/1724); this proportion is lower than in 1994/95, when 57% of cases referred to the coroner had autopsies. The other 91 cases were hospital ('consent') autopsies, representing 11% of the total number.

When relatives refuse a hospital autopsy, the case is often referred to the coroner. This approach should not be used to set aside the family's wishes. A coroner may order an autopsy for his own lawful purposes, even if the next of kin opposes this. The coroner must perform a balancing act between the wishes of the relatives and the coroner's duty to society. In overriding the wishes of the family, the coroner's actions must be 'proportionate'. Within the current system the clinical curiosity of a surgeon, by itself, would not be a sufficient reason for a coroner to override the wishes of the family.

We received 596 autopsy reports, 70% of the 857 examinations performed. The pathology advisors reviewed a random sample of 499 reports. This sample was 84% of the reports received (499/596) or 58% of all the autopsies performed (499/857).

> **Cases in which no autopsy was performed may not have been fully investigated.**

The lack of autopsy in 59% of cases raises the question of whether the investigation and audit of these deaths were complete [37]. Many recent studies have highlighted that autopsies still reveal unexpected findings, even in the age of high-technology medicine [37-40]. This fact is also demonstrated by many of the vignettes in this report.

Case Study 81

A laparotomy was performed on a patient with a distended tender abdomen and air under the diaphragm. The SpR4 who performed the operation noted multiple perforations of the right colon with faecal contamination of the peritoneum. The patient died in recovery. Autopsy showed the cause to be an obstructing carcinoma of the sigmoid colon. There were also liver metastases. Neither of these findings was observed during the laparotomy.

THE QUALITY OF THE AUTOPSY REPORT

Clinical history

A clinical history was absent from 11% (55/499) of all coroners' cases. This finding may reflect the requirement of some coroners that the autopsy report does not contain a clinical history, as highlighted previously [2]. Of the 444 cases with a clinical history, it was considered to be of an acceptable standard in 90% (400/444), a similar proportion to the previous year [2]. The other 44 cases fell below a satisfactory standard, usually because the clinical history was too brief to allow appreciation of a complex clinical picture.

Description of external appearances

In 31% (154/499) of cases, scars or incisions were described but not measured, despite guidelines recommending this practice [36,37]. The height was recorded in 60% (301/499) and the weight in 45% (226/499). These proportions are similar to last year [2]. The height and weight should be recorded in all cases because they are important objective measurements of body build and allow sensible interpretation of organ weights. Overall, the external description was graded as below a satisfactory standard in 9% (43/499), often because important information about the operation site was omitted.

Gross description of internal organs and operation sites

The gross description of internal organs was considered unsatisfactory in 18% (89/499) of reports. The usual reason was that the description was too brief to allow full clinicopathological correlation. In particular, there was failure to adequately describe the operation site; Tables 7.1 and 7.2 show that in 18% (91/499) of reports the operation site was not described or the description was inappropriate.

Table 7.1	Is the operation site described?
Operation site described	2000/01
Yes	420 (84%)
No	59 (12%)
Not applicable	20 (4%)
Total	**499**

Table 7.2	Is the gross examination of the operation site appropriate to the clinical problem?
Gross examination appropriate	2000/01
Yes	388 (92%)
No	32 (8%)
Total	**420**

As in last year's report [2], most cases in which the operation site was not adequately described were orthopaedic procedures. However other specialties were not immune from this failing.

Case Study 82

A check cystoscopy in a male with superficial transitional cell carcinoma of the bladder was complicated postoperatively by acute retention. A transurethral catheter could not be passed, so a suprapubic catheter was inserted. Unfortunately, bowel contents passed via the catheter. A cystoscopy under local anaesthesia confirmed misplacement of the catheter associated with a tear in the bladder. A laparotomy to repair the ileum and bladder was performed. However, the patient also had severe chronic obstructive airways disease and it proved impossible to wean him off the ventilator.

In the autopsy report, the external examination did not include the suprapubic catheter site. The internal examination described the small intestine and bladder as 'normal' with no mention of the repairs that had been performed.

Although most pathologists weigh the major organs, as required by the guidelines [36,37] there remains a minority that do not (Table 7.3).

Table 7.3	Organs that were examined by pathologist but NOT weighed
Organ	Number of cases
Brain	34
Lungs	38
Heart	14
Liver	48
Spleen	56
Kidneys	50

The autopsy was limited in 6% (29/499) of cases, most being coroners' cases in which examination of the brain was omitted. In only a minority was this because the next of kin had expressed a desire for limited examination, despite recent adverse media comment on autopsy practice. It would appear that relatives are not generally withholding consent for full autopsy, but it will be important to monitor any trend in this direction in the future.

Retention of autopsy material

Histological specimens were retained in 27% (134/499) of cases, compared to 28% last year and 23% in 1994/95 [2,3]. However, the retained tissue was itemised in under half of these 134 autopsy reports, despite recent recommendations that tissues or organs retained should be clearly stated [41]. In nine cases, material was retained for other tests, usually microbiology. In only four reports was there a statement that the relatives had refused consent for retention of organs and/or tissue.

A description of the histology was included in only 66% (88/134) of cases in which histology was taken. Of the reports in which the description of histology was missing, all but one were coroners' cases. The histology reports were considered satisfactory in 92% (81/88). Of the cases with no histology report, its absence was considered to detract significantly from the value of the report in 21% (87/411), a similar proportion to the previous year [2].

Case Study 83

A 78-year-old, female patient with a choledochoduodenal fistula underwent an ERCP and biliary tract stenting, following which she was discharged from hospital. Four days later she was readmitted with small bowel obstruction and a laparotomy was planned for the following day. She had suffered a MI 15 years earlier and was known to have an abdominal aortic aneurysm. On admission she had shortness of breath, basal lung crepitations and an ejection systolic murmur. An ECG diagnosed LVH, a chest X-ray revealed a right basal effusion and serum biochemistry showed elevated troponin levels and renal impairment (urea 20.4 mmol/l, creatinine 157 micromol/l). A medical referral (grade unknown) provided an opinion that the murmur was not significant and no echocardiography was performed. General anaesthesia included arterial and venous pressure monitoring. Anaesthesia was complicated by

ST segment depression and haemodynamic instability. Laparotomy showed small bowel ischaemia with no lesion obstructing the bowel lumen. Postoperatively she was managed on an ICU, the troponin level was higher than preoperatively and she died the following day.

The autopsy description of the heart stated that there was asymmetrical thickening of the interventricular septum with areas of scarring that the pathologist interpreted as hypertrophic obstructive cardiomyopathy. There was also triple-vessel atherosclerosis of the coronary arteries with thrombotic occlusion of the right coronary artery. No histology was taken. The cause of death was given as 'ischaemic heart disease and hypertrophic cardiomyopathy'.

The lack of histology in this case was considered a serious fault by the Pathology Advisors. There are genetic implications to a diagnosis of hypertrophic cardiomyopathy, and tissue should have been retained to confirm this diagnosis. In the opinion of the Advisors, it seems likely that the changes described in the report could all be due to ischaemic heart disease.

Summary of lesions, clinicopathological correlation and cause of death

A summary of lesions was present in 17% (83/499) of cases, continuing the downward trend in the number of reports with this feature observed last year [2]. A summary of lesions is a useful device in complex cases, but a comprehensive and accurate clinicopathological correlation is more important and can encompass all the major and incidental findings with a discussion of their relevance.

A clinicopathological correlation was present in 68% (341/499), a higher proportion than previously [2,3]. It was satisfactory in 81% (276/341); the usual reason for the remainder being less than satisfactory was excessive brevity.

Cause of death

An Office for National Statistics (ONS) cause of death was given in all but four cases. In the 495 reports detailing a cause of death it followed ONS formatting rules in 96% (473/495). However, it included reference to the operation in only 50%

(246/495), an even lower proportion than the 76% found in the previous year [2]. Although in a few cases it seemed appropriate to omit the operation from the cause of death, there were far more cases where the operation was at least a contributory factor, and should have been mentioned in part II of the ONS cause of death; in some cases, there was no mention of the operation even though it should have been in part I. Examples of appropriate formats might be (these examples are fictitious):

I(a)   Cerebral metastases
I(b)   Adenocarcinoma of the colon
          (excised 5 January 2002)

or

I(a)   Coronary artery thrombosis
I(b)   Coronary artery atherosclerosis

II   Above-knee amputation for peripheral
          vascular disease

The date in the first example is to comply with the request of the ONS and World Health Organisation that the date of removal of primary malignant tumours should be recorded, in addition to the site and histological type [42].

Failure to mention the operation in the ONS cause of death was one of the most frequent criticisms made by the Pathology Advisors, and has been raised as a problem in previous NCEPOD reports [2, 43]. Perhaps pathologists think that by including the operation there is an implication that the surgery was below standard or inappropriate, or that by omitting the operation from the cause of death that an inquest can be avoided. However, an inquest should not be necessary simply because the operation is recorded. Coroners are required to hold an inquest if there is reasonable cause to suspect that the deceased died an unnatural death, but the criteria by which a death can be classified as unnatural are not well defined. It has been suggested that *"... an 'unnatural death' is one which is wholly or partly caused, or accelerated, by any act, intervention or omission other than a properly executed measure intended to prolong life.... If, however, because of a hopeless prognosis, treatment is undertaken with a known and substantial risk, it may be likely that treatment has shortened life. Provided that no safer method of dealing with the case offered itself, this is still a death due to natural causes for practical purposes"* [44]. By these criteria, many deaths following operation can be classified as natural. Furthermore, even if the death is not natural, this does not of itself imply negligence.

Case Study 84

A female with advanced breast carcinoma had an axillobifemoral graft performed for occlusion of the distal aorta. The graft occluded and she was taken back to theatre where thrombectomy was initially successful but was quickly followed by re-occlusion. Extensive ischaemic changes in both lower limbs developed and she died about 24 hours after the initial graft operation.

The cause of death was given as 'ischaemic heart disease and peripheral vascular disease'; there was no mention of the operation in any part of the ONS cause of death. Breast carcinoma was included in part II.

Problems with the ONS cause of death in some of these cases are a cause for concern. The quality of death certification in general was criticised in a recent study [42], and pathologists have an important role in improving matters. Any paternalistic attempt to spare the relatives of the deceased any extra distress by omitting the operation from the cause of death is likely to be misguided in an era when the public expect openness and honesty from the medical profession.

The principal cause of death is shown in Table 7.4. The left-hand column shows the cause given on the autopsy report, while the other shows the cause that, in the opinion of the Pathology Advisors, was most likely (on the evidence of the autopsy report together with the other material supplied to NCEPOD). A difference of opinion is evident in some cases. Traumatic causes, primary postoperative haemorrhage and aspiration pneumonia were possibly under-reported by pathologists – could this be because they believe that an inquest will be avoided if they are not recorded on the death certificate?

Table 7.4 shows that ischaemic heart disease is by an order of magnitude the most important disease process causing death in these patients. Pulmonary embolism remains a significant cause despite prophylactic measures. Many of the 'gastrointestinal disease' cases were bowel infarcts.

Table 7.4	Principal cause of death *(answers may be multiple, n=499)*	
Cause of death	Autopsy report	Pathology Advisor
Sepsis	34	33
Malignant disease	45	45
Ischaemic heart disease	208	197
Pulmonary embolism	29	28
Other cardiovascular disease (non-malignant)	66	66
Cerebrovascular disease	8	6
Pneumonia (excluding aspiration)	25	22
Aspiration pneumonia	3	5
Other lung disease (non-malignant)	9	11
Gastrointestinal disease	46	58
Primary postoperative haemorrhage	22	28
Trauma	36	54
Other	25	33
Not stated	2	0
Not known	0	1

Case Study 85

A 57-year-old male presented with a swelling in the thigh and pyrexia. There was a past medical history of lobectomy for lung carcinoma, Crohn's disease and coeliac disease. The diagnosis of an abscess related to Crohn's disease was entertained, and a laparotomy was performed at which a psoas haematoma was drained. Postoperatively, his haemoglobin fell markedly and there was excessive blood in the drain. Re-laparotomy found a raw area in the left iliac fossa that was packed. However, blood continued to 'pour' into the drain. Despite all resuscitative efforts, including 13 units of blood, he died. The autopsy report gave a good description of the internal findings, and histology of the mass in the thigh unexpectedly demonstrated anaplastic large cell lymphoma.

Case Study 86

A 99-year-old female died on the operating table following haemorrhage. A staff grade orthopaedic surgeon carried out the operation for fixation of a fractured neck of femur with a locum consultant available by telephone. A spinal anaesthetic was inserted and the operation commenced at 11.30. An hour and a quarter later it was necessary to convert to general anaesthesia as the spinal was wearing off. Fixation was difficult as the fracture was severely comminuted and the equipment available was limited. Eventually a dynamic hip screw was inserted but additional stability was required and at 14.30 attempts were made to pass a wire around the femur. This resulted in a rapid haemorrhage requiring 9 units of blood, 4 units of FFP, 4 litres of Gelofusine and 1.5 litres of Hartmanns. The vascular surgeons came to help, identified the bleeding as being from the profunda femoris artery, and this was ligated. The blood pressure was stated to be low throughout this period but there is no charted value after a recording of 70 mmHg at 14.50. Although the surgeon suggests that 'all seemed stable and closure of the wounds was in progress' when the patient arrested, the anaesthetist describes that the blood pressure was difficult to maintain despite the fluids and bolus of epinephrine. The patient had an EMD arrest at 16.25.

The autopsy identified that the coronary arteries showed very severe atheroma and calcification. The right coronary was completely occluded about 1 cm from its origin and the anterior descending coronary showed 90-95% occlusion near its origin. The myocardium showed diffuse fibrosis. The pathologist gave the cause of death as:
I (a) Coronary occlusion
I (b) Coronary artery atheroma
and went on to conclude that in his/her opinion, the fracture and operation were not material factors in the death.

In the first of these two cases, the Pathology Advisors considered that primary postoperative haemorrhage was the immediate cause of death, even though the operation had been performed well. However, the ONS cause of death did not mention either the haemorrhage or the operation. Nor was there any clinicopathological correlation. Therefore, an otherwise good autopsy that had revealed an unexpected diagnosis was classified as poor overall. In the second case, there was an intra-operative haemorrhage which, as a result of the underlying cardiac condition, could not be tolerated and death occurred. Was it the cardiac condition or the haemorrhage that should be blamed?

Overall score for the autopsy

> Autopsies continue to provide useful information and are an important part of auditing perioperative deaths. However some of these examinations were unsatisfactory and did not explain the death. Problems included undue brevity, failure to properly examine the operation site, failure to make appropriate clinicopathological correlation and failure to take histology. These findings demonstrate that pathologists often under-investigated postoperative deaths.

Table 7.5 shows the overall score for the autopsy reports analysed. It shows that 35% were below a satisfactory standard. This proportion is slightly higher than last year [2], when 30% were judged poor or unsatisfactory, and considerably higher than 1994/95 when 12% were classified as poor or unsatisfactory. There may be two reasons for this: either the quality of reports is getting worse, or the standards set by the Pathology Advisors have risen. Although the latter is possible, we cannot test this hypothesis by reviewing cases from previous years because the data are destroyed after the review is complete. Nevertheless, we believe our standards are reasonable and it is disappointing that so many cases fall below a satisfactory standard. Common reasons include undue brevity of the report, failure to describe the operation site, failure to make adequate clinicopathological correlation, failure to take histology when indicated and failure to record

the operation in the ONS cause of death. Just one of these occurrences did not necessarily make an otherwise satisfactory report poor in our judgement, but two or more were likely to do so.

Case Study 87

A 93-year-old male with a fractured neck of femur due to a fall had a dynamic hip screw repair. Spinal anaesthesia was used in view of the presence of severe chronic obstructive airways disease. Hypotension was a problem during and after the operation. The postoperative haemoglobin level was 4.8 mg/dl, and a blood transfusion was given. Pulmonary oedema developed and the patient died.

The ONS cause of death was given as 'I (a) Acute pulmonary oedema with massive hydrothorax, due to I (b) General and coronary atherosclerosis, II Possible chronic hypertensive disease.'

The autopsy report described the internal findings in just 13 lines of text. There was no description of the operation site and apparently no attempt to determine the cause of the postoperative fall in haemoglobin. There was no clinicopathological correlation.

The cause of death includes neither the recent operation nor the fall, and does not accurately reflect the clinicopathological picture. Furthermore, the death was classified as natural even though the sequence of events leading to death was initiated by a fall. This autopsy added almost nothing to the investigation of the death and was classified as unacceptable.

Table 7.5	Quality of autopsies		
Quality of autopsy	**2000/01**	**1994/95**	**1999/00**
Unacceptable, laying the pathologist open to serious professional criticism	11 (2%)	8 (2%)	8 (2%)
Poor	167 (33%)	48 (10%)	96 (28%)
Satisfactory	202 (40%)	204 (43%)	150 (43%)
Good	93 (19%)	193 (41%)	73 (21%)
Excellent, meeting all the standards set by the RCPath guidelines	26 (5%)	17 (4%)	19 (5%)
Total	**499**	**470**	**346**

As can be seen in Table 7.6, the detection of unexpected findings at autopsy reiterates the importance of this process in clinical mortality audit. In 102 cases (20%) there was a major discrepancy between clinical diagnosis and autopsy, and in a further 34 cases (7%) there was a minor discrepancy or interesting incidental finding. In 75 cases (15%) there was a failure to explain some important aspect of the case, although in 26 of these, the autopsy was felt to have been conducted satisfactorily.

Table 7.6	History, ante-mortem clinical diagnosis and cause of death compared with autopsy findings (answers may be multiple n=499)			
	Coroners'	Hospital	Total 2000/01	1999/00
Confirmation of essential clinical findings	357	17	374 (75%)	262 (76%)
A discrepancy in the cause of death or in a major diagnosis, which if known, might have affected treatment, outcome or prognosis	30	1	31 (6%)	29 (8%)
A discrepancy in the cause of death or in a major diagnosis, which if known, would probably not have affected treatment, outcome or prognosis	69	2	71 (14%)	52 (15%)
A minor discrepancy or interesting incidental finding	33	1	34 (7%)	30 (9%)
A failure to explain some important aspect of the clinical problem, as a result of a satisfactory autopsy	24	2	26 (5%)	22 (6%)
A failure to explain some important aspect of the clinical problem, as a result of an unsatisfactory autopsy	48	1	49 (10%)	35 (10%)

The proportions in each category are very similar to those observed last year [2]. Common reasons for failure to explain some aspect of the clinical problem as a result of an unsatisfactory autopsy included failure to describe the operation site adequately and failure to take material for further analysis.

LIAISON WITH CLINICIANS

Attendance of the clinical team at the autopsy

In only 27% (234/857) of cases in which an autopsy occurred were the clinical team informed of the date and time, and in only 50% (117/234) of these cases did a member of the clinical team attend. The usual reason given by clinicians was that they were unavailable or had other commitments (67%), a difficulty that is bound to be compounded if the autopsy is held outside the hospital where the death occurred. This is a common situation for coroner's autopsies.

The Pathology Advisors believe that the clinical team should normally attend to observe the findings as part of the educational and audit functions of the autopsy. Local arrangements should be in place to make this possible. However, this is obviously not happening in the majority of cases. This is a longstanding problem that has been raised in previous NCEPOD reports [2,3,43]. Given the preponderance of coroner's autopsies, it is to the coroner's pathologist that we should look to for change and improvement in this area.

Communication of the autopsy findings to the clinical team

> **Autopsy reports should be sent to all clinicians providing a case summary to the pathologist. There are agreed standards for this practice but the requirements of some coroners often restrict the communication necessary for good mortality audit.**

Of all the autopsy reports, 71% (610/857) were received by the clinical team. This figure is similar to last year [2], but is less than in 1994/95 when 78% of reports were received. Of those clinicians who gave a timescale for receipt of the report, 73% (267/365) received it within a month of the examination.

In 97 cases, the surgeon stated in the NCEPOD questionnaire that the autopsy had not confirmed the clinical impression; in a further 82 cases, even though the overall clinical impression had been confirmed, the surgeon indicated that unexpected findings had been revealed. Thus, in 21% (179/857) of cases, surgeons stated that the autopsy added significant information, an example of which is given in Case Study 30 in Chapter 4.

Autopsy in this case revealed the cause of the acute abdomen to be a perforated gangrenous appendix. The appendix was anterior to the ileum, which was considered to account for the unusual clinical course. Histology showed adrenal infarction, acute tubular necrosis, diffuse alveolar damage and hypoxic changes in brain and liver.

When an autopsy takes place after a perioperative death, good practice should include the following points:

- The often complex clinical picture should be clear to the pathologist.

- The autopsy should be a complete examination of all major organs and include the operation site.

- Tissue for histology or other investigations should be kept where appropriate.

- The report should give enough detail so that the pathological changes and their relationship to the clinical picture are clear.

- Previously taken surgical specimens, and the histology, should be referred to in the clinical correlation and conclusions.

- The ONS cause of death should be clear and accurately reflect the pathological findings, including the operation where appropriate.

- The findings should be available to the clinicians in good time, and the relevance of the pathological changes should be clearly stated in a clinicopathological correlation in the report.

- The findings should be available to the relatives of the deceased.

> **The structure of the coroner's autopsy sometimes conflicts with the requirements of a full investigation into perioperative deaths. In particular, the flow of information between clinicians and pathologists can be severely inhibited.**

However, these features are not always present in autopsies analysed for NCEPOD; this raises the question 'why?' One problem, highlighted in a previous report [2], is the potential conflict between the purposes of a coroner's autopsy and the need for full examination of the death for audit. For example:

- The purpose of a coroner's autopsy is to ascertain cause of death; any further investigation is not strictly part of the examination. In particular, Rule 9 of the Coroners' Rules [45] states that tissue may only be retained for histology if it is needed to ascertain the cause of death; investigations for any other reason require consent from the next of kin. In practice, the result is that pathologists do not take tissue when it would be indicated to analyse other pathological processes.

- A coroner's autopsy is often held in a public mortuary not attached to the hospital where the death occurred, preventing busy clinicians from attending the autopsy and inhibiting interaction between pathologists and clinicians. A possible result is pathologists failing to understand the clinical picture, while clinicians do not benefit from the examination. Moreover, some coroners prohibit communication between pathologist and clinician; sometimes surgeons write in the NCEPOD questionnaires that they are not meant to be present at coroner's autopsies.

- The report of a coroner's autopsy belongs to the coroner. This fact can inhibit the use of the report in audit and education. For example, this statement or something similar is boldly emblazoned on most reports: 'This report is confidential and should not be disclosed to a third party without the coroner's consent.' We have also encountered reports endorsed with: 'Not to be filed in patient's notes.' Others have: 'This copy of this report is provided with the approval of HM Coroner for the information of the deceased patient's consultant and his/her immediate medical colleagues. It must not be copied or used for any other purpose. Its use and distribution are controlled by the Coroners' Rules 1984.' Some coroners actively prevent the dissemination of information derived from autopsies.

Case Study 88

The following extracts from an exchange of letters relate to an infant who died during a repair of a complete atrioventricular septal defect.

Letter to HM Coroner from the consultant cardiothoracic surgeon: 'I would like permission to forward a copy of the postmortem report on X to the National Confidential Enquiry into Perioperative Deaths. They have asked me to fill in their usual questionnaire and, in particular, to enclose an autopsy report if one is available.'

Reply signed pp on behalf of the Coroner: 'Thank you for your letter...regarding release of the Post Mortem (sic) report on X to the National Confidential Enquiry into Perioperative Deaths. In my opinion, this authority is not an "Interested Person" within the meaning of the Coroner's (sic) Rules. If they require a copy Post Mortem (sic), they need to apply directly to my office, stating their reason for wanting a copy.'

In reply to the question on the NCEPOD surgical questionnaire, 'If a surgeon did not attend the postmortem, why not?' the surgeon wrote 'Our Coroner does not permit communication between his pathologist and the surgeon unless the surgeon has a specific question.'

Many reports suffer from excessive brevity, failure to describe important features such as the operation site, and lack of clinicopathological correlation. It may be that busy pathologists with a large number of coroner's autopsies to perform are unable to spend adequate time on the examination of these often-complex cases. In addition, the Coroner's Officer may have different priorities from the clinicians interested in the case.

Case Study 89

A fit 75-year-old male was treated for small recurrences of his bladder tumour at check cystoscopy. He made an excellent recovery from the anaesthetic and returned to the ward. In the early hours of the following morning, he had what was presumed to be a large haematemesis; resuscitation was unsuccessful.

The coroner was contacted and the surgeon anticipated an autopsy would be necessary, as the cause of the haematemesis was not known. However, he records that 'the Coroner's Officer pressurised the junior medical staff into giving a putative cause of death and an autopsy was declined.' The surgeon contacted the acting coroner to complain but no autopsy was performed.

The autopsy of a perioperative death needs to go beyond simply establishing the cause of death because of its potential value as an audit tool. Since the great majority of autopsies in perioperative deaths are for the coroner (89% this year), this is an important issue. These problems need addressing in the light of the Home Office-led review of death certification and the coronial system in England and Wales [46].

Another matter is the audit of the overall quality of autopsy reports. We have found the standard varies widely. Autopsies are not audited in the same way as other clinical and pathological activities (e.g. quality control in biochemistry and cytology) and perhaps the Royal College of Pathologists should consider this issue. One area in which there is a particular need for education is in formulating ONS causes of death; the evidence of NCEPOD is that many pathologists are not doing so correctly.

We also need to remember the relatives of the deceased [47]. Feeding back the findings of the autopsy will improve their understanding of the circumstances of the death and, incidentally, the value of the autopsy [48,49]. There may be a place for pathologists in carrying out this task [50].

THE CLINICIANS' PERSPECTIVE

> The autopsy should be seen as an essential and fundamental part of the on-going examination of clinical practice. Coroners should understand their responsibility in supporting this requirement.

Given the focus within this report on examining the progress of surgical patients through their hospital care, in that every patient considered here died, how did the actions of pathologists and coroners link with the process as a whole?

The place and purpose of an autopsy in current practice is becoming increasingly debatable. This is largely due to the high percentage of coroner's examinations, which by their nature are governed by the Coroners' Act (1988) and Coroners' Rules (1984). For the relatives of a patient, particularly in the case of the death of a younger surgical patient, it can be an enormous emotional load. For the NHS, the time involved and the cost are also significant factors. If autopsies are to be performed then, to be justified, their purpose must be clearly defined.

Current practice

Case Study 90

An elderly female with longstanding Crohn's disease was admitted to a medical bed with a developing pneumonia. Eight days later she was transferred to the care of the surgeons as she had peritonitis. Preoperatively the anaesthetist recorded that her condition was very poor. Her blood pressure was 90/50 mmHg, pulse rate 102, respiratory rate 28-30 and she was receiving 50% oxygen by mask. A laparotomy was performed starting at 19.30, and a perforation of the caecum was found with faecal peritonitis. A subtotal colectomy was performed with an ileostomy. Despite active measures by the anaesthetist, her systolic blood pressure never rose above 100 throughout the operation, which lasted until 21.10. Subsequently the patient was transferred to the ICU where she died five hours later.

An autopsy was done and the report is brief, consisting mainly of boxes, which have been filled in. These are not easy for the uninitiated to decipher. Whilst coronary arteries 2 and aorta 3 may be taken to refer to the degree of arterial atheroma, lungs 2 and veins 4 are more difficult to comprehend. Nowhere is there an explanation of the coding system. The cause of death is given as:

I (a) Perforation of colon (Treated)
I (b) Chronic idiopathic inflammatory bowel disease

Was the autopsy of value in understanding the reason why this patient died? If we accept that one of the principles of the autopsy is to increase our understanding about the underlying disease and the effects of treatment, then the answer in this case is probably 'No'. While the cause of death may have been correct, neither the clinical nor pathology advisors could verify this because the internal findings were given as numerical codes (which were not explained), rather than free text, and a clinicopathological correlation (which could have put the findings in context) was absent. This autopsy report communicated nothing of value to the clinicians.

In drawing attention to this case, the purpose is not to criticise but to ask how we can avoid the situation where the clinicians, the coroner and the pathologist all act in total isolation.

Whatever else may be the purpose of an autopsy, whether a hospital or coroner's autopsy, it is to be expected that it will try to establish a cause of death. As medicine progresses and becomes ever more complex this becomes much less simple. 45% (853/1911) of these patients died in a critical care bed. The progression to death in these cases is complex and accompanied by multiple interventions. The intensivist refers to a death being the result of multi-organ failure but on the autopsy report this often translates into bronchopneumonia. Is there a widening gap in understanding between the critical care doctor and the pathologist?

> **When an autopsy is to be performed, arrangements for communication between clinicians and the pathologist need to be formalised. Clinicians involved should provide a case summary to the pathologist prior to the autopsy and include details as to how they can be contacted for further discussion.**

Case Study 91

An 87-year-old female was admitted under the care of the physicians. Her admission notes show that she had had nausea and vomiting for six days prior to admission. Her abdomen was mildly distended and she had constipation. Conservative treatment was ordered. Five days following admission she was referred to the surgeons. Her condition was of concern to the anaesthetists, she was recorded as ASA 3/4, and a consultant, a staff grade and an SHO were all present at the laparotomy. A surgical registrar performed the operation. An obstructing carcinoma of the sigmoid was found and resected, no metastases were seen. Postoperatively the patient was taken to the ICU where she was ventilated and required increasing inotropic support, as she became septic and cardiovascularly unstable. Eventually it was decided, following discussion with the relatives, to withdraw inotropic support and the patient died on the third postoperative day from multi-organ failure.

The death was reported to the coroner and an autopsy was ordered. Nothing that could not have been anticipated was found and the cause of death was given as:

I (a)   Bronchopneumonia
I (b)   Carcinoma of the colon (operated)

In identifying these as being the diseases or conditions directly leading to death, the form adds the footnote that 'this does NOT mean the mode of dying, such as (e.g.) heart failure, asphyxia, asthenia, etc. It means the disease, injury or complication, which caused death'. This phrase comes from the ONS death certificate.

Whilst it might be seen as pedantic to dwell on the difference between the intensivist's and pathologist's view as to the cause of death, bronchopneumonia resulting in death following shortly after a surgical operation for the resection of a sigmoid carcinoma without metastases might suggest sub-standard care. In reality the patient was in a poor state to withstand the operation and died despite maximum postoperative intervention. To the clinician giving multi-organ failure as the cause of death makes this very much clearer. To the pathologist, the finding of florid bronchopneumonia at autopsy may represent the final 'coup-de-grace' in the patient's inexorable downward-spiralling course and may, to him/her, be a perfectly acceptable immediate cause of death. Such differences of opinion should be overcome by discussions between the pathologists and clinicians both before and after the autopsy. However, the degree to which a pathologist is permitted to make his/herself aware of the clinical background to a patient's management appears to be very variable. As our pathologists have illustrated, this may be due to the attitude of some coroners who positively discourage communication. Such obstruction to the flow of information must limit the function of the pathologist and the quality of the information he can contribute to the understanding of a case. The following clinical vignette illustrates this point.

Case Study 92

An elderly male with severe Parkinson's disease was admitted for incision and drainage of an abscess in the groin. A spinal anaesthetic was administered with some difficulty due to the patient's rigidity. The ECG showed marked S-T segment depression but the systolic blood pressure was stable at 145 mmHg. Twenty-five minutes into the procedure the abscess had been drained and the wound was being cleaned with betadine and hydrogen peroxide when the patient underwent a sudden collapse. Initially there was a bradycardia and glycopyrrolate 200 micrograms together with ephedrine 12 mg were given. About a minute later, the blood pressure and pulse disappeared; epinephrine 1:10,000 was given in two boluses of 5ml. An LMA was inserted and 100% oxygen administered.

When, to improve venous access, a 14 G cannula was inserted into the left external jugular vein gas bubbles were aspirated in large amounts. The anaesthetist also noted the appearance of the face and veins to be suggestive of superior mediastinal obstruction. In view of the age and general state of the patient's health, it was decided that further resuscitation should not be attempted.

The case was reported to the coroner who decided that an autopsy was required. Despite the events described above, no specific actions were taken to identify gas in the circulation and the cause of death was given as:

I (a)   *Abscess of right groin (operated) due to*

I (b)   *Right Richter's femoral hernia & small bowel obstruction*

II   *Myocardial ischaemia; coronary atherosclerosis*

The pathologist went on to make the following conclusions:

'Death was due fundamentally to the effects of a large groin abscess, which was under operation for drainage. This abscess arose over a right femoral hernia sac. Also present was undoubted small bowel obstruction with fluid faeces retained back to the stomach. This was the result of adhesion and kinking of the small bowel in

relation to the neck of the hernia. A knuckle of bowel wall had probably been incarcerated in the neck of the hernia. This represented an incomplete or Richter's hernia with chronic adhesion and probably intermittent partial herniation initially. The hernia was substantially reduced at autopsy examination but haemorrhage and inflammation in part of the bowel wall was consistent with recent herniation. Inflamed bowel was the likely source of infection and the cause of the abscess.

The anaesthetist observed an undoubted episode of gas embolism with gas bubbles drained from the neck veins. The likely source of this was small veins in the wall of the abscess cavity. There was no breach of any major vessel. This gas embolic episode coincided with the final collapse.

However, there was no evidence of gas embolism of fatal degree. The patient was profoundly ill with major sepsis and small bowel obstruction. He also had severe myocardial ischaemia owing to severe coronary artery disease.

Gas embolism was present to some undeterminably extent and was coincident with the collapse and cardiac arrest. It may have precipitated the cardiac arrest. However, the embolism was consequent upon the operative procedure, which was properly carried out. Gas embolism was a minor and indirect factor in the death, which was fundamentally due to sepsis and intestinal obstruction.

Small bowel obstruction was not diagnosed in life but Richter's hernia is notoriously difficult to diagnose owing to incomplete closure of the bowel. Bowel was not present in the hernial sac and pus was not in continuity between the peritoneal cavity and the abscess space.

There was no evidence of failure of care contributing to the death. The medical and surgical notes were detailed and exemplary'.

The pathologist's conclusion in this case study, might be construed as setting out to exonerate the clinicians, as has been mentioned in **"The Pathologist's Perspective"** at the beginning of this chapter. However, the clinicians had no doubt of the significance of the gas embolism and the clinical events surrounding the death support their view that it was the cause of death. Hydrogen peroxide causing gas embolism and death is of very considerable significance. Clearly this was a complex case, illustrating that differences of opinion may persist despite the very full discussions, which had taken place.

The complexities of modern clinical care challenge many pathologists, particularly those with forensic training only, who may have a limited understanding of recent advances in critical care. Some will have trained in clinical medicine in the early days of intensive care units. For surgeons and anaesthetists not directly engaged in critical care, it is often difficult to keep abreast of developments. How much more difficult is this for the pathologist?

It is accepted that the pathologist's opinion on the cause of death will, on some occasions, differ from that of the clinicians and often the autopsy will elucidate or discover factors that were unknown to the clinicians. However, there are examples where the pathologist appears to be unaware of the clinical circumstances of death (see Case Studies 85 and 86 earlier in this chapter). When this happens, there is an impression of clinicians, pathologist and coroners each acting in total isolation. From whichever perspective one chooses to view this process, the current approach to autopsies (the majority of which are coroner's examinations) demonstrates the urgent need for better communication between all parties involved.

When there is better communication and a comprehension of the significance of clinical events things can be very much better.

Case Study 93

A 70-year-old female had septicaemia requiring intensive care and was subsequently admitted for a nephrectomy to remove the kidney that was the source of infection. Her general health was poor and in particular she had a history of ischaemic heart disease and cardiac failure and was receiving lisinopril and digoxin. An echocardiogram was performed and this showed an ejection fraction of 11%. The consultant anaesthetist noted the echo findings as 'mod/severe LV impairment' in the preoperative note. The operation was completed in under an hour and the patient was returned to the ward after 10 minutes in recovery.

The following morning she had a good urine output and was apyrexial and stable. During the afternoon her urine output deteriorated and at 20.30 she suffered an EMD arrest from which she was resuscitated. Post-arrest, the serum potassium was 7.0 mEq/L and glucose and insulin were given. However, she remained unresponsive with dilated pupils and it was decided that further resuscitation was not indicated and she died at 01.30.

The excellent autopsy report notes that the histopathologist discussed the case with the anaesthetist

prior to the autopsy. The events leading to death are clearly described. Examination of the heart showed that 'most of the anterior wall of the left ventricle and two-thirds of the septum have been severely scarred and damaged by previous myocardial infarct'. 'The coronary arteries displayed severe atheroma throughout'. In particular the anterior descending branch was almost completely occluded for most of its course and the right coronary artery had 'severe confluent calcified atheromatous plaques'. The cause of death was given as:

I (a)   Acute on chronic cardiac failure

I (b)   Severe ischaemic heart disease and mitral valve stenosis

I (c)   Severe coronary atheroma and thrombosis

Interestingly, this autopsy report could be criticised for not recording the operation in part II of the ONS cause of death.

> **Pathologists and clinicians should hold multidisciplinary audit meetings.**
>
> **Findings from autopsies need to be part of the process of learning from deaths at morbidity and mortality meetings. Pathologists undertaking autopsies should attend such meetings not only for the benefit of the clinical discussion but also as part of the pathologist's continuing professional development.**

As the proportion of autopsies performed for the coroner has increased and the number of hospital autopsies has declined, the autopsy has become a process that appears, in many cases, to have lost its link with clinical medicine. This may result from poor communication between the clinician and the pathologist and a failure in understanding by the pathologist of the role of the often-complex clinical events leading to death. There is a need to bridge this gap by insisting that there is proper communication between clinicians and the pathologist prior to the autopsy. This should be a requirement which, through the use of formal summaries from the clinicians to the pathologist, would ensure that the clinical situation prior to death was understood by the pathologist; it would also discourage the arbitrary dismissal of clinical factors by the pathologist, as sometimes happens at present. Such a system cannot be put in place unless the current coronial system is altered. The quality of clinical summaries may also be an issue; the submission of incomplete, inadequate or misleading information would not be acceptable. Once the principle of shared information was accepted then the separate but linked issue of quality could be addressed.

In addition, pathologists undertaking autopsies need to be very much more aware of the clinical interventions taking place prior to death, particularly for those patients dying in intensive care units. For this to happen, the pathologist should form part of multidisciplinary morbidity and mortality discussions that take place following surgical deaths, with the opportunity to amend the cause of death and conclusions in the light of these discussions.

All aspects of medicine are being subjected to external audit; there is no reason why aspects of current practice in relation to autopsies should not receive similar scrutiny. The quality of these examinations should be assessed and audited by independent groups that include clinicians whose patients are undergoing autopsy. There is, from the cases examined by NCEPOD, evidence of inconsistency in the way in which individual coroners are ordering autopsies. In that the performance of an autopsy can be stressful to relatives and expensive, the decision-making process applied by coroners could be improved and monitored. How can a coroner, who has many duties, consider in detail the large number of deaths which will be reported to him on a daily basis from the area within his jurisdiction?

This of course presupposes that a coroner can find a pathologist to do the work. Anecdotal evidence indicates that coroners may often experience problems in finding a suitable pathologist to do some autopsies, especially those requiring specialist expertise. The Royal College of Pathologists' current workforce figures show that 16% (173/1071) of consultant histopathologist posts and a similar percentage (7/42) of paediatric pathologist posts across the UK are vacant (personal communication).

For autopsies to be of a broader value to modern practice, those performing them and the conclusions they reach need to be more fully integrated into multidisciplinary medical practice.

REFERENCES

1. *Learning from Bristol.* The Report of the Public Inquiry into children's heart surgery at the Bristol Royal Infirmary 1984-1995. The Stationery Office, 2001.

2. *Changing the way we operate.* The 2001 Report of the National Confidential Enquiry into Perioperative Deaths. NCEPOD. London, 2001. **www.ncepod.org.uk**

3. *The Report of the National Confidential Enquiry into Perioperative Deaths 1994/95.* NCEPOD. London, 1996.

4. Hammond P. *The death of the autopsy.* NHS Magazine. June 2002; 28.

5. Poloniecki JD, Roxburgh JC. *Performance data and the mortuary register.* Ann R Coll Surg Engl 2000; **82:**401-404.

6. *Data Remember.* Audit Commission. London, 2001. **www.audit-commission.gov.uk**

7. *Step Guide to Improving Operating Theatre Performance.* Department of Health. July 2002. **www.modern.nhs.uk**

8. *Hospital Building Note 26.* Section 4.37. Department of Health. 1991. **www.nhsestates.gov.uk**

9. *Guidelines for the Provision of Anaesthetic Services.* Royal College of Anaesthetists. London, 1999. **www.rcoa.ac.uk**

10. *Isolated Acute Medical Services.* Report of a working party of the Royal College of Physicians. London, 2002. **www.rcplondon.ac.uk**

11. Intensive Care Society, *Standards for Intensive Care Units,* Intensive Care Society. London, 1997. **www.ics.ac.uk**

12. *National Minimum Standards Regulations, Independent Health Care.* Department of Health. London, 2002. **www.doh.gov.uk**

13. *Recommendations for standards of monitoring during anaesthesia and recovery,* Association of Anaesthetists of Great Britain and Ireland. London, 2000. **www.aagbi.org**

14. Goodacre S, Irons R. *ABC of clinical electrocardiography:atrial arrhythmias.* BMJ 2002; **7337:** 594-7.

15. *Implementing and ensuring safe sedation practice for healthcare procedures in adults.* Academy of Medical Royal Colleges. London, 2001. **www.aocrc.org.uk**

16. *Day case cataract surgery.* SIGN publication No. 53, 2001. **www.show.scot.nhs.uk/SIGN**

17. *Local anaesthesia for intraocular surgery.* Royal College of Anaesthetists and Royal College of Ophthalmologists, London, 2001. **www.rcoa.ac.uk www.rcophth.ac.uk**

18. *Pre-operative assessment – the role of the anaesthetist.* Association of Anaesthetists of Great Britain and Ireland. London, 2001. **www.aagbi.org**

19. *Early management of patients with a head injury.* SIGN publication No. 46, 2000. **www.show.scot.nhs.uk/SIGN**

20. *Report of the working party on the management of patients with head injuries.* Royal College of Surgeons of England. London, 1999. **www.rcseng.ac.uk**

21. *Safe neurosurgery.* Society of British Neurosurgeons. London, 1993.

22. *Making the best use of a department of clinical radiology.* Guidelines for doctors. 4th Edition. Royal College of Radiologists. London, 1998. **www.rcr.ac.uk**

23. Munro J, Booth A, Nicholl J. *Routine pre-operative testing: a systematic review of the evidence.* Health Technology Assessment 1197; 1:12. **www.hta.nhsweb.nhs.uk**

24. Eagel KA, Berger PB, Calkins H, Chaitman BR, Ewy GA, Fleishmmann KE, Fleisher LA, Froehlich JB, Gusberg RJ, Leppo JA, Ryan T, Schlant RC, Winters WLJr. *ACC/AHA guideline update on perioperative cardiovascular evaluation for noncardiac surgery: a report of the American College of Cardiology/American Heart Association Task Force on Practice Guidelines (Committee to update the 1996 Guidelines on Perioperative Cardiovascular Evaluation for Noncardiac Surgery).* American College of Cardiology. 2002. **www.acc.org**

25. Lee TH, Marcantonio ER, Mangione CM, Thomas EJ, Polanczyk CA, Cook EF, Sugarbaker DJ, Donaldson MC, Poss R, ho KKL, Ludwig LE, Pendan A, Goldman L. *Derivation and prospective validation of a simple index for prediction of cardiac risk of major noncardiac surgery.* Circulation 1999, **100**: 1043-9.

26. *Extremes of Age.* The 1999 Report of the National Confidential Enquiry into Perioperative Deaths. NCEPOD. London, 1999.

27. *Pharmacy Technicians carrying out a final check for accuracy of a dispensed medicine.* Policy statement No:005. Guild of Healthcare Pharmacists. 2001. **www.ghp.org.uk**

28. *Good Medical Practice.* General Medical Council. London, 2001. **www.gmc-uk.org**

29. *Clinical Risk Management Standards.* NHS Litigation Authority. London, 2002. **www.nhsla.com**

30. Crawford JR, Beresford TP, Lafferty KL. *The CRABEL score – a method for auditing medical records.* Ann R Coll Surg Engl, 2001; **83**: 65-8.

31. *Setting the Records Straight.* Audit Commission. London, 1995. www. audit-commission.gov.uk

32. *Basic Surgical Training.* The Royal College of Surgeons of England. London, 1999. **www.rcseng.ac.uk**

33. *Good Surgical Practice.* The Royal College of Surgeons of England. London, 2000. **www.rcseng.ac.uk**

34. Hoile RW. *Are we fit to make decisions?* Clinician in Management 1998; **7**:38-40.

35. Watkin D. *Patients must consider potential serious complications.* BMJ 2002; **325**:339.

36. *Guidelines for Postmortem Reports.* Royal College of Pathologists. London, 1993. **www.rcpath.org**

37. Start RD, Cross SS. *Pathological investigation of deaths following surgery, anaesthesia and medical procedures.* J Clin Pathol 1999; **52**:640-652.

38. Nichols L, Aronica P, Babe C. *Are autopsies obsolete?* Am J Clin Pathol 1998; **110**:210-218.

39. Jennings CR, Bradley PJ. *Are autopsies useful? Do premorbid findings predict postmortem results in head and neck cancer patients?* Ann R Coll Surg Engl 2002; **84**:133-136.

40. Rutty GN, Duerden RM, Carter N, Clark JC. *Are Coroners' necropsies necessary? A prospective study examining whether a "view and grant" system of death certification could be introduced into England and Wales.* J Clin Pathol 2001; **54**:279-284.

41. *Guidelines for the Retention of Tissues and Organs at Post-mortem Examination.* Royal College of Pathologists. London, 2000. **www.rcpath.org**

42. Swift B, West K. *Death certification: an audit of practice entering the 21st century.* J Clin Pathol 2002; **55**:275-279.

43. *Then and Now.* The 2000 Report of the National Confidential Enquiry into Perioperative Deaths. London, 2000.

44. Pilling HH. *Natural and unnatural deaths.* Med Sci Law 1967; **7**:59-62.

45. *Coroners' Rules (1984) Rule 9: Preservation of material.* HMSO, London, 1984.

46. *Fundamental review of the Coroner's system.* Home Office. 2002. **www.coronersreview.org.uk**

47. Rankin J, Wright C, Lind T. *Cross sectional survey of parents' experience and views of the postmortem examination.* Brit Med J 2002; **324**:816-818.

48. McPhee SJ, Bottles K, Lo B, Saika G, Crommie D. *To redeem them from death. Reactions of family members to autopsy.* Am J Med 1986; **80**:665-671.

49. Start RD, Saul CA, Cotton K, Mathers NJ, Underwood JCE. *Public perceptions of necropsy.* J Clin Pathol 1995; **48**:497-500.

50. Vanezis P, Leadbeatter S. *Next of kin clinics: a new role for the pathologist.* J Clin Pathol 2000; **53**:646.

APPENDIX A

REPORTED DEATHS BY TRUST/HOSPITAL GROUP

The following tables show the number of deaths reported to NCEPOD in 2000/01 compared to deaths reported in 1999/00 and the participation rate of trusts/hospitals. The tables also show the number of reported lost notes by each hospital and the number of cases where no reason was given for the non-return of the questionnaire. Other reasons for non-return include consultants no longer working at hospital, hospitals unable to identify clinicians involved in the care of patient and consultants on long-term leave.

ENGLAND

Trust name	Deaths reported		Surgical questionnaires				Anaesthetic questionnaires			
	2000/01	1999/00	Sent	Received	Notes reported missing	No reason given for non-return	Sent	Received	Notes reported missing	No reason given for non-return
Addenbrooke's NHS Trust	24	42	6	5	-	1	6	6	-	-
Aintree Hospitals NHS Trust	141	87	15	12	-	3	14	13	1	-
Airedale NHS Trust	1	81	0	-	-	-	0	-	-	-
Ashford & St Peter's Hospital NHS Trust	79	50	12	11	-	1	8	6	-	2
Barking, Havering and Redbridge Hospitals NHS Trust	235	257	23	23	-	-	20	18	-	2
Barnet and Chase Farm Hospitals NHS Trust	108	124	18	16	-	2	19	19	-	-
Barnsley District General Hospital NHS Trust	121	101	14	11	-	2	11	11	-	-
Barts and the London NHS Trust	191	216	24	21	-	2	14	10	1	3
Basildon & Thurrock General Hospitals NHS Trust	45	28	12	12	-	-	12	11	-	-
Bedford Hospital NHS Trust	119	88	7	6	-	1	6	6	-	-
Birmingham Children's Hospital NHS Trust	18	11	7	6	-	-	7	7	-	-
Birmingham Heartlands & Solihull NHS Trust	252	266	30	26	1	2	29	28	1	-
Birmingham Women's Healthcare NHS Trust	3	1	1	0	-	1	1	1	-	-
Blackburn, Hyndburn & Ribble Valley Healthcare NHS Trust	57	111	10	9	1	-	7	6	-	1
Blackpool, Fylde and Wyre Hospitals NHS Trust	300	253	17	14	-	3	15	14	1	-
Bolton Hospitals NHS Trust	129	105	12	12	-	-	11	11	-	-
Bradford Hospitals NHS Trust	194	194	20	18	-	2	19	18	-	1
Brighton & Sussex University Hospitals NHS Trust	198	180	23	22	-	1	17	17	-	-
Bromley Hospitals NHS Trust	80	4	7	4	-	3	5	5	-	-
Burnley Health Care NHS Trust	1	2	0	-	-	-	0	-	-	-
Burton Hospitals NHS Trust	12	44	2	2	-	-	1	1	-	-
Calderdale & Huddersfield NHS Trust	140	172	9	8	-	1	9	8	1	-

Trust name	Deaths reported		Surgical questionnaires				Anaesthetic questionnaires			
	2000/01	1999/00	Sent	Received	Notes reported missing	No reason given for non-return	Sent	Received	Notes reported missing	No reason given for non-return
Cardiothoracic Centre Liverpool NHS Trust	62	55	9	7	-	1	8	8	-	-
Central Manchester/ Manchester Children's University Hospitals NHS Trust	74	61	14	13	1	-	14	13	-	-
Chelsea & Westminster Healthcare NHS Trust	15	25	4	4	-	-	4	3	-	1
Chesterfield & North Derbyshire Royal Hospital NHS Trust	62	68	10	10	-	-	10	10	-	-
Chorley & South Ribble NHS Trust	34	47	7	6	-	-	7	7	-	-
Christie Hospital NHS Trust	3	5	0	-	-	-	0	-	-	-
City Hospitals Sunderland NHS Trust	207	215	18	16	-	1	18	16	-	-
Countess of Chester Hospital NHS Trust	131	92	9	8	-	1	8	8	-	-
Dartford & Gravesham NHS Trust	65	46	6	6	-	-	4	4	-	-
Doncaster and Bassetlaw Hospitals NHS Trust	156	160	17	16	1	-	15	15	-	-
Dudley Group of Hospitals NHS Trust (The)	125	No deaths reported	13	10	-	2	1	1	-	-
Ealing Hospital NHS Trust	8	26	1	1	-	-	1	0	-	1
East & North Hertfordshire NHS Trust	18	81	5	4	-	1	5	5	-	-
East Cheshire NHS Trust	31	30	6	6	-	-	6	6	-	-
East Kent Hospitals NHS Trust	312	252	30	28	-	2	25	21	2	2
East Somerset NHS Trust	26	41	6	6	-	-	6	6	-	-
East Sussex Hospitals NHS Trust	158	205	18	17	1	-	18	17	-	1
Epsom & St Helier NHS Trust	116	106	14	13	-	1	12	12	-	-
Essex Rivers Healthcare NHS Trust	143	139	10	9	-	1	10	10	-	-
Frimley Park Hospitals NHS Trust	64	72	12	11	_	1	11	10	-	1
Gateshead Health NHS Trust	77	74	10	9	-	1	10	10	-	-
George Eliot Hospital NHS Trust	67	63	10	7	-	2	9	4	1	4
Gloucestershire Hospitals NHS Trust	398	384	31	30	-	-	27	25	1	1

Trust name	Deaths reported		Surgical questionnaires				Anaesthetic questionnaires			
	2000/01	1999/00	Sent	Received	Notes reported missing	No reason given for non-return	Sent	Received	Notes reported missing	No reason given for non-return
Good Hope Hospital NHS Trust	84	95	11	10	1	-	11	10	-	1
Great Ormond Street Hospital for Children NHS Trust (The)	36	47	10	10	-	-	10	10	-	-
Guy's & St Thomas' Hospital Trust	79	161	15	11	-	4	14	14	-	-
Hammersmith Hospitals NHS Trust	148	46	15	12	-	3	14	14	-	-
Harrogate Health Care NHS Trust	89	72	5	5	-	-	5	5	-	-
Heatherwood & Wexham Park Hospitals NHS Trust	143	60	18	14	-	4	18	13	2	2
Hereford Hospitals NHS Trust	12	15	5	5	-	-	5	5	-	-
Hillingdon Hospital NHS Trust	30	45	5	5	-	-	5	5	-	-
Hinchingbrooke Health Care NHS Trust	61	59	9	8	-	1	5	5	-	-
Homerton University Hospital NHS Trust	33	18	4	4	-	-	3	3	-	-
Hull and East Yorkshire Hospitals NHS Trust	177	143	21	20	1	-	21	19	-	2
Ipswich Hospital NHS Trust	148	181	12	12	-	-	9	9	-	-
Isle of Wight Healthcare NHS Trust	74	68	6	5	-	1	0	-	-	-
James Paget Healthcare NHS Trust	101	120	11	11	-	-	10	10	-	-
Kettering General Hospital NHS Trust	114	135	14	12	-	1	14	14	-	-
Kings College Hospital NHS Trust	134	120	15	11	-	2	11	3	-	8
King's Lynn & Wisbech Hospitals NHS Trust	91	67	8	5	-	3	7	7	-	-
Kingston Hospital NHS Trust	17	49	3	2	-	1	3	1	-	2
Leeds Teaching Hospitals NHS Trust (The)	517	521	56	39	1	9	43	27	3	13
Lewisham Hospital NHS Trust (The)	116	115	12	9	-	2	12	12	-	-
Liverpool Women's Hospital NHS Trust	4	5	0	-	-	-	0	-	-	-
Luton & Dunstable Hospital NHS Trust	50	40	7	5	-	2	6	5	-	1
Maidstone & Tunbridge Wells NHS Trust	207	217	21	21	-	-	17	15	-	2

Trust name	Deaths reported		Surgical questionnaires				Anaesthetic questionnaires			
	2000/01	1999/00	Sent	Received	Notes reported missing	No reason given for non-return	Sent	Received	Notes reported missing	No reason given for non-return
Mayday Healthcare NHS Trust	60	67	10	10	-	-	10	8	-	1
Medway NHS Trust	134	127	14	13	-	-	7	7	-	-
Mid Cheshire Hospitals NHS Trust	164	148	14	10	1	3	11	5	1	5
Mid-Essex Hospital Services NHS Trust	94	100	12	12	-	-	11	11	-	-
Mid Staffordshire General Hospitals NHS Trust	77	56	11	9	-	2	10	8	-	2
Mid Yorkshire Hospitals NHS Trust	217	210	25	23	1	1	22	22	-	-
Milton Keynes General NHS Trust	30	35	8	8	-	-	8	7	-	1
Moorfields Eye Hospital NHS Trust	0	0	-	-	-	-	-	-	-	-
Morecombe Bay Hospitals NHS Trust	119	121	16	14	-	2	15	15	-	-
Newcastle upon Tyne Hospitals NHS Trust (The)	440	373	43	34	1	6	35	29	1	4
Newham Healthcare NHS Trust	41	50	6	6	-	-	6	6	-	-
Norfolk & Norwich University Hospital NHS Trust	264	257	22	19	-	2	22	19	3	-
North Bristol NHS Trust	179	119	32	25	1	4	31	28	-	3
North Cheshire Hospitals NHS Trust	39	108	5	4	-	1	3	3	-	-
North Cumbria Acute Hospitals NHS Trust	73	122	11	10	-	1	8	7	-	1
North Durham Healthcare NHS Trust	58	123	8	8	-	-	8	7	-	-
North Hampshire Hospitals NHS Trust	56	48	11	10	-	1	11	9	-	2
North Middlesex University Hospital NHS Trust	93	No deaths reported	12	9	-	1	12	12	-	-
North Staffordshire Hospital NHS Trust	79	117	16	12	3	1	16	16	-	-
North Tees and Hartlepool NHS Trust	99	118	13	13	-	-	14	14	-	-
North West London Hospitals NHS Trust	127	114	14	13	-	-	14	14	-	-
Northampton General Hospital NHS Trust	65	91	10	9	-	1	10	10	-	-
Northern Devon Healthcare NHS Trust	64	75	7	6	-	1	5	4	-	-
Northern Lincolnshire & Goole Hospitals NHS Trust	83	110	13	10	1	1	7	6	1	-

Trust name	Deaths reported		Surgical questionnaires				Anaesthetic questionnaires			
	2000/01	1999/00	Sent	Received	Notes reported missing	No reason given for non-return	Sent	Received	Notes reported missing	No reason given for non-return
Northumbria Healthcare NHS Trust	144	154	18	18	-	-	16	16	-	-
Nottingham City Hospital NHS Trust	75	107	14	13	-	-	13	13	-	-
Nuffield Orthopaedic Centre NHS Trust	6	2	1	1	-	-	1	1	-	-
Oxford Radcliffe Hospitals NHS Trust	269	291	35	32	-	3	33	31	2	-
Papworth Hospital NHS Trust	107	94	7	7	-	-	7	7	-	-
Pennine Acute Hospitals NHS Trust (The)	239	232	30	27	-	1	30	28	-	1
Peterborough Hospitals NHS Trust	134	115	17	17	-	-	16	14	2	-
Plymouth Hospitals NHS Trust	326	206	37	29	-	6	33	23	1	8
Poole Hospital NHS Trust	152	No deaths reported	10	8	-	2	0	-	-	-
Portsmouth Hospitals NHS Trust	114	37	16	14	-	2	12	9	-	3
Preston Acute Hospitals NHS Trust	121	90	12	9	1	1	7	4	1	2
Princess Alexandra Hospital NHS Trust (The)	3	44	0	-	-	-	0	-	-	-
Princess Royal Hospital NHS Trust (The)	11	14	5	4	-	1	5	5	-	-
Queen Elizabeth Hospital NHS Trust	67	89	5	5	-	-	4	4	-	-
Queen Mary's Sidcup NHS Trust	2	16	0	-	-	-	0	-	-	-
Queen's Medical Centre Nottingham University Hospital NHS Trust	326	321	30	29	-	1	27	26	1	-
Queen Victoria Hospital NHS Trust (The)	16	22	2	2	-	-	2	2	-	-
Robert Jones/Agnes Hunt Orthopaedic Hospital NHS Trust	2	3	2	2	-	-	2	2	-	-
Rotherham General Hospitals NHS Trust	132	135	11	11	-	-	10	10	-	-
Royal Berkshire & Battle Hospitals NHS Trust	22	33	9	7	-	2	7	7	-	-
Royal Bournemouth & Christchurch Hospitals NHS Trust	96	94	12	11	-	1	11	10	1	-
Royal Brompton & Harefield NHS Trust	137	145	15	10	-	5	15	13	1	-

Trust name	Deaths reported		Surgical questionnaires				Anaesthetic questionnaires			
	2000/01	1999/00	Sent	Received	Notes reported missing	No reason given for non-return	Sent	Received	Notes reported missing	No reason given for non-return
Royal Cornwall Hospitals Trust	224	102	17	13	-	3	16	16	-	-
Royal Devon & Exeter Healthcare NHS Trust	267	271	19	19	-	-	17	16	-	1
Royal Free Hampstead NHS Trust	128	30	13	8	-	5	11	5	-	6
Royal Liverpool & Broadgreen University Hospitals NHS Trust	221	194	20	20	-	-	12	12	-	-
Royal Liverpool Children's NHS Trust (The)	22	24	3	3	-	-	3	3	-	-
Royal Marsden NHS Trust (The)	27	24	2	1	-	-	2	0	1	1
Royal National Orthopaedic Hospital NHS Trust	10	5	2	1	-	1	2	2	-	-
Royal Orthopaedic Hospital NHS Trust (The)	5	7	3	3	-	-	3	3	-	-
Royal Shrewsbury Hospitals NHS Trust	22	14	7	6	1	-	7	7	-	-
Royal Surrey County Hospital NHS Trust	38	62	9	9	-	-	9	9	-	-
Royal United Hospital Bath NHS Trust	3	24	0	-	-	-	0	-	-	-
Royal West Sussex NHS Trust (The)	68	95	10	9	-	1	10	9	-	1
Royal Wolverhampton Hospitals NHS Trust (The)	136	155	13	12	-	1	13	13	-	-
Salford Royal Hospitals NHS Trust	156	143	18	16	1	1	16	15	1	-
Salisbury Health Care NHS Trust	40	28	10	10	-	-	10	10	-	-
Sandwell & West Birmingham Hospitals NHS Trust	218	259	24	19	1	4	23	20	-	-
Scarborough & North East Yorkshire Health Care NHS Trust	101	96	8	7	-	-	8	8	-	-
Sheffield Children's Hospital NHS Trust	15	13	3	2	-	1	3	3	-	-
Sheffield Teaching Hospitals NHS Trust	364	319	40	38	1	-	33	33	-	-
Sherwood Forest Hospitals NHS Trust	117	118	10	10	-	-	9	9	-	-
South Buckinghamshire NHS Trust	47	51	7	6	1	-	6	5	1	-
South Devon Healthcare NHS Trust	58	106	7	7	-	-	7	6	-	1

Trust name	Deaths reported		Surgical questionnaires				Anaesthetic questionnaires			
	2000/01	1999/00	Sent	Received	Notes reported missing	No reason given for non-return	Sent	Received	Notes reported missing	No reason given for non-return
South Durham Healthcare NHS Trust	71	60	10	9	-	1	10	10	-	-
South Manchester University Hospitals NHS Trust	95	124	17	16	-	-	17	16	-	1
South Tees Hospitals NHS Trust	248	293	30	30	-	-	25	25	-	-
South Tyneside Healthcare Trust	54	68	7	5	-	2	7	7	-	-
South Warwickshire General Hospitals NHS Trust	79	57	10	8	1	1	10	10	-	-
Southampton University Hospitals NHS Trust	282	9	34	30	-	1	30	26	-	3
Southend Hospital NHS Trust	116	112	13	12	1	-	10	7	1	2
Southern Derbyshire Acute Hospitals NHS Trust	129	142	13	13	-	-	13	13	-	-
Southport & Ormskirk Hospital NHS Trust	114	81	9	9	-	-	9	9	-	-
St George's Healthcare NHS Trust	289	290	29	22	-	3	22	15	2	5
St Helens & Knowsley Hospitals NHS Trust	131	156	15	12	1	1	14	13	-	1
St Mary's NHS Trust	40	75	10	9	-	1	8	5	1	2
Stockport NHS Trust	74	68	12	11	1	-	12	12	-	-
Stoke Mandeville Hospital NHS Trust	42	49	4	4	-	-	4	4	-	-
Surrey & Sussex Healthcare NHS Trust	No deaths reported	95	0	-	-	-	0	-	-	-
Swindon & Marlborough NHS Trust	93	82	14	14	-	-	9	9	-	-
Tameside & Glossop Acute Services NHS Trust	50	73	10	10	-	-	11	9	-	2
Taunton & Somerset NHS Trust	24	38	3	3	-	-	3	3	-	-
Trafford Healthcare NHS Trust	24	28	2	2	-	-	2	2	-	-
United Bristol Healthcare NHS Trust	72	89	19	14	1	4	17	16	-	-
United Lincolnshire Hospitals NHS Trust	218	276	28	23	1	4	24	23	-	1
University College London Hospitals NHS Trust	160	154	22	16	1	4	22	15	4	1
University Hospital Birmingham NHS Trust	182	185	27	26	1	-	21	16	1	4

Trust name	Deaths reported		Surgical questionnaires				Anaesthetic questionnaires			
	2000/01	1999/00	Sent	Received	Notes reported missing	No reason given for non-return	Sent	Received	Notes reported missing	No reason given for non-return
University Hospitals Coventry & Warwickshire NHS Trust	133	217	21	16	1	4	22	20	-	1
University Hospitals of Leicester NHS Trust	279	234	38	31	3	4	35	32	2	1
Walsall Hospitals NHS Trust	111	147	13	11	-	2	12	11	-	1
Walton Centre for Neurology & Neurosurgery NHS Trust	26	29	4	4	-	-	4	2	1	1
West Dorset General Hospitals NHS Trust	71	113	7	7	-	-	7	7	-	-
West Hertfordshire Hospitals NHS Trust	152	144	19	16	2	1	18	14	1	3
West Middlesex University Hospital NHS Trust	34	20	5	4	-	-	5	5	-	-
West Suffolk Hospitals NHS Trust	94	98	15	13	-	-	13	13	-	-
Weston Area Health Trust	54	61	4	4	-	-	3	3	-	-
Whipps Cross University Hospital NHS Trust	112	90	13	9	3	1	13	7	5	1
Whittington Hospital NHS Trust	45	41	6	6	-	-	5	5	-	-
Winchester & Eastleigh Healthcare NHS Trust	27	63	4	4	-	-	4	4	-	-
Wirral Hospital NHS Trust	175	175	17	17	-	-	16	14	2	-
Worcestershire Acute Hospitals NHS Trust	95	169	12	11	-	-	11	11	-	-
Worthing & Southlands Hospitals NHS Trust	128	136	15	14	1	-	13	12	1	-
Wrightington, Wigan & Leigh NHS Trust	129	107	16	16	-	-	14	11	1	2
York Health Services NHS Trust	97	94	12	12	-	-	11	10	1	-

WALES

Trust name	Deaths reported		Surgical questionnaires				Anaesthetic questionnaires			
	2000/01	1999/00	Sent	Received	Notes reported missing	No reason given for non-return	Sent	Received	Notes reported missing	No reason given for non-return
Bro Morgannwg NHS Trust	10	6	2	2	-	-	1	1	-	-
Cardiff & Vale NHS Trust	29	174	6	5	-	1	1	1	-	-
Carmarthenshire NHS Trust	72	112	11	11	-	-	10	10	-	-
Ceredigion & Mid Wales NHS Trust	28	26	5	5	-	-	5	5	-	-
Conwy & Denbighshire NHS Trust	89	106	14	13	-	-	14	14	-	-
Gwent Healthcare NHS Trust	230	220	28	26	1	1	24	22	1	1
North East Wales NHS Trust	89	100	10	10	-	-	10	9	-	1
North Glamorgan NHS Trust	46	35	7	6	-	-	7	5	1	1
North West Wales NHS Trust	87	79	14	13	-	1	14	14	-	-
Pembrokeshire & Derwen NHS Trust	43	44	5	5	-	-	5	5	-	-
Pontypridd & Rhondda NHS Trust	76	100	7	6	-	1	7	7	-	-
Swansea NHS Trust	218	215	32	30	1	1	24	17	-	5

NORTHERN IRELAND

Trust name	Deaths reported		Surgical questionnaires				Anaesthetic questionnaires			
	2000/01	1999/00	Sent	Received	Notes reported missing	No reason given for non-return	Sent	Received	Notes reported missing	No reason given for non-return
Altnagelvin Hospitals Health & Social Services Trust	12	12	3	3	-	-	2	2	-	-
Belfast City Hospital Health & Social Services Trust	58	50	8	7	-	1	8	8	-	-
Causeway Health & Social Services Trust	11	12	2	2	-	-	2	2	-	-
Craigavon Area Hospital Group Trust	43	51	6	6	-	-	6	6	-	-
Down Lisburn Health & Social Services Trust	23	19	2	2	-	-	2	2	-	-
Green Park Healthcare Trust	4	3	1	1	-	-	1	1	-	-
Mater Hospital Belfast Health & Social Services Trust	30	22	5	5	-	-	5	5	-	-
Newry & Mourne Health & Social Services Trust	30	16	3	3	-	-	1	1	-	-
Royal Group of Hospitals & Dental Hospitals & Maternity Hospitals Trust	106	100	18	14	-	2	15	10	4	1
Sperrin Lakeland Health & Social Care NHS Trust	9	16	4	4	-	-	4	3	-	1
Ulster Community & Hospitals NHS Trust	55	35	7	7	-	-	6	5	-	1
United Hospitals Health & Social Services Trust	18	24	4	2	2	-	4	2	1	-

OTHER HOSPITALS

Trust name	Deaths reported		Surgical questionnaires				Anaesthetic questionnaires			
	2000/01	1999/00	Sent	Received	Notes reported missing	No reason given for non-return	Sent	Received	Notes reported missing	No reason given for non-return
Guernsey	22	14	3	3	-	-	3	2	-	-
Isle of Man	26	22	3	3	-	-	3	3	-	-
Jersey	21	31	4	4	-	-	4	3	-	1
DSCA – The Princess Mary's Hospital, Cyprus	No deaths reported	No deaths reported	-	-	-	-	-	-	-	-

INDEPENDENT HOSPITAL GROUPS

Hospital / Group name	Deaths reported		Surgical questionnaires				Anaesthetic questionnaires			
	2000/01	1999/00	Sent	Received	Notes reported missing	No reason given for non-return	Sent	Received	Notes reported missing	No reason given for non-return
Aspen Healthcare	2	0	1	1	-	-	1	1	-	-
Benenden Hospital Trust (The)	0	1	0	-	-	-	0	-	-	-
BMI Healthcare	78	87	22	18	-	2	21	17	-	4
BUPA	31	33	6	6	-	-	6	5	-	1
Capio Healthcare UK	12	19	4	4	-	-	4	3	1	-
HCA International	37	47	4	4	-	-	4	2	-	2
King Edward VII Hospital	3	5	0	-	-	-	0	-	-	-
King Edward VII's Hospital Sister Agnes	2	5	0	-	-	-	0	-	-	-
London Clinic (The)	13	14	3	2	-	1	3	3	-	-
Nuffield Hospitals	16	20	4	3	-	1	4	4	-	-

ASA 3: A patient with severe systemic disease that limits activity but is not incapacitating.

ASA 4: A patient with incapacitating systemic disease that is a constant threat to life.

ASA 5: A moribund patient who is not expected to survive for 24 hours with or without an operation.

* The definitions are those in use during 2000/01. The wording of ASA grades 3-5 was modified and a sixth grade added in 1999, but was changed too late for inclusion in this study.

Classification of operation (NCEPOD definition)

EMERGENCY: Immediate life-saving operation, resuscitation, simultaneous with surgical treatment (e.g. trauma, ruptured aortic aneurysm). Operation usually within one hour.

URGENT: Operation as soon as possible after resuscitation (e.g. irreducible hernia, intussusception, oesophageal atresia, intestinal obstruction, major fractures). Operation within 24 hours.

SCHEDULED: An early operation but not immediately life-saving (e.g. malignancy). Operation usually within three weeks.

ELECTIVE: Operation at a time to suit both patient and surgeon (e.g. cholecystectomy, joint replacement).

Recovery and special care areas (Association of Anaesthetists of Great Britain and Ireland definitions)

HIGH DEPENDENCY UNIT: A high dependency unit (HDU) is an area for patients who require more intensive observation, treatment and nursing care than can be provided on a general ward. It would not normally accept patients requiring mechanical ventilation, but could manage those receiving invasive monitoring.

INTENSIVE CARE UNIT: An intensive care unit (ICU) is an area to which patients are admitted for treatment of actual or impending organ failure, especially when mechanical ventilation is necessary.

RECOVERY AREA: A recovery area is an area to which patients are admitted from an operating theatre, and where they remain until consciousness has been regained, respiration and circulation are stable and postoperative analgesia is established.

APPENDIX B

GLOSSARY

Definition of the 1994/95, 1999/00 and 2000/01 sample groups

1994/95: The first occurrence within the year for each surgeon of a death within 3 days of surgery.

1999/00: A random sample of 10% of reported deaths.

2000/01: The first occurrence within the year for each surgeon of a death within 3 days of surgery.

Admission category (NCEPOD definitions)

ELECTIVE: At a time agreed between the patient and the surgical service.

URGENT: Within 48 hours of referral/consultation.

EMERGENCY: Immediately following referral/consultation, when admission is unpredictable and at short notice because of clinical need.

American Society of Anesthesiologists (ASA) classification of physical status*

ASA 1: A normal healthy patient.

ASA 2: A patient with mild systemic disease.

APPENDIX C

ABBREVIATIONS

A&E	Accident & Emergency
AAA	Abdominal aortic aneurysm
AF	Atrial fibrillation
AQ	Anaesthetic questionnaire
ARDS	Acute respiratory distress syndrome
ASA	American Society of Anesthesiologists
BP	Blood pressure
CABG	Coronary artery bypass grafts
CCF	Congestive cardiac failure
CNST	Clinical negligence scheme for trusts
COPD	Chronic obstructive pulmonary disease
CT	Computed tomography
CVA	Cerebrovascular accident
CVP	Central venous pressure
CXR	Chest X-ray
DGH	District general hospital
DHS	Dynamic hip screw
DIC	Disseminated intravascular coagulation
DoH	Department of Health
DVT	Deep vein thrombosis
ECG	Electrocardiogram
EMD	Electromechanical dissociation
ENT	Ear, nose and throat
ERCP	Endoscopic retrograde cholangiopancreatography

EUA	Examination under anaesthetic
FFP	Fresh frozen plasma
GA	General anaesthesia
GCS	Glasgow coma score
GI	Gastrointestinal
HDU	High dependency unit
HES	Hospital episode statistics
HO	House officer
ICU	Intensive care unit
IHD	Ischaemic heart disease
INR	International normalised ratio
IV	Intravenous
IVU	Intravenous urogram
JVP	Jugular venous pressure
LMA	Laryngeal mask airway
LV	Left ventricle
LVF	Left ventricular failure
LVH	Left ventricular hypertrophy
MI	Myocardial infarction
MRI	Magnetic resonance imaging
MRSA	Methicillin resistant staphylococcus aureus
NCCG	Non-consultant career grade
NHS	National Health Service
NIBP	Non-invasive blood pressure
NICE	National Institute for Clinical Excellence
NIDDM	Non-insulin dependent diabetes mellitus
NMR	Nuclear magnetic resonance
ONS	Office of National Statistics
PE	Pulmonary embolus
PEG	Percutaneous endoscopic gastrostomy
PICU	Paediatric intensive care unit
PND	Paroxysmal nocturnal dyspnoea
PVD	Peripheral vascular disease
RIF	Right iliac fossa
SASM	Scottish Audit of Surgical Mortality
SHO 1,2	Senior house officer, year 1 or 2
SOB	Shortness of breath
SpR 1,2,3,4	Specialist registrar, year 1, 2, 3 or 4
SQ	Surgical questionnaire
SVT	Supraventricular tachycardia
TIA	Transient ischaemic attack
TKR	Total knee replacement
VF	Ventricular fibrillation
VT	Ventricular tachycardia
WBC	White blood count

APPENDIX D

NCEPOD CORPORATE STRUCTURE

The National Confidential Enquiry into Perioperative Deaths (NCEPOD) is an independent body to which a corporate commitment has been made by the Associations, Colleges and Faculties related to its areas of activity. Each of these bodies nominates members of the Steering Group.

Steering Group
(as at 31 July 2002)

Members

Dr S. Bridgman (Faculty of Public Health Medicine)

Dr M. Burke (Royal College of Pathologists)

Dr J.F. Dyet (Royal College of Radiologists)

Prof I.T. Gilmore (Royal College of Physicians)

Mr B. Keogh (Royal College of Surgeons of England)

Mr G.T. Layer (Association of Surgeons of Great Britain and Ireland)

Prof. D.M. Luesley (Royal College of Obstetricians and Gynaecologists)

Dr J.M. Millar (Royal College of Anaesthetists)

Dr P. Nightingale (Royal College of Anaesthetists)

Dr M. Pearson (Royal College of Physicians)

Mr B.F. Ribeiro (Royal College of Surgeons)

Dr P.J. Simpson (Royal College of Anaesthetists)

Mr L.F.A. Stassen (Faculty of Dental Surgery, Royal College of Surgeons of England)

Mr M.F. Sullivan (Royal College of Surgeons of England)

Prof T. Treasure (Royal College of Surgeons of England)

Dr D. Whitaker (Association of Anaesthetists of Great Britain and Ireland)

Mrs M. Wishart (Royal College of Ophthalmologists)

APPENDICES

Observers

Mrs M. Ibbetson (Lay representative)

Dr P.A. Knapman (Coroners' Society of England and Wales)

Prof P. Littlejohns (National Institute for Clinical Excellence)

Ms M. McElligott (Royal College of Nursing)

Mr P. Milligan (Institute of Healthcare Management)

NCEPOD is a company, limited by guarantee and a registered charity, managed by Trustees.

Trustees

Mr J.Ll. Williams (Chairman)

Mr M.F. Sullivan (Treasurer)

Dr P.J. Simpson

Prof T. Treasure

Clinical Co-ordinators

The Steering Group appoint the Principal Clinical Co-ordinators for a defined tenure. The Principal Clinical Co-ordinators lead the review of the data relating to the annual sample, advise the Steering Group and write the reports. They may also from time to time appoint Clinical Co-ordinators. All Co-ordinators must be engaged in active academic/clinical practice (in the NHS) during the full term of office.

Principal Clinical Co-ordinators

Anaesthesia	**Dr G.S. Ingram**
Surgery	**Mr R.W. Hoile**

Clinical Co-ordinators

Anaesthesia	**Dr A.J.G. Gray**
	Dr K.M. Sherry
Surgery	**Mr K.G. Callum**
	Mr I.C. Martin

Funding

The total annual cost of NCEPOD was approximately £550,000 in 2000/01. We are pleased to acknowledge the support of the following organisations, who contributed to funding the Enquiry in 2000/2001.

National Institute for Clinical Excellence

Welsh Office

Health and Social Services Executive (Northern Ireland)

States of Guernsey Board of Health States of Jersey

Department of Health and Social Security, Isle of Man Government

Aspen Healthcare

Benenden Hospital

BMI Healthcare

BUPA

Community Hospitals Group

HCA International

King Edward VII Hospital, Midhurst

King Edward VII's Hospital Sister Agnes

Nuffield Hospitals

The Heart Hospital

The London Clinic

This funding covers the total cost of the Enquiry, including administrative salaries and reimbursements for Clinical Co-ordinators, office accommodation charges, computer and other equipment as well as travelling expenses for the Co-ordinators, Steering Group and Advisory Groups.

APPENDIX E

DATA COLLECTION & REVIEW METHODS

The National Confidential Enquiry into Perioperative Deaths (NCEPOD) reviews clinical practice and aims to identify remediable factors in the practice of anaesthesia, all types of surgery and other invasive procedures. The Enquiry considers the quality of the delivery of care and not specifically causation of death. The commentary on the reports is based on peer review of the data, questionnaires and notes submitted; it is not a research study based on differences against a control population, and does not attempt to produce any kind of comparison between clinicians or hospitals.

From April 1 2002, NCEPOD will review clinical practice across all specialities not just anaesthetics and surgery.

Scope

All National Health Service and Defence Secondary Care Agency hospitals in England and Wales and Northern Ireland, and public hospitals in Guernsey, Jersey and the Isle of Man are included in the Enquiry, as well as the majority of hospitals in the independent healthcare sector. From April 1 2002, it is mandatory for independent hospitals to participate as part of the National Minimum Standards Regulations introduced by the National Care Standards Commission.

Reporting of deaths

NCEPOD collects basic details on all deaths in hospital within 30 days of a surgical procedure (with some exceptions – see Appendix I), through a system of local reporting. The Local Reporters (Appendix F) in each hospital are often consultant clinicians, but this role is increasingly being taken on by information and clinical audit departments who are able to provide the data from hospital information systems. When incomplete information is received, the NCEPOD administrative staff contact the appropriate medical records or information officer, secretarial or clinical audit staff.

Deaths of patients in hospital within 30 days of a surgical procedure (excluding maternal deaths) are included. If Local Reporters are aware of postoperative deaths at home they also report them. A surgical procedure is defined by NCEPOD as:
"any procedure carried out by a surgeon or gynaecologist, with or without an anaesthetist, involving local, regional or general anaesthesia or sedation."

Local Reporters provide the following information:

- Name of trust/hospital
- Sex/hospital number/NHS number of patient
- Name of hospital in which the death occurred (and hospital where surgery took place, if different)
- Dates of birth, final operation and death
- Surgical procedure performed
- Name of consultant surgeon
- Name of anaesthetist

Sample for more detailed review

The data collection year runs from 1 April to 31 March. Each year, a sample of the reported deaths is reviewed in more detail. The sample selection varies for each data collection year, and is determined by the NCEPOD Steering Group (see Appendix D).

NCEPOD may, on occasion, collect data about patients who have survived more than 30 days after a procedure. These data are used for comparison with the data about deaths, or to review a specific aspect of clinical practice. Data from other sources may also be used.

The perioperative deaths, which fell within the sample group for 2000/01, occurred within the first three days following the operative procedure. Only the first death for each surgeon was sampled. For each sample case, questionnaires were sent to the consultant surgeon or gynaecologist and consultant anaesthetist. These questionnaires were identified only by a number, allocated in the NCEPOD office. Copies of operation notes, anaesthetic records, fluid balance charts and autopsy reports were also requested. Surgical questionnaires were sent directly to the consultant surgeon or gynaecologist under whose care the patient was at the time of the final operation before death. When the Local Reporter had been able to identify the relevant consultant anaesthetist, the anaesthetic questionnaire was sent directly to him or her. However, in many cases this was not possible, and the local tutor of the Royal College of Anaesthetists was asked to name a consultant to whom the questionnaire should be sent. Copies of the questionnaires used in 2000/01 are available from the NCEPOD office on request.

Since the introduction of clinical governance in April 1999, participation in the confidential enquiries has become a mandatory requirement for clinicians in the NHS and has been mandatory for independent hospitals since April 2002. Trusts/hospitals are therefore now kept informed of their participation levels on a quarterly basis.

Consultants

NCEPOD holds a database, regularly updated, of all consultant anaesthetists, gynaecologists and surgeons in England, Wales and Northern Ireland.

Analysis and review of data

The NCEPOD administrative staff manage the collection, recording and analysis of data. The data are aggregated to produce the tables and information in the reports; further unpublished aggregated data is available from the NCEPOD office on request. All data are aggregated to regional or national level only, so that individual trusts and hospitals cannot be identified.

Advisory groups

The NCEPOD Clinical Co-ordinators (see Appendix D), together with the Advisory Groups for anaesthesia and surgery, review the completed questionnaires and the aggregated data. The members of the Advisory Groups are drawn from hospitals in England, Wales and Northern Ireland. The Advisory Group in pathology reviews autopsy data from the surgical questionnaires.

Production of the report

The Advisory Groups comment on the overall quality of care within the speciality and on any particular issues or individual cases which merit attention. These comments form the basis for the published report, which is prepared by the Co-ordinators, with contributions from the Advisors. The report is reviewed and agreed by the NCEPOD Steering Group prior to publication.

Confidentiality

NCEPOD is registered with the Data Protection Registrar and abides by the Data Protection Principles. All reporting forms, questionnaires and other paper records relating to the sample are shredded once an individual report is ready for publication. Similarly, all identifiable data are removed from the computer database.

Before review of questionnaires by the Clinical Co-ordinators or any of the Advisors, all identification is removed from the questionnaires and accompanying papers. The source of the information is not revealed to any of the Co-ordinators or Advisors. The Chief Executive of NCEPOD is the Caldicott Guardian for all information held.

APPENDIX F

LOCAL REPORTERS

As at 1 September 2001 (i.e. the close of the sample collection), with NHS trusts listed according to regional divisions in place at that date.

We appreciate that there are many clinical audit and information departments involved in providing data, although we have named only the individual nominated as the Local Reporter.

Eastern

Addenbrooke's NHS Trust
Dr D. Wight

Basildon & Thurrock General Hospitals NHS Trust
Dr A.K. Abdulla

Bedford Hospital Trust
Mrs S. Blackley

East & North Hertfordshire NHS Trust
Dr A. Fattah (Queen Elizabeth II Hospital & Hertford County Hospital)
Dr D.J. Madders (Lister Hospital)

Essex Rivers Healthcare NHS Trust
Mrs E. Pudney

Hinchingbrooke Health Care NHS Trust
Dr M.D. Harris

Ipswich Hospital NHS Trust
Mr I. Lennox

James Paget Hospital Healthcare NHS Trust
Dr M.J. Wilkinson

King's Lynn & Wisbech Hospitals NHS Trust
Mr D.J. Sildown
Luton & Dunstable Hospital NHS Trust
Dr D.A.S. Lawrence

Mid-Essex Hospital Services NHS Trust
Mr P. Dziewulski

Norfolk & Norwich University Hospital NHS Trust
Dr A.J.G. Gray

Papworth Hospital NHS Trust
Dr M. Goddard

Peterborough Hospitals NHS Trust
Dr P.M. Dennis

Princess Alexandra Hospital NHS Trust
Dr R.G.M. Letcher

Southend Hospital NHS Trust
Ms W. Davis

West Hertfordshire Hospitals NHS Trust
Dr R. Smith (Watford General Hospital & Mount Vernon Hospital)

Dr A.P. O'Reilly (*St Albans City Hospital & Hemel Hempstead General Hospital*)

West Suffolk Hospitals NHS Trust
Mrs V. Hamilton

London

Barking, Havering and Redbridge
Hospitals NHS Trust
Mrs D. Jago (*Oldchurch Hospital & Harold Wood NHS Trust Hospital*)
Dr P. Tanner (*King George Hospital*)

Barnet and Chase Farm Hospitals NHS Trust
Dr W.H.S. Mohamid (*Chase Farm Hospital*)
Dr J. El-Jabbour (*Barnet General Hospital*)

Barts and the London NHS Trust
Dr K. Wark (*London Chest Hospital*)
Dr D.J. Wilkinson (*St Bartholomew's Hospital*)
Dr P.J. Flynn (*Royal London Hospital*)

Bromley Hospitals NHS Trust
Dr A. Turvey

Chelsea & Westminster Healthcare NHS Trust
Ms I. Penny

Ealing Hospital NHS Trust
Dr C. Schmulian

Epsom and St Helier NHS Trust
Dr L. Temple (*Epsom General Hospital*)
Dr F. Anderson (*St Helier Hospital*)

Great Ormond Street Hospital for Children
NHS Trust
Dr A. Mackersie

Guy's & St Thomas' Hospital Trust
Mr W.J. Owen (*St Thomas' Hospital*)
No named reporter (*Guy's Hospital*)

Hammersmith Hospitals NHS Trust
Professor G.W.H. Stamp

Hillingdon Hospital NHS Hospital
Dr F.G. Barker

Homerton University Hospital NHS Trust
Mrs S. Kimenye

King's College Hospital NHS Trust
Mrs S. Bowler

Kingston Hospital NHS Trust
Mr P. Willson

Lewisham Hospital NHS Trust
Dr G. Phillip

Mayday Healthcare NHS Trust
Mr C. Fernandez

Moorfields Eye Hospital NHS Trust
Professor P. Luthert

Newham Healthcare NHS Trust
Dr C. Grunwald

North Middlesex University Hospital NHS Trust
Dr K.J. Jarvis

North West London Hospitals NHS Trust
Dr C.A. Amerasinghe (*Central Middlesex Hospital*)
Dr G. Williams (*Northwick Park Hospital & St Mark's Hospital*)

Queen Elizabeth Hospital NHS Trust
Mr S. Asher

Queen Mary's Sidcup NHS Trust
Dr E.J.A. Aps

Royal Brompton & Harefield NHS Trust
Mrs S. Da Silva (*Harefield Hospital*)
Professor D. Denison (*Royal Brompton Hospital*)

Royal Free Hampstead NHS Trust
Dr J.E. McLaughlin

Royal Marsden NHS Trust
Dr J. Williams

Royal National Orthopaedic Hospital NHS Trust
Mrs K. Harris

St George's Healthcare NHS Trust
Dr C.M. Corbishley

St Mary's NHS Trust
Ms R.A. Hittinger

University College London Hospitals NHS Trust
Ms R. Farquharson (*National Hospital for Neurology & Neurosurgery*)
Ms F. Johnson (*University College Hospital & Middlesex Hospital*)

West Middlesex University Hospital NHS Trust
Dr R.G. Hughes

Whipps Cross University Hospital NHS Trust
Ms P. Hewer

Whittington Hospital NHS Trust
Dr S. Ramachandra

North West

Aintree Hospitals NHS Trust
Dr W. Taylor

Blackburn, Hyndburn & Ribble Valley
Healthcare NHS Trust
Mr R.W. Nicholson

Blackpool Fylde and Wyre Hospitals NHS Trust
Dr K.S. Vasudev

Bolton Hospitals NHS Trust
Dr S. Wells

Burnley Health Care NHS Trust
Mr D.G.D. Sandilands

Cardiothoracic Centre Liverpool NHS Trust
Dr M. Jackson

Central Manchester/Manchester Children's
University Hospitals NHS Trust
Dr M. Newbould (*Booth Hall Children's Hospital &
Royal Manchester Children's Hospital*)
Dr E.W. Benbow (*Manchester Royal Infirmary*)

Chorley & South Ribble NHS Trust
Dr M. Calleja

Christie Hospital NHS Trust
Miss S.T. O'Dwyer

Countess of Chester Hospital NHS Trust
Dr W.E. Kenyon

East Cheshire NHS Trust
Dr A.R. Williams

Liverpool Women's Hospital NHS Trust
Mr T. Caine

Mid Cheshire Hospitals NHS Trust
Miss H. Moulton

Morecambe Bay Hospitals NHS Trust
Dr R.W. Blewitt (*Royal Lancaster Infirmary*)
Dr V.M. Joglekar (*Furness General Hospital*)

North Cheshire Hospitals NHS Trust
Dr K. Strahan (*Halton General Hospital*)
Dr M.S. Al-Jafari (*Warrington Hospital*)

Pennine Acute Hospitals NHS Trust
Ms M. Ince (*Bury General Hospital, Fairfield General
Hospital*)
Dr D. Butterworth (*North Manchester General
Hospital*)
Mrs V. Davies (*The Royal Oldham Hospital*)
Dr M. Bradgate (*Birch Hill Hospital, Rochdale
Infirmary*)

Preston Acute Hospitals NHS Trust
Mrs N. Leahey

Royal Liverpool & Broadgreen University Hospitals
NHS Trust
Ms R. Dean

Royal Liverpool Children's NHS Trust
Mrs P.A. McCormack

Salford Royal Hospitals NHS Trust
Mrs E. Craddock

South Manchester University Hospitals NHS Trust
Dr J. Coyne

Southport and Ormskirk Hospital NHS Trust
Dr S.A.C. Dundas

St Helens & Knowsley Hospitals NHS Trust
Mr M. Atherton

Stockport NHS Trust
Dr M.W.J. Cutts

Tameside and Glossop Acute Services NHS Trust
Dr A.J. Yates

Trafford Healthcare NHS Trust
Ms S. Mountain

Walton Centre for Neurology & Neurosurgery NHS
Trust
Dr J. Broome

Wirral Hospital NHS Trust
Dr M.B. Gillett

Wrightington, Wigan & Leigh NHS Trust
Mrs P. Sharkey (*Royal Albert Edward Infirmary*)
Dr J.M. Frayne (*Wrightington Hospital*)

Northern & Yorkshire

Airedale NHS Trust
Dr J.J. O'Dowd

Bradford Hospitals NHS Trust
Dr C.A. Sides

Calderdale & Huddersfield NHS Trust
Mr R.J.R. Goodall (*Calderdale Royal Hospital*)
Mr A.W.F. Milling (*Huddersfield Royal Infirmary*)

City Hospitals Sunderland NHS Trust
Miss K. Ramsay

Gateshead Health NHS Trust
Dr A. McHutchon

Harrogate Healthcare NHS Trust
Miss A.H. Lawson

Hull and East Yorkshire Hospitals NHS Trust
Mrs J. Fountain (*Hull Royal Infirmary & Princess Royal Hospital*)
Mr G. Britchford (*Westwood Hospital & Castle Hill Hospital*)

Leeds Teaching Hospitals NHS Trust
Dr C. Abbott (*Leeds General Infirmary*)
Mr S. Knight (*St James's University Hospital*)

Mid Yorkshire Hospitals NHS Trust
Dr P. Gudgeon (*Dewsbury & District Hospital*)
Dr I.W.C. Macdonald (*Pontefract General Infirmary, Pinderfields General Hospital*)

Newcastle upon Tyne Hospitals NHS Trust
Miss D. Wilson (*Royal Victoria Infirmary & Newcastle General Hospital*)
Dr M.K. Bennett (*Freeman Hospital*)

North Cumbria Acute Hospitals NHS Trust
Mr B. Earley (*West Cumberland Hospital*)
Dr P. Stride (*Cumberland Infirmary*)

North Durham Healthcare NHS Trust
Miss S. Green

North Tees and Hartlepool NHS Trust
Mr I.L. Rosenberg (*University Hospital of North Tees*)
Mrs A. Lister (*University Hospital of Hartlepool*)

Northumbria Healthcare NHS Trust
Dr A. Coleman (*Hexham General Hospital*)
Dr S. Johri (*North Tyneside General Hospital*)
Dr J. Rushmer (*Wansbeck General Hospital*)

Scarborough & North East Yorkshire Health Care NHS Trust
Dr A.M. Jackson

South Durham Healthcare NHS Trust
Mr K. Naylor

South Tees Hospitals NHS Trust
Ms S. Goulding (*The James Cook University Hospital, Middlesborough General Hospital*)
Dr D.C. Henderson (*Friarage Hospital*)

South Tyneside Healthcare Trust
Dr K.P. Pollard

York Health Services NHS Trust
Dr C. Bates

South East

Ashford & St Peter's Hospital NHS Trust
Mrs B. Driver (*Ashford Hospital*)
Mrs E. Simmonds (*St Peter's Hospital*)

Brighton & Sussex University Hospitals NHS Trust
Mr M. Renshaw (*Royal Sussex County Hospital, Brighton General Hospital, Royal Alexandra Children's Hospital*)
Dr P.A. Berresford (*Princess Royal Hospital*)
Mr P.J. Ward (*Hurstwood Park Neurological Centre*)

Dartford & Gravesham NHS Trust
Mrs R. Ballentyne

East Kent Hospitals NHS Trust
Ms M. Harvey

East Sussex Hospitals NHS Trust
Mrs P. Jones (*Eastbourne General Hospital, All Saints Hospital*)
Mr S. Ball (*Conquest Hospital, Bexhill Hospital*)

Frimley Park Hospitals NHS Trust
Dr G.F. Goddard

Heatherwood and Wexham Park Hospitals NHS Trust
Ms J. Hartley

Isle of Wight Healthcare NHS Trust
Ms S. Wilson

Maidstone & Tunbridge Wells NHS Trust
Mr N. Munn

Medway NHS Trust
Mrs J.L. Smith

Milton Keynes General NHS Trust
Dr S.S. Jalloh

North Hampshire Hospitals NHS Trust
Ms A. Timson

Northampton General Hospital NHS Trust
Dr A.J. Molyneux

Nuffield Orthopaedic Centre NHS Trust
Dr P. Millard

Oxford Radcliffe Hospitals NHS Trust
Dr P. Millard *(John Radcliffe Hospital & Radcliffe Infirmary)*
Dr N.J. Mahy *(Horton Hospital)*

Portsmouth Hospitals NHS Trust
Dr N.J.E. Marley *(St Mary's Hospital & Queen Alexandra Hospital)*
Dr Y. Ansah Boaeteng *(Royal Hospital)*

Queen Victoria Hospital NHS Trust
Mrs D.M. Helme

Royal Berkshire & Battle Hospitals NHS Trust
Dr R. Menai-Williams

Royal Surrey County Hospital NHS Trust
Mrs G. Willner

Royal West Sussex NHS Trust
Mr J.N.L. Simson

South Buckinghamshire NHS Trust
Dr M.J. Turner

Southampton University Hospitals NHS Trust
Mrs S. Milne

Stoke Mandeville Hospital NHS Trust
Dr A.F. Padel

Surrey & Sussex Healthcare NHS Trust
Mrs M. Stoner

Winchester & Eastleigh Healthcare NHS Trust
Dr R.K. Al-Talib

Worthing & Southlands Hospitals NHS Trust
Mrs M. Miles

South West

East Somerset NHS Trust
Dr J.P. Sheffield

Gloucestershire Hospitals NHS Trust
Dr P. Sanderson *(Gloucestershire Royal Hospital)*
Dr W.J.Brampton *(Cheltenham General Hospital)*

North Bristol NHS Trust
Dr N.B.N. Ibrahim *(Frenchay Hospital)*
Ms T. Lucas *(Southmead Hospital)*

Northern Devon Healthcare NHS Trust
Dr J. Davies

Plymouth Hospitals NHS Trust
Dr C.B.A. Lyons

Poole Hospital NHS Trust
Mr P. Stebbings

Royal Bournemouth & Christchurch Hospitals NHS Trust
Mrs E. Hinwood

Royal Cornwall Hospitals Trust
Mrs M. Manser

Royal Devon & Exeter Healthcare NHS Trust
Dr R.H.W. Simpson

Royal United Hospital Bath NHS Trust
Ms L. Hobbs

Salisbury Healthcare NHS Trust
Dr S.M. Khan

South Devon Healthcare NHS Trust
Dr N.G. Ryley

Swindon & Marlborough NHS Trust
Mr M.H. Galea

Taunton & Somerset NHS Trust
Dr B. Browne

United Bristol Healthcare NHS Trust
Dr M. Ashworth *(Bristol Royal Hospital for Sick Children)*
Mr J. Murdoch *(St Michael's Hospital)*
Mr R.A. Harrad *(Bristol Eye Hospital)*
Dr E.A. Sheffield *(Bristol General Hospital & Bristol Royal Infirmary)*

West Dorset General Hospitals NHS Trust
Dr A. Anscombe

Weston Area Health Trust
Dr M.F. Lott

Trent

Barnsley District General Hospital NHS Trust
Dr M.A. Longan

Chesterfield & North Derbyshire Royal Hospital
NHS Trust
Dr R.D. Start

Doncaster and Bassetlaw Hospitals NHS Trust
Dr G. Kesseler *(Montagu Hospital & Doncaster Royal
Infirmary)*
Dr S. Beck *(Bassetlaw District General Hospital)*

Kettering General Hospital NHS Trust
Dr J.A.H. Uraiby

Northern Lincolnshire & Goole Hospitals NHS
Trust
Dr W.M. Peters *(Diana Princess of Wales Hospital)*
Dr C.M. Hunt *(Goole & District Hospital & Scunthorpe
General Hospital)*

Nottingham City Hospital NHS Trust
Mrs C. Wright

Queen's Medical Centre Nottingham University
Hospital NHS Trust
Dr J.A. Jones

Rotherham General Hospitals NHS Trust
Ms H. Gooch

Sheffield Children's Hospital NHS Trust
Dr I. Barker

Sheffield Teaching Hospitals NHS Trust
Dr S.K. Suvarna

Sherwood Forest Hospitals NHS Trust
Mr P. Bend *(King's Mill Hospital)*
Dr I. Ross *(Newark Hospital)*

Southern Derbyshire Acute Hospitals NHS Trust
Mr J.R. Nash

United Lincolnshire Hospitals NHS Trust
Dr J.A. Harvey *(Lincoln County Hospital)*
Dr D. Clark *(Grantham and District Hospital)*
Ms S. Sinha *(Pilgrim Hospital)*

University Hospitals of Leicester NHS Trust
Mr M.J.S. Dennis *(Leicester General Hospital)*
Mr S. Hainsworth *(Leicester Royal Infirmary)*
Mrs S. Clarke *(Glenfield Hospital)*

West Midlands

Birmingham Children's Hospital NHS Trust
Dr P. Ramani

Birmingham Heartlands & Solihull NHS Trust
Dr M. Taylor

Birmingham Women's Healthcare NHS Trust
Dr M. Mitze

Burton Hospitals NHS Trust
Dr N. Kasthuri

Dudley Group of Hospitals NHS Trust
Mr G. Stevens

George Eliot Hospital NHS Trust
Dr D. Bose
Good Hope Hospital NHS Trust
Dr J. Hull

Hereford Hospitals NHS Trust
Dr F. McGinty

Mid Staffordshire General Hospitals NHS Trust
Dr V. Suarez

North Staffordshire Hospital NHS Trust
Dr T.A. French

Princess Royal Hospital NHS Trust
Dr R.A. Fraser

Robert Jones & Agnes Hunt Orthopaedic Hospital
NHS Trust
Mrs C. McPherson

Royal Orthopaedic Hospital NHS Trust
Mr A. Thomas

Royal Shrewsbury Hospitals NHS Trust
Dr R.A. Fraser

Royal Wolverhampton Hospitals NHS Trust
Dr J. Tomlinson

Sandwell & West Birmingham Hospitals NHS Trust
Mrs I. Darnley *(Sandwell General Hospital)*
Dr S.Y. Chan *(City Hospital)*

South Warwickshire General Hospitals NHS Trust
Dr R. Brown

University Hospitals Birmingham NHS Trust
Professor E.L. Jones

University Hospitals of Coventry and Warwickshire
NHS Trust
Dr J. Macartney

Walsall Hospitals NHS Trust
Dr Y.L. Hock

Worcestershire Acute Hospitals NHS Trust
Ms S. Lisseman

Northern Ireland

Altnagelvin Hospitals Health & Social Services
Trust
Dr J.N. Hamilton

Armagh & Dungannon Health & Social Services
Trust
Mr B. Cranley

Belfast City Hospital Health & Social Services Trust
Mrs A. McAfee

Causeway Health & Social Services Trust
Dr C. Watters

Craigavon Area Hospital Group Trust
Mr B. Cranley

Down Lisburn Health & Social Services Trust
Dr B. Huss (*Lagan Valley Hospital*)
Dr N. Storey (*Downe Maternity Hospital*)
Dr M. Milhench (*Downe Hospital*)

Green Park Healthcare Trust
Dr J.D.R. Connolly

Mater Hospital Belfast Health & Social Services
Trust
Dr P. Gormley

Newry & Mourne Health & Social Services Trust
Mr B. Cranley

Royal Group of Hospitals & Dental Hospitals &
Maternity Hospitals Trust
Mr M. McDonald

Sperrin Lakeland Health & Social Services Trust
Dr W. Holmes (*Erne Hospital*)
Dr F. Robinson (*Tyrone County Hospital*)

Ulster Community & Hospitals NHS Trust
Dr T. Boyd

United Hospitals Health & Social Services Trust
Mr I. Garstin (*Antrim Hospital*)
Mr D. Gilroy (*Whiteabbey Hospital*)
Mr P.C. Pyper (*Mid Ulster Hospital*)

Wales

Bro Morgannwg NHS Trust
Dr A. Dawson (*Neath General Hospital*)
Dr A.M. Rees (*Princess of Wales Hospital*)

Cardiff and Vale NHS Trust
Dr A.G. Douglas-Jones (*University Hospital of Wales*)
Dr R. Attanoos (*Llandough Hospital*)
Mrs M. Keenor (*Cardiff Royal Infirmary*)

Carmarthenshire NHS Trust
Dr R.B. Denholm (*West Wales General Hospital*)
Dr L. Murray (*Prince Philip Hospital*)

Ceredigion & Mid Wales NHS Trust
Mrs C. Smith

Conwy & Denbighshire NHS Trust
Dr B. Rogers

Gwent Healthcare NHS Trust
Dr M. Rashid (*Royal Gwent Hospital*)
Dr G. Evans (*Nevill Hall Hospital*)

North East Wales NHS Trust
Dr A.H. Burdge

North Glamorgan NHS Trust
Mrs A. Shenkorov

North West Wales NHS Trust
Dr A.W. Caslin

Pembrokeshire & Derwen NHS Trust
Dr G.R. Melville Jones

Pontypridd & Rhondda NHS Trust
Dr D. Stock

Swansea NHS Trust
Dr S. Williams (*Singleton Hospital*)
Dr A. Dawson (*Morriston Hospital*)

Defence Secondary Care Agency

Princess Mary's Hospital
Sqdn Ldr J.M. Lewis-Russell

Guernsey/Isle of Man/Jersey

Guernsey
Ms J. Ellyatt

Isle of Man
Ms E. Clark

Jersey
Dr H. Goulding

Abbey Hospitals Ltd.

Abbey Caldew Hospital
Ms V. Holliday

Abbey Gisburne Park Hospital
Ms A. Cooke

Abbey Park Hospital
Ms J. Colyer

Abbey Sefton Hospital
Mr A. Stewart

Aspen Healthcare

Holly House Hospital
Ms J. Row

Parkside Hospital
Ms H. Bradbury

BMI Healthcare

Alexandra Hospital
Mrs P. Enstone

Bath Clinic
Mrs E.M. Jones

Beardwood Hospital
Ms S. Greenwood

Beaumont Hospital
Mrs C. Power

Bishops Wood Hospital
Ms D. Dorken

Blackheath Hospital
Mrs V. Power

Chatsworth Suite, Chesterfield & N Derbyshire
Ms S. Darbyshire

Chaucer Hospital
Mrs G. Mann

Chelsfield Park Hospital
Ms C. Poll

Chiltern Hospital
Ms J. Liggitt

Clementine Churchill Hospital
Ms S. Latham

Droitwich Spa Hospital
Mrs P. Fryer

Esperance Hospital
Mrs S. Mulvey

Fawkham Manor Hospital
Miss C. Stocker

Garden Hospital
Ms J. Benson

Goring Hall Hospital
Mrs A. Bailey

Hampshire Clinic
Mrs R. Phillips

Harbour Hospital
Ms S. Prince

Highfield Hospital
Ms P. Shields

Kings Oak Hospital
Mrs C. Le May

London Independent Hospital
Mrs U. Palmer

Manor Hospital
Mrs S. Otter

Meriden Wing, Walsgrave Hospital
Ms C. Ayton

Nuneaton Private Hospital
Mrs A. Garner

Paddocks Hospital
Ms S. Hill

Park Hospital
Mrs S. Quickmire

Princess Margaret Hospital
Mrs J. Gough

Priory Hospital
Dr A.G. Jacobs

Ridgeway Hospital
Mrs R. Butler

Runnymede Hospital
Mrs P. Hill

Sandringham Hospital
Mr S. Harris

Sarum Road Hospital
Ms Y.A. Stoneham

Saxon Clinic
Mrs V. Shiner

Shelburne Hospital
Mrs M. Jones

Shirley Oaks Hospital
Mrs S. White

Sloane Hospital
Miss J. Matthews

Somerfield Hospital
Mrs M. Lewis

South Cheshire Private Hospital
Mrs A. Peake

Thornbury Hospital
Mrs J. Cooper

Three Shires Hospital
Mrs C. Beaney

Werndale Hospital
Mrs A. Morgan

Winterbourne Hospital
Mrs S. Clark

BUPA

BUPA Alexandra Hospital
Mrs J. Witherington

BUPA Belvedere Hospital
Mrs E. Vincent

BUPA Cambridge Lea Hospital
Miss M. Vognsen

BUPA Chalybeate Hospital
Miss M. Falconer

BUPA Dunedin Hospital
Ms E. Prior

BUPA Fylde Coast Hospital
Mrs D. Hodgkins

BUPA Gatwick Park Hospital
Mrs A-M. Hanley

BUPA Hartswood Hospital
Ms S. Fraser-Betts

BUPA Hastings Hospital
Mrs S. Parsons

BUPA Hospital Bristol
Miss M. O'Toole

BUPA Hospital Bushey
Mrs J. Salmon

BUPA Hospital Cardiff
Dr A. Gibbs

BUPA Hospital Clare Park
Ms M. Wood

BUPA Hospital Elland
Ms V. Cryer

BUPA Hospital Harpenden
Ms S. Ryan

BUPA Hospital Hull & East Riding
Mrs K. Newton

BUPA Hospital Leeds
Mr D. Farrell

BUPA Hospital Leicester
Mrs C.A. Jones

BUPA Hospital Little Aston
Mrs J. Moore

BUPA Hospital Manchester
Ms A. McArdle

BUPA Hospital Norwich
Ms J. Middows

BUPA Hospital Portsmouth
Mrs J. Ward

BUPA Methley Park Hospital
Mrs J. Shaw

BUPA Murrayfield Hospital
Miss J.C. Bott

BUPA North Cheshire Hospital
Mrs A. Parry

BUPA Parkway Hospital
Mrs M.T. Hall

BUPA Redwood Hospital
Miss A.M. Hanley

BUPA Regency Hospital
Ms D. Davies

BUPA Roding Hospital
Mrs D. Britt

BUPA South Bank Hospital
Ms C. Stubbs

BUPA St Saviour's Hospital
Mr N. Bradley

BUPA Tunbridge Wells Hospital
Mrs B. Thorp

BUPA Washington Hospital
Ms J. Davis

BUPA Wellesley Hospital
Mrs P. Stellon

BUPA Yale Hospital
Mrs J. Bidmead

Community Hospitals Group

Ashtead Hospital
Ms R. Hackett

Berkshire Independent Hospital
Ms J. McCrum

Duchy Hospital
Ms D. Martin

Euxton Hall Hospital
Ms B. Dickinson

Fitzwilliam Hospital
Ms S. Needham

Fotheringhay Suite
Ms G. Jones

Fulwood Hall Hospital
Ms C. Aucott

Mount Stuart Hospital
Ms J. Abdelrahman

New Hall Hospital
Ms H.L. Cole

North Downs Hospital
Mrs M. Middleton

Oaklands Hospital
Mrs I. Russell

Oaks Hospital
Ms M. Gallifent

Park Hill Hospital
Ms D. Abbott

Pinehill Hospital
Ms K. Elliott

Renacres Hall Hospital
Ms A. Shannon

Rivers Hospital
Ms K. Handel

Rowley Hall Hospital
Ms L. Serginson

Springfield Hospital
Ms J. Inggs

West Midlands Hospital
Ms F. Allinson

Winfield Hospital
Ms M. Greaves

Woodland Hospital
Ms L. Hutchings

Yorkshire Clinic
Ms J. Sands

HCA International

Harley Street Clinic
Ms S. Thomas

Lister Hospital
Mrs J. Norman

London Bridge Hospital
Ms Y. Terry

Portland Hospital for Women and Children
Miss A.D. Sayburn

Princess Grace Hospital
Mrs D. Hutton

Wellington Hospital
Mr R. Hoff

Nuffield Hospitals

Acland Hospital
Miss C. Gilbert

Birmingham Nuffield Hospital
Ms E. Loftus

Bournemouth Nuffield Hospital
Mrs E. Cornelius

Cheltenham & Gloucester Nuffield Hospital
Ms J.T. Cassidy

Chesterfield Nuffield Hospital
Mr P. Garrett

Cleveland Nuffield Hospital
Ms V. Lacey

Duchy Nuffield Hospital
Mrs T. Hampson

East Midlands Nuffield Hospital
Mrs C. Williams

Essex Nuffield Hospital
Mrs P. Turner

Exeter Nuffield Hospital
Mrs T. Starling

Grosvenor Nuffield Hospital
Mrs J.L. Whitmore

Guildford Nuffield Hospital
Mrs I. Houghton

HRH Princess Christian's Hospital
Ms S. Fisher

Huddersfield Nuffield Hospital
Ms B. Woodrow

Hull Nuffield Hospital
Mrs B. Menham

Lancaster & Lakeland Nuffield Hospital
Mrs K. McKay

Leicester Nuffield Hospital
Ms M. Damant

Lincoln Nuffield Hospital
Mrs E. Ashpole

Mid Yorkshire Nuffield Hospital
Miss M. Falconer

Newcastle Nuffield Hospital
Mrs D. Thornton

North London Nuffield Hospital
Ms B. Harrison

North Staffordshire Nuffield Hospital
Mrs S. Gowers

Nottingham Nuffield Hospital
Ms R. Bradbury

Plymouth Nuffield Hospital
Ms G. Mansfield

Purey Cust Nuffield Hospital
Mrs S.A. Brown

Shropshire Nuffield Hospital
Mrs S. Crossland

Somerset Nuffield Hospital
Mrs J.A. Dyer

Suffolk Nuffield Hospital
Ms S. Verow

Sussex Nuffield Hospital
Mrs F. Booty

Thames Valley Nuffield Hospital
Ms H. Dob

Tunbridge Wells Nuffield Hospital
Ms R. Stephens

Warwickshire Nuffield Hospital
Mrs J. Worth

Wessex Nuffield Hospital
Mrs V. Heckford

Woking Nuffield Hospital
Ms K. Barham

Wolverhampton Nuffield Hospital
Mr B. Lee

Wye Valley Nuffield Hospital
Mrs W.P. Mawdesley

Other Independent Hospitals

Benenden Hospital
Mr D. Hibler

Foscote Private Hospital
Mrs L. Tuzzio

Heart Hospital
Ms A. Harvey

King Edward VII Hospital
Dr J. Halfacre

King Edward VII's Hospital Sister Agnes
Mrs J. Jordan-Moss

London Clinic
Mrs K. Perkins

St Anthony's Hospital
Ms C. Hagan

St Joseph's Hospital
Sister Bernadette Marie

APPENDIX G

PARTICIPANTS

Consultant anaesthetists

These consultant anaesthetists returned at least one questionnaire relating to the period 1 April 2000 to 31 March 2001. We are not able to name all of the consultants who have done so, as their names are not known to us.

Abbas S.
Abbott M.A.
Abernethy S.
Acharya P.A.
Acharya S.A.
Adams H.G.
Adams T.J.
Adejumo G.
Agyare K.
Ahmed K.
Ahmed M.
Ainley T.C.
Ainsworth Q.
Akinpelu O.E.
Al-Shaikh B.Z.
Alcock R.
Alderson J.D.
Alexander J.
Alexander R.
Ali M.A.
Ali S.
Allan M.W.B.
Allen J.G.
Allen R.
Allman K.G.
Allsop E.A.
Amin M.
Ammar T.A.A.
Anderson I.
Anderson J.
Anderson S.K.
Andrews C.J.H.
Andrews J.I
Appadu B.
Appleby J.N.
Arif M.H.
Armstrong R.F.
Arrigoni P.B.
Arrowsmith J.
Ashby M.W.
Ashurst N.H.
Aslan S.
Aspbury J.N.
Atherton A.M.J.
Atherton P.
Atkinson S.
Aung M.
Aveling W.
Babatola O.
Backs P.J.
Bacon R.
Badami A.J.
Baguley I.
Bailey C.R.
Bainton A.B.
Baker G.M.
Balachandra K.

Ball A.J.
Ballance P.G.
Bamber P.A.
Bamigbade T.
Bapat P.
Barham C.J.
Barker J.P.
Barnard M.
Barnardo P.
Barr C.
Barrera-Groba C.
Barrett R.F.
Barrie J.
Bass S.
Bastiaenen H.L.R.
Bastian B.
Batchelor A.M.
Bavister P.H.
Baxter R.C.H.
Bayley P.
Bayoumi M.
Beacham K.
Bedford T.
Beechey A.P.G.
Beers H.T.B.
Beeton C.
Behl S.P.
Bell J.
Bell J.K.
Bell K.
Bellin J.M.
Bellis D.
Bennett J.
Bennett M.W.R.
Berry C.
Berthoud M.C.
Bewley J.
Bhandari S.
Bhasin N.
Bhaskar H.K.
Bhaskaran N.C.
Bhatti T.H.
Bird T.M.
Biswas A.
Blancke W.
Blayney M.R.
Block R.
Blossfeldt P.
Blues C.
Boaden R.W.
Board P.
Boden J.L.
Boira B.
Bolton D.T.
Bonner S.
Booker P.D.
Borman E.

Bose D.
Botha R.A.
Bourne J.A.
Bourne T.M.
Bousfield J.D.
Bowman R.A.
Bowry A.
Boyden J.
Boys J.E.
Brampton W.
Brandner B.
Braude N.
Bray R.J.
Breckenridge J.L.
Breeze C.
Brewin M.D.
Broadway P.
Brocklehurst I.C.
Brocklesby S.
Brook J.
Brooks N.C.
Brooks R.J.
Broomhead C.
Brosnan S.
Brown M.
Browne D.
Browning M.
Brownlie G.
Bryant J.D.
Bryden D.C.
Buckley P.M.
Buckoke D.
Buggy D.
Buist R.J.
Bukht M.D.G.
Bull P.T.
Burchett K.R.
Burden R.J.
Burke S.
Burlingham A.N.
Burnell J.C.
Burns A.
Burt D.
Burt G.
Butler J.
Butt W.
Byrne A.
Byrne A.J.
Bywater N.J.
Caddy J.M.
Calder I.
Caldicott L.D.
Callander C.
Calleja M.A.
Campbell D.
Campbell J.
Caranza R.

Carden D.
Carnie J.C.
Carr B.
Carson D.
Carter A.
Carter J.A.
Carter J.A.
Cartwright D.P.
Cartwright P.D.
Casey W.F.
Cavill G.
Ch'ng K.T.
Chaderton N.
Chadwick I.S.
Chaffe A.G.
Chakrabarti P.
Chalmers E.P.D.
Chamberlain M.E.
Chambers P.H.
Chapman J.M.
Chapman M.G.
Charlton G.A.
Charway C.L.
Chater S.N.
Chesshire N.
Chestnutt W.N.
Chetty S.
Childs D.
Chin C.
Chitkara N.
Chitra G.
Choksey F.
Choudhry A.
Chrispin P.S.
Christian A.S.
Christie I.W.
Chung R.A.
Church J.J.
Clark G.P.M.
Clark G.S.
Clark R.
Clarke C.
Clarke J.T.
Clarke P.
Clarke T.N.S.
Claydon P.
Clements E.A.F.
Clift J.
Clifton P.J.M.
Coates M.B.
Cobner P.G.
Cockroft S.
Cody M.
Coe A.J.
Coghill J.C.
Coghlan S.
Cohen R.

Cole A.
Coleman N.
Coleman P.
Collie J.
Collingborn M.
Collins C.
Collins J.
Collins P.D.
Colville L.J.
Colvin M.P.
Coniam S.W.
Conn D.
Conroy P.T.
Conyers A.B.
Cook J.H.
Cook P.R.
Cooke R.A.
Cooper A.E.
Cooper D.
Cooper R.
Cooper R.
Cope R.
Corser G.C.
Cossham P.S.
Cotton B.R.
Counsell D.
Craig R.
Cranston A.J.
Crighton I.
Crighton S.
Cross G.D.
Cross R.
Cudworth P.
Culbert B.
Da Costa F.
Dakin M.
Dalgleish J.G.
Daniels M.
Dasey N.
Dash A.
Dashfield A.
Daum R.E.O.
Davey A.J.
Davidson A.
Davidson R.
Davies C.
Davies E.
Davies G.
Davies G.K.
Davies H.
Davies J.S.S.
Davies M.
Davies M.H.
Davies N.J.H.
Davies S.
Davis A.
Davis I.

Davis M.
Day C.
Day C.D.
De J.
Deacock S.
Deakin C.
Deane M.
Denny N.M.
Dent H.
Derbyshire D.R.
Desborough J.P.
Deshpande S.
Deulkar U.V.
Dhond G.
Dichmont E.V.
Dickson D.
Dierick A.
Digby S.J.
Dimond J.
Dinsmore J.
Dobson P.M.S.
Dodd P.
Dolenska S.
Donald F.
Dowdall J.W.
Down M.P.
Downer J.P.
Doyle A.
Doyle L.
Doyle P.
Drage M.
Dravid R.
Drummond R.S.
Dryden C.
Dua R.
Duane D.
Dubash D.H.
Dulimie K.
Duncan F.
Duncan P.W.
Dunkley C.
Dunn S.R.
Dunnet J.
Dunnett I.A.R.
Dunnill R.P.H.
Dyar O.
Dye D.J.
Eadsforth P.
Earnshaw G.
Eccersley P.S.
Eckersall S.
Edmondson W.C.
Edwards A.E.
Edwards G.
Edwards R.
Edwards R.
Edwards S.

El-Behesy B.
Eldabe S.
Eldridge A.J.E.
Elegbe E.
Elliott D.J.
Elliott R.H.
Elton R.J
England A.
Enright S.M.
Erwin D.C.
Eskander A.
Esmail M.
Espinet A.J.
Evans F.E.
Evans G.
Evans G.S.
Evans J.A.
Evans K.
Evans M.L.
Evans P.
Evans R.D.
Evans R.J.C.
Ewah B.N.
Fahy L.T.
Fairbrass M.J.
Falconer R.
Fale A.
Farling P.A.
Farnsworth G.
Fawcett W.
Fazackerley E.J.
Fearnley S.J.
Felgate M.
Fell L.
Feneck R.O.
Fenner S.
Fenton R.
Fergusson N.V.
Fernandez-Jimenez P.
Ferres C.J.
Findlow D.
Firn S.
Fischer H.B.J.
Fitz-Henry J.
Fitzpatrick D.C.
Flatt N.
Fletcher A.
Foley M.
Forde S.
Forrest E.
Foster S.
Fox A.
Francis G.A.
Francis J.
Francis R.N.
Frazer R.S.
Freeman J.

Freeman R.
French G.
Friend J.
Frost A.R.
Fryer J.M.
Fryer M.E.
Furniss P.
Fuzzey G.J.J.
Gabbott D.A.
Gallagher L.B.S.
Gallagher T.
Gammanpila S.W.
Ganado A.
Gandhi S.
Ganepola S.R.
Garrett C.P.O.
Gasser J.
Gaston J.H.
Gedney J.
Gell I.R.
George A.
Geraghty I.F.
Gerrish S.P.
Ghaly R.G.
Ghobrial E.
Ghoorun S.
Ghosh S.
Gibson J.S.
Gill N.
Gill R.
Gillespie I.A.
Gilliland H.
Girling K.
Glaisyer H.
Glavina M.J.
Goldsack C.
Goldsmith A.L
Goodman N.
Gordon H.L.
Gormley W.P.
Gothard J.W.W.
Gough M.B.
Goulden M.
Goulden P.
Goulding S.
Gouldson R.
Govenden V.
Grady A.K.
Graham D.
Graham F.
Graham I.F.M.
Grant I.C.
Gray A.J.G.
Gray D.
Gray H.S.J.
Gray P.
Gray S.

Grebenik C.R.
Green C.P.
Green D.
Greenslade G.L.
Greenwell S.K.
Gregory M.
Gregory M.A.
Greig D.G.
Grewal M.S.
Griffith N.G.
Griffiths D.E.
Griffiths R.B.
Grounds M.
Groves R.
Grummitt R.
Gruning T.
Grunwald C.
Guerin D.
Guest C.
Gupta V.L.
Guratsky B.P.
Gwinnutt C.L.
Haden R.M.
Hadi N.G.
Hahn A.
Haigh A.
Hall B.
Hall P.J.
Hall R.M.
Hambly P.
Hamilton-Davies C.
Hamilton-Farrell M.R.
Hammond J.
Hanning C.D.
Haq A.
Hardwick M.
Hardy P.A.J.
Hare J.
Harle C.
Harling D.H.
Harper C.
Harper K.W.
Harper N.
Harpin R.
Harris D.N.F.
Harris J.W.
Harris R.W.
Harris T.J.B.
Harrison G.
Harrison S.J.
Harrod S.
Hartley M.
Hartopp I.K.
Harvey D.C.
Harvey P.B.
Hasan M.A.
Hassani A.

Hawkins D.J.
Hawkins S.
Hawley S.K.
Hawthorne L.
Haycock J.C.
Hayes M.
Heath K.J.
Hegarty J.E.
Heggie N.M.
Heidelmeyer C.
Heining M.P.D.
Helwa S.A.I.
Hemming A.E.
Henderson K.
Heneghan C.P.H.
Heriot J.
Hewlett A.M.
Hicks I.R.
Hill A.
Hill H.
Hill R.
Hill S.
Hill S.
Hinds C.J.
Hoad D.J.
Hobbs A.
Hodgson C.A.
Holden D.
Holgate P.
Holland H.
Hollis J.N.
Hollywood P.G.
Holmes W.
Hood G.
Hopkinson J.M.
Hopton P.
Horsman E.L.
Horton W.
Hough M.B.
Howard R.P.
Howell E.
Howell P.J.
Howes D.
Howie J.
Howsam S.
Hoyal R.H.A.
Huddy N.C.
Hughes A.
Hughes D.G.
Hughes J.
Hughes J.A.
Hughes K.R.
Hugo S.
Hull J.
Hulme G.
Hunt P.C.W.
Hunt T.M.

Hunter D.	Jones R.E.	Kraayenbrink M.A.	Lockie J.
Hunter J.D.	Jones S.E.F.	Kulkarni A.	Lockwood G.
Hunter S.J.	Joshi R.	Kulkarni P.R	Loh L.
Hurst J.	Judkins K.	Kumar C.M.	Long D.H.
Hussein A.	Kalia P.	Kutarski A.A.	Lord B.
Hussein M.H.A.	Kalmanovich D.V.A.	Lacasia C.	Loughnan B.
Hutchings P.J.G.	Kamath B.S.K.	Lahoud G.	Loveland R.
Hutchinson G.	Kandasamy R.	Lamb A.S.T.	Lowe D.
Hutchinson H.T.	Kapila A.	Lamb J.	Lowrie A.
Hutchinson J.	Kapoor V.	Lamplugh G.	Loyden C.F.
Hutchison G.	Kavan R.	Lanham P.R.W.	Ludgrove T.
Hutton P.	Kearns C.F.	Lanigan C.	Lung C.P.C.
Imrie M.M.	Keays R.	Lassey P.D.	Luthman J.A.
Ingram K.S.	Keeler J.	Lauder G.	Luxton M.C.
Iossifidis I.	Kelleher A.	Laurie P.	Lynch M.V.
Isaac J.L.	Kelly E.P.	Lavies N.G.	Macartney N.
Ismail F.	Kelsall P.	Lawes E.G.	Macaulay D.
Ismail K.	Kendall A.P.	Lawton G.	Maccario M.
Jack R.D.	Kennedy D.J.	Layfield D.J.	MacDonnell S.
Jackson A.P.F.	Kennedy N.	Leach A.	MacIntosh K.
Jackson D.M.	Kennedy S.	Leadbeater M.J.	Mackay J.H.
Jackson H.	Kent A.P.	Leary J.	Mackintosh G.
Jackson I.J.B.	Keogh B.F.	Lee J.	MacLachlan K.
Jaidev V.C.	Kershaw E.J.	Lee K.G.	MacLeod G.F.
Jaitly V.	Kesseler G.	Lee P.	Madden A.P.
James J.	Kessell G.	Leech R.	Madhavan G.
James P.D.	Kettern M.A.	Lehane J.	Maennl U.
James R.H.	Khalil A.	Leigh J.	Maher O.A.
Jameson P.	Khalil H.R.I.	Leith S.	Mahmood N.
Jamieson J.R.	Khan A.A.	Leng C.	Mahoney A.
Jardine A.D.	Kiff K.	Lenz R.J.	Mahroo A.R.
Jash K.	Kilpatrick S.M.	Lesser P.J.A.	Maile C.J.D.
Jayamaha J.E.L.	King D.H.	Letheran M.	Main A.
Jayamaha S.	King N.W.	Levison A.	Majeed A.
Jayaratnasingam S.	King T.A.	Levy D.M.	Malaiya A.K.
Jayaweera R.	Kingsbury Q.D.	Lewis D.G.	Mallinson C.
Jeffs N.G.	Kini K.J.	Lewis I.	Manji M.
Jena N.M.	Kinsella M.	Lewis P.	Mann R.A.M.
Jenkins B.J.	Kinsella T.J.	Lewis R.P.	Mann S.
Jenkins I.	Kipling R.M.	Liban B.	Markham K.
Jenkins J.R.	Kirby I.J.	Liddle A.	Marsh A.M.
Jennings F.O.	Kirby S.A.	Liddle M.	Marshall A.G.
Jesuthasan M.	Kirk D.	Lilburn K.	Marshall C.
Jewell W.	Kirk P.	Liley A.	Marshall F.P.F.
Jewkes C.	Knibb A.A.	Lilley J.P.	Marshall P.
Jeyapalan I.	Knights D.	Lillywhite N.	Marthi R.
Jingree M.	Kocan M.	Lin E.S.	Martin A.J.
Johnson A.	Koehli N.	Lindop M.J.	Martin D.
Johnson G.	Kohli V.	Lindsay F.R.	Martin J.L.
Johnson I.	Kong A.	Linsley A.	Masri Z.
Johnson M.	Kong K.L.	Lintin D.J.	Massey S.R.
Johnson T.W.	Konieczko K.M.	Linton R.A.F.	Master B.R.
Johnston P.	Kotak D.	Littlejohn I.H.	Masters A.P.
Johnston P.	Kotak P.	Littler C.	Matheson K.H.
Jones H.M.	Kotur C.F.	Lloyd D.R.	Matta B.
Jones I.W.	Koussa F.	Lloyd-Thomas A.	Matthews P.
Jones R.A.	Kouzel A.S.	Lockhart A.S.	Matthews P.J.

Matthews R.F.J.
Maxwell B.
Mayall M.
Mayne D.J.
Mazumder J.K.
Mc Court K.C.
McAndrew P.
McAuley F.
McBride R.J.
McCallum M.I.D.
McCartney C.
McClymont C.
McCoy E.
McCrory J.W.
McDonald P.
McFadzean W.A.
McGeachie J.F.
McGinty M.
McGowan W.A.W.
McHugh P.
McHutchon A.
McIndoe A.
McKay A.C.
McKinney M.
McKnight C.K.
McLeod T.J.
McNamara J.
McQuillan P.
McVey F.
Meadows D.P.
Meikle R.J.
Mendham J.
Mendonca L.M.
Mercer N.P.
Messant M.
Messih M.N.A.
Mettam I.
Michel M.
Micklewright R.
Milaszkiewicz R.M.
Millett S.V.
Millican D.L.
Milligan K.R.
Milligan N.S.
Mills K.
Mills P.J.
Milne I.S.
Milne M.R.
Milner A.R.
Mishra K.P.
Misra U.
Mitchell J.
Mitchell M.D.
Mitchell R.W.D.
Mitchell V.
Mobley K.A.
Mohammed L.

Mohan H.
Monk C.
Moody R.A.
Moony R.N.E.
Moore C.A.
Moore K.C.
Moore N.A.
Morcos W.E.
Moriarty A.
Morris A.
Morris G.N.
Morris J.E.
Morris P.J.
Morris S.
Morrison W.
Morton A.K.
Moscuzza F.
Moss R.
Mottart K.
Mousdale S.
Mowbray M.J.
Moyle J.T.B.
Muldonn O.T.
Mullen P.
Mulrooney P.
Mumtaz T.
Munn J.
Muralitharan V.
Murphy J.
Murphy N.
Murphy P.G.
Murray R.
Murthy B.
Murthy B.
Musto P.
Myerson K.R.
Myint H.
Nalliah R.S.C.
Nancekievill M.L.
Nandakumar C.G.
Nandi K.
Nandwani N.
Naqushbandi K.
Nash J.
Nathanson M.H.
Naunton A.
Navapurkar V.U.
Nelson R.
Nesbitt G.A.
Newman P.
Newson C.
Nicholl A.D.J.
Nicholson G.
Nicol A.
Nicol M.
Nicoll J.M.V.
Nicoll S.

Nithianandan S.
Noden J.
Norley I.
Normandale J.P.
Norton A.C.
Norton P.M.
Notcutt W.G.
Nunez J.
O'Beirne H.A.
O'Connor B.
O'Connor M.
O'Donoghue B.
O'Dwyer C.A.
O'Dwyer J.
O'Hanlon J.
O'Keeffe N.
O'Neill M.P.
O'Sullivan G.M.
O'Sullivan K.A.
Oldham T.
Oomman G.J.
Orr D.A.
Osborne M.A.
Osborne N.
Ousta B.
Pais W.A.
Paix A.
Palmer J.
Palmer M.
Palmer R.
Panayioutou S.
Pandit J.
Pandya K.S.
Pannell M.
Pappachan V.J.
Park J.
Park W.G.
Parmar M.
Parr S.
Parry H.M.
Patel A.
Patel A.
Patel H.T.
Patel P.
Patel P.I.
Paterson I.
Pathirana D.U.S.
Patient P.S.
Patrick M.R.
Patten M.
Pattison J.
Pavlou S.P.
Payne J.F.
Payne N.E.S.
Peacock J.E.
Pead M.
Pemberton C.J.

Penfold N.
Pennefather S.H.
Pereira N.H.
Perrera C.
Peters T.
Phillips A.
Phillips G.H.
Phillips K.
Phillips K.A.
Phillips P.D.
Pickford F.J.
Pickworth A.J.
Pinchin R.M.E.
Pinnock C.
Platt N.
Plummer R.B.
Pollock C.G.
Poobalasingam N.
Poole D.
Poon A.
Porter A.
Potter F.A.
Pottinger K.A.
Powell D.R.
Powroznyk A.V.V.
Price C.
Price K.
Price M.L.
Price W.
Pridie A.K.
Priest T.
Prince G.D.
Proctor E.A.
Prosser D.
Pryn S.J.
Puddy B.R.
Pullman M.
Purcell-Jones G.
Purday J.P.
Puttick N.
Quader M.A.
Quiney N.F.
Quinlan J.
Qureshi S.M.
Rabey P.
Radhakrishna S.
Rafferty M.P.
Raftery S.M.
Ralph C.
Ralph S.
Ralston C.
Ramachandra V.
Ramirez A.
Rampton A.J.
Ramsay T.M.
Ranasinghe D.
Randall N.P.C.

Randall P.J.
Rao J.J.
Rao P.J.
Raphael G.
Rasanayagam R.
Rashid Z.
Rawal S.B.
Rawlinson W.A.L.
Ray S.
Reed P.A.
Reed P.N.
Reid M.F.
Reilly C.S.
Restall J.
Rich P.
Richards D.C.
Richardson J.
Richmond C.
Richmond M.N.
Richmond S.M.
Riddell G.S.
Riddell P.
Riddell P.L.
Riedel A.
Rigg J.
Riley B.
Ritchie P.A.
Robbins P.
Roberts C.
Roberts J.
Roberts W.O.
Robins D.W.
Robinson B.
Robinson D.
Robinson D.J.C.
Robinson P.N.
Robson E.
Rogers C.M.
Rogers S.O.
Rollin A.M.
Romer H.
Rooney M.J.
Ross M.T.
Ross S.
Rothwell M.P.
Rouse J.M.
Routh G.S.
Roysam C.
Royston D.
Ruff S.J.
Ruiz K.
Rush E.
Rushmer J.
Rushton A.
Russell G.
Rutter D.V.
Rutter J.M.

Ryan D.W.
Ryder I.
Rylah L.T.A.
Saddler J.M.
Sage M.
Saha D.
Sainsbury M.
Sajjad T.
Salem M.G.D.
Salib Y.
Salmon N.P.
Samaan A.K.
Sammut M.
Sanchez A.
Sanders G.
Sanderson P.
Sanehi O.
Sanikop S.
Sansome A.
Sashidharan R.
Saunders D.A.
Saunders P.
Saunders P.
Scallan M.J.H.
Schwarz P.A.
Scott A.D.
Scott M.
Scott R.
Scriven P.M.
Scull T.
Scullion D.
Scully S.A.
Seager S.J.
Sear J.
Secker C.
Sekar M.
Selim A.
Sellwood W.G.
Selsby D.S.
Seth N.
Sewell J.
Seymour A.H.
Shah D.
Shaikh L.
Shaikh R.
Shajar M.
Shambrook A.S.
Shannon P.
Shanthaklimar R.E.
Sharpe R.
Shaw I.H.
Shaw T.C.
Shawket S.
Shepherd D.
Shepherd J.E.
Shepherd T.P.
Sherry O.

Sherwood N.
Shlugman D.
Shukla A.C.
Sides C.A.
Silva S.
Simpson P.J.
Sinclair J.R.
Sinclair M.
Sinden M.
Singa K.
Singh A.
Singh S.
Siriwardhana S.A.
Sivalingam T.
Sivayokan P.
Sizer J.
Skinner H.
Skinner T.
Skoyles J.R.
Slade J.
Slater A.
Smith B.A.
Smith B.L.
Smith D.
Smith I.
Smith J.B.
Smith J.E.
Smith M.
Smith M.
Smith M.B.
Smith P.
Smith P.A.
Smith P.D.
Smith Q.
Smith S.
Smith S.
Smith S.
Smithers E.
Snape S.
Somanathan S.
Songhurst L.Z.
Soppitt A.J.
Southern D.
Sowden G.R.
Spargo P.
Spelina K.R.
Spiers S.P.W.
Spittal M.
Sprigge J.S.
Squires S.J.
Stack C.G.
Stambach T.
Stanford B.J.
Stanley J.
Stannard C.
Stapleton C.L.
Steer B.

Stewart J.
Stocks G.
Stoddart A.P.
Stoilova T.M.
Stoker M.
Stokes M.
Stone J.
Stone P.G.
Stoneham M.
Stonham J.
Stratford N.
Strube P.
Stubbing J.F.
Summerfield R.J.
Summors A.
Susay S.
Sutcliffe N.
Swales H.
Swanepoel A.
Swanevelder J.L.C.
Swanson L.
Swayamprakasam A.
Sweeney B.P.
Swinhoe C.F.
Symington M.
Szafranski J.S.
Tandon B.
Tannett P.G.
Tarpey J.J.
Taylor A.J.
Taylor C.
Taylor C.
Taylor E.A.S.
Taylor M.
Taylor N.
Taylor P.
Teale K.
Teasdale A.
Telford R.
Thacker A.
Thind J.
Thomas D.I.
Thomas D.L.
Thomas V.L.
Thompson D.G.
Thompson E.M.
Thompson H.
Thompson M.C.
Thoms G.
Thomson S.
Thorn J.L.
Thornberry A.
Thorniley A.
Thornley B.
Thornton P.
Thorpe C.
Thorpe S.

Till C.
Timmis P.
Tinloi S.F.
Tipping T.
Tobias M.A.
Tofte B.C.
Tolhurst-Cleaver C.L.
Tomlinson J.H.
Tomlinson P.
Toomey P.
Tordoff S.
Train J.
Trask M.D.
Tring I.C.
Trotter T.
Tufft N.
Turrell A.
Turvey A.
Tweedie D.G.
Twohey L.C.
Twohig M.M.
Uddin S.M.K.
Umerah E.
Uncles D.R.
Underwood S.
Urquhart J.
Utting H.J.
Vaidya A.
Valentine J.
van Miert M.
Varley S.C.
Vaughan S.T.A.
Veness A.M.
Venkat N.
Venkataraman P.
Verma R.
Vernon J.M.
Vernon M.S.
Vickers A.P.
Victoria A.
Vijay V.
Vohra S.
Voice A.
Wace J.R.
Wadsworth R.
Wagle A.
Wainwright A.C.
Wakeling H.G.
Waldmann C.S.
Walker C.P.R.
Walker G.
Walker I.
Walker M.A.
Wall T.
Wallbank I.W.
Walton M.
Ward J.

Ward M.E.
Ward P.
Ward R.M.
Ward S.
Ward-McQuaid J.M.C.
Wark K.J.
Warnell I.H.
Waterland J.
Waters B.
Waters J.H.
Watson D.
Watson D.A.
Watson D.M.
Watson D.M.
Watson P.J.Q.
Watson-Jones E.
Watt J.
Watt N.
Watts A.
Weaver M.K.
Webb A.
Webb T.B.
Wee L.
Weir P.
Weitkamp B.F.
Weldon O.G.W.
Wenstone R.
West K.J.
Westbrook J.
Weston G.A.
Wheatley E.
Wheatly S.
Whelan E.
Whitaker A.J.
Whitaker D.K.
White A.
White E.O.
White M.J.
Whitehead I.
Whitehead J.P.
Whiteley S.
Wielogorski A.K.
Wignarajah A.
Wilkey A.D.
Wilkins A.
Wilkins C.J.
Wilkinson D.A.
Wilkinson M.B.
Will R.
Willatts D.G.
Williams B.
Williams C.
Williams D.J.M.
Williams E.G.N.
Williams I.
Williams K.N.
Williams L.J.

Williams N.
Williams N.J.
Williams P.
Williamson S.
Willis B.A.
Wilson A.J.
Wilson A.M.
Wilson A.T.
Wilson C.M.
Wilson K.
Wilson P.T.J.
Wilson S.
Wilton H.J.
Withers M.
Wolff A.
Wood A.
Wood D.W.
Wood K.
Wood P.J.
Woodall N.M.
Woodham M.
Woods I.
Woods J.M.
Woods L.
Woodsford P.V.
Wooldridge W.
Woolf R.
Wragg S.D.
Wright J.
Wright M.M.
Wroth R.P.
Wyatt R.
Wyse M.
Yanny H.
Yanny W.A.
Yardy N.
Yate B.
Yates D.W.
Yau K.W.
Yeoman P.
Yetton R.
Yoganathan S.
Yogasakaran B.S.
Young J.D.
Zideman D.A.

APPENDIX H

PARTICIPANTS

Consultant surgeons and gynaecologists

These consultant surgeons and gynaecologists returned at least one questionnaire relating to the period 1 April 2000 to 31 March 2001.

Abercrombie J.F.
Abrams P.
Abulafi A.M.
Adair H.M.
Adam I.J.
Adeyemi O.
Adhikari A.R.
Adiseshiah M.
Adjepong S.
Afify S.E.
Afshar F.
Agrawal S.
Ahiaku E.
Ahmad S.M.
Ahmed B.
Ahmed M.
Akoh J.A.
Al-Dabbagh A.K.R.
Al-Dadah Q.
Al-Khatib M.
Al-Mufti R.
Al-Sabti A.
Albert D.
Albert J.S.
Alderman P.M.
Alexander D.J.
Ali D.
Ali S.H.
Allan D.
Allan S.M.
Allardice G.E.
Allardice J.
Allcock S.
Allen C.L.O.
Allen D.R.
Allen M.
Allen S.
Allsopp R.
Allum R.L.
Allum W.H.
Alpar E.K.
Alun-Jones T.
Alwitry M.
Amaku E.O.
Amamilo S.
Amarah S.
Ambrose N.S.
Ammori B.
Amrani M.
Anandaram P.S.
Anderson D.R.
Anderson G.H.
Anderson I.D.
Anderson J.
Anderson J.A.
Anderson R.J.L.
Anderson R.S.

Anderton J.M.
Andrew D.R.
Andrew J.G.
Andrews B.
Andrews C.M.
Andrews N.
Andrews S.
Angelini G.D.
Anikin V.
Anson K.
Antrobus J.N.
Antrum R.M.
Anyanwu L.
Apakama I.G.
Appleton G.V.N.
Apthorpe H.
Arafa M.
Archer T.J.
Argano V.
Arkell D.G.
Armistead S.H.
Armitage N.C.
Armitage T.G.
Armstrong C.P.
Arnold R.
Asaad S.S.
Asante D.K.
Ashour H.
Ashpole R.D.
Aston N.O.
Atkins R.
Atrah S.G.
Attara G.A.
Attwood S.E.A.
Au J.
Auchincloss J.M.
Audisio R.
Aukland A.
Aukland P.
Auld B.J.
Ausobsky J.R.
Avill R.
Aziz T.
Babar A.
Backhouse C.M.
Badenoch D.F.
Badger I.
Bailey I.
Bainbridge E.T.
Baird R.N.
Bajekal R.
Baker A.R.
Baldwin D.L.
Balfour T.W.
Bamford D.
Bamford P.N.
Bancewicz J.

Banks A.J.
Bannister G.C.
Bannister J.J.
Baqai A.N.
Baraka M.E.
Bardsley A.F.
Bardsley D.
Barkeji M.
Barker J.R.
Barker S.G.E.
Barlow C.
Barnard S.P.
Barr H.
Barrett A.M.
Barrett D.
Barrington R.L.
Barron D.
Barros D'Sa A.A.B.
Barsoum G.
Basheer A.M.M.
Bashir T.
Bassili F.S.
Bassuini M.M.
Bastawrous S.
Bates C.A.
Bates T.
Bateson P.G.
Batra H.C.
Battersby R.D.E.
Bawarish A.
Baxandall R.C.
Baxter J.N.
Bdesha A.
Beacon J.P.
Beard J.D.
Beard R.C.
Bearn P.
Beck R.
Beckdash B.
Beckingham I.J.
Bedford A.F.
Beeby D.I.
Bell B.A.
Bell J.R.
Bell N.J.
Bell P.R.F.
Benfield J.
Benhamida A.J.
Benjamin I.S.
Benjamin J.C.
Benson J.
Bentley P.G.
Benzinger H.
Berry A.R.
Berry D.
Berstock D.A.
Bett N.J.

Betts C.D.
Bevis C.R.A.
Bewick M.
Beynon J.
Bhamra M.S.
Bhattacharya S.
Bhatti T.
Bhoora I.
Bhullar T.P.S.
Billings P.J.
Binfield P.M.
Birch N.
Bircher M.D.
Birchill M.
Bird R.
Birtwistle S.
Bishop C.C.R.
Biswas S.P.
Black J.
Black P.R.M.
Black R.J.
Blackburn N.
Blackburne J.S.
Blackett R.L.
Blackford H.N.
Blair P.
Blair S.D.
Blake G.
Blamey R.W.
Blauth C.
Bleach N.R.
Bliss R.
Blower A.
Blunt R.J.
Boardman K.P.
Bodey W.N.
Bolger B. (deceased)
Bolton J.P.
Bolton-Maggs B.G.
Bonnici A.V.
Bonser R.
Boome R.
Borowsky K.
Bose P.
Bostock S.H.
Botha A.
Boulos P.B.
Bourke J.B.
Bowsher W.G.
Bowyer G.
Bracey D.J.
Bradbrook R.A.
Bradburn M.
Bradbury A.
Bradley P.J.
Bradnock B.
Braithwaite B.D.

Braithwaite P.A.
Bramble F.J.
Bransom C.J.
Brar A.
Brawn W.J.
Brayley J.
Brearley S.
Brennan J.
Brett M.
Brewood A.F.M.
Brewster N.
Brewster S.F.
Bridgewater B.
Bridle S.H.
Briffa N.
Briggs P.J.
Bristol J.B.
Britton B.J.
Britton J.M.
Britton J.P.
Bromage J.D.
Broodryk A.P.
Brooke N.
Brooks C.H.
Brooks M.
Brooks S.
Brooks S.G.
Broome G.
Brough R.
Brough W.A.
Broughton A.C.
Browell D.
Brown A.
Brown A.A.
Brown C.
Brown H.
Brown M.G.
Brown R.J.
Brown T.H.
Browne A.O.J.
Browne T.
Browning M.
Browning N.
Brownson P.
Browse D.
Bryan R.M.
Bryan S.
Bryant P.A.
Brydon H.L.
Buch K.
Buchanan J.
Buchanan J.M.
Buckels J.A.C.
Bucknill T.M.
Buick R.G.
Bullen B.R.
Bullock P.

Bunce C.
Bunker T.D.
Burgess N.A.
Burgess P.
Burke D.A.
Burke M.
Burkitt D.
Burnand K.G.
Butler C.
Butt M.S.
Buxton T.
Byrne P.O.
Cade D.
Cadoux-Hudson T.
Cain D.
Cairns D.W.
Calder D.A.
Cale A.R.J.
Callam M.J.
Callear A.B.
Callum K.C.
Calvert C.H.
Calvert P.T.
Cameron C.R.
Campbell C.S.
Campbell D.
Campbell D.J.
Campbell J.B.
Campbell J.K.
Campbell R.
Campbell W.B.
Campbell W.J.
Cant P.
Carey D.
Carey J.
Carlson G.L.
Carpenter R.
Carter P.S.
Carter S.R.
Carty N.J.
Carvell J.E.
Casha J.
Casula R.P.
Cavanagh S.P.
Cave-Bigley D.J.
Cawthorn S.J.
Chadwick C.J.
Chadwick D.R.
Chadwick S.
Chakrabarti A.
Chan C.
Chan H.Y.
Chan P.
Chan R.N.W.
Chandrasekaran V.
Chang D.
Chang R.W.S.

Channon G.M.	Collin J.	Cunningham C.	Dickson G.H.
Chapman M.A.S.	Collins F.J.	Curley P.J.	Dihmis W.C.
Chapman P.	Collins R.E.C.	Curran F.T.	Dilworth G.R.
Chappatte O.A.	Conboy V.	Currie I.	Dingle A.F.
Chare M.J.B.	Cook A.	Curwen C.	Dixon A.R.
Charnley G.J.	Cook A.I.M.	Cuschieri R.J.	Dixon J.H.
Charnley R.M.	Cooke R.S.	Cusick E.	Dodds S.
Chatterji S.	Cooke T.J.C.	Da Silva A.	Dodenhoff R.M.
Chaudrey T.A.	Cooke W.M.	Dahar N.A.	Doig R.L.
Chave H.	Coombes G.B.	Dan A.N.	Dolan S.
Chawdhery M.Z.	Cooper G.J.	Daoud R.	Dolan T.G.
Cheah K.	Cooper J.C.	Darby C.R.	Donaldson D.R.
Cheatle T.R.	Cooper M.J.	Darke S.G.	Donaldson P.J.
Checketts R.G.	Cooper Wilson M.	Darzi A.	Donell S.
Cheema I.A.	Coorsh J.C.	Das S.	Donnachie N.J.
Cherry R.J.	Copeland S.A.	David H.G.	Donovan A.G.
Cheshire N.	Corbett C.R.R.	Davies C.J.	Donovan I.A.
Cheslyn-Curtis S.	Corbett W.A.	Davies M.	Doran A.
Chilvers A.S.	Corder A.	Davies N.	Doran J.
Chinegwundoh F.I.	Corless D.J.	Davies R.M.	Dormandy J.A.
Chitkara D.	Corlett M.P.	Davies S.J.M.	Dorricott N.J.
Choy A.	Cornaby A.	Davis C.H.G.	Dorudi S.
Chugh S.	Cornell M.	Dawson J.L.	Dorward N.
Citron N.D.	Corner N.	Dawson J.W.	Dos Remedios I.
Ciulli F.	Corson J.	Dawson K.	Dowell J.K.
Clague M.B.	Costello C.B.	Dawson P.M.	Downes E.M.
Clark A.W.	Coveney E.	Day A.C.	Downing R.
Clark D.	Cox G.J.	De Boer P.G.	Drabble E.
Clark D.W.	Cox P.J.	de Cossart L.M.	Drake D.P.
Clark G.W.B.	Cox R.	De Friend D.	Drakeley M.J.
Clark J.	Crabbe D.C.G.	de Kiewiet G.P.	Drummond P.M.
Clark K.	Craig D.M.	de Leval M.	Duffy J.P.
Clarke D.	Craigen M.A.C.	De Sousa B.A.	Duffy T.J.
Clarke J.	Cranley B.	Deacon P.B.	Duggan E.
Clarke J.M.F.	Crate I.D.	Deane A.M.	Dunkley A.
Clarke N.W.	Crawford D.J.	Deans G.	Dunlop P.
Clarke R.W.	Crawshaw C.C.	Debrah S.	Dunn J.
Clason A.E.	Creedon R.	Dega R.	Dunnett W.
Clasper J.	Crick M.D.	Deiraniya A.	Dunning J.
Clay N.R.	Crighton I.L.	Delicata R.J.	Dunning P.G.
Clayson A.	Crinnion J.N.	Delrievere L.	Durning P.
Cleak D.K.	Cripps N.P.J.	Dempster D.W.	Durrans D.
Clegg J.F.	Cripps N.	Denton G.W.L.	Duthie G.S.
Clements D.A.	Crisp J.C.	Denton J.S.	Duthie J.S.
Clements W.	Crisp W.J.	Derodra J.	Dutta B.K.
Clifford R.P.	Crockard H.A.	Derry C.D.	Dworkin M.J.
Clothier P.R.	Croft R.J.	Desai A.	Dyke G.W.
Coady M.S.E.	Cross A.T.	Desai K.	Dyson P.H.P.
Coates C.J.	Cross F.W.	Deshmukh R.	Earnshaw J.J.
Cobb J.P.	Cruickshank D.J.	Deville de Goget J.	Eaton S.
Cobb R.A.	Cruickshank G.	Dhillon R.	Ebbs S.R.
Cochrane J.P.S.	Crumplin M.K.H.	Dhorajiwala J.M.	Edge A.J.
Cohen G.	Cullen P.J.	Di Salvo C.	Edmondson S.
Coker A.O.	Cullen P.T.	Diamond T.	Edwards J.A.
Coker T.P.	Cullimore J.E.	Dias P.S.	Edwards J.L.
Colin J.F.	Cumming J.	Dickinson A.J.	Edwards P.R.
Collier S.	Cunliffe W.J.	Dickinson I.K.	El-Barghouti N.

El-Hasani S.
El-Safty M.M.
Elder J.B.
Ellenbogen S.
Elliott D.
Elliott J.R.M.
Elliott M.J.
Ellis D.J.
Ellis S.
Emmerson K.
England P.C.
Epstein H.P.
Evans D.A.
Evans F.
Evans G.H.
Evans H.J.R.
Evans S.C.
Everitt N.J.
Eyers P.S.
Eyres K.
Fahmy N.R.M.
Fairbank A.C.
Fairbrother B.J.
Fansa M.
Farhan M.J.
Farooqi A.
Farouk M.
Farrands P.A.
Farrar M.
Farrell R.
Farrington W.T.
Fawcett D.P.
Fayaz M.
Fenton J.
Ferguson C.J.
Ferguson G.H.
Ferguson J.
Ferrie B.G.
Fewster S.
Fiddian N.J.
Field J.
Fiennes A.
Finch D.R.A.
Finnis D.
Firth J.L.
Fisher E.W.
Flannigan G.M.
Fleetcroft J.P.
Fletcher M.S.
Fligelstone L.
Flint G.
Flood B.M.
Flook D.
Flowerdew A.F.
Floyd A.
Flynn N.A.K.
Fogg A.J.B.

Foley R.
Fontaine C.J.
Ford T.F.
Fordham M.
Fordyce M.J.F.
Formela L.J.
Forrest J.F.
Forrest L.
Forsyth A.A.
Fortes Mayer K.D.
Fossard D.P.
Foster M.E.
Fountain S.W.
Fowlis G.A.
Fox A.D.
Fox J.N.
Foy M.A.
Foy P.
Fozard J.B.J.
Fraser I.D.
Fraser S.
Freeman R.M.
Fugleholm K.
Fyfe I.S.
Gajraj H.
Galea M.
Galinanes M.
Gallagher P.
Galland R.B.
Gallegos N.C.
Gana H.B.
Gannon M.X.
Gardecki T.I.M.
Gardiner J.
Gardiner K.
Garg S.K.
Garnham A.
Gartell P.C.
Garth R.J.N.
Garvan N.
Gateley C.
Gateley D.
Gaunt M.E.
Gayner A.D.
Geary N.P.J.
Gee A.
Geeranavar S.S.
George P.P.
Georgekutty K.A.
Gerber C.
Germon T.
Geroulakos G.
Geutjens G.
Ghareeb E.
Ghosh S.
Gibb P.
Gibbon A.J.

Gibbons C.L.M.
Gibbons C.P.
Gibbs S.
Gibson A.
Gibson R.A.
Gibson R.J.
Giddings A.E.B.
Gie G.A.
Gilbert J.M.
Gilbert L.
Gilbert P.
Gill P.J.
Gill S.S.
Gilling-Smith G.L.
Glasgow M.M.S.
Glass R.E.
Glazer G.
Glenville B.E.
Godfrey K.A.
Golash A.
Gold D.
Goldman M.D.
Goldstraw P.
Goodier D.
Goodman A.J.
Goodwin M.I.
Gordon A.
Gosling D.C.
Gough A.L.
Gough M.J.
Goulbourne I.A.
Gourevitch D.
Gower R.L.
Grace D.L.
Graham T.R.
Grange W.J.
Grant A.J.
Gray L.
Gray M.R.
Greaney M.G.
Greatorex R.A.
Green T.
Greenall M.J.
Greenhalgh R.M.
Greenstein D.
Gregory R.J.H.
Gregson P.
Griffin S.C.
Griffin S.M.
Griffith C.D.M.
Griffith J.
Griffiths A.B.
Griffiths D.A.
Griffiths E.
Griffiths N.J.
Griffiths R.W.
Griffiths W.E.G.

Grocott E.
Groenewald C.
Grotte G.J.
Gryf-Lowczowski J.
Gudgeon M.
Guest J.
Gull S.E.
Gullan R.W.
Gunasekera L.
Gunn R.S.
Gunning K.
Gurusinghe N.T.
Guvendik L.
Guy A.J.
Guy P.J.
Gwynn B.R.
Haddad F.S.
Hadjiminas D.
Hahn D.M.
Hall A.W.
Hall C.
Hall J.H.
Hall R.I.
Hallan R.
Hallett J.P.
Halliday A.W.
Hallissey M.T.
Halliwell M.
Ham R.J.
Hambidge J.E.
Hamer A.J.
Hamer D.B.
Hamilton G.
Hamilton H.
Hamilton J.R.L.
Hamlyn P.J.
Hammad Z.
Hammer A.J.
Hammonds J.C.
Hampal S.
Handley R.
Hands L.J.
Hannon R.J.
Hanson D.R.
Haray P.N.
Hardee P.
Harding S.P.
Hardy S.C.
Hargest R.
Hargreaves D.
Harkness W.F.J.
Harland R.N.L.
Harley J.M.
Harper W.M.
Harrington P.
Harris P.L.
Harris T.M.

Harrison B.J.	Hocken D.B.	Hussain S.T.	Jenner R.E.
Harrison D.J.	Hodder S.	Hutchins P.M.	Jewkes A.
Harrison I.D.	Hoddinott H.C.	Hutchinson R.	Jibril J.A.
Harrison J.D.	Hodgkinson J.P.	Hyde I.D.	John T.G.
Harrison R.A.	Hoile R.W.	Iftikhar S.Y.	Johnson A.G.
Harrison T.A.	Holcombe C.	Imman I.	Johnson A.O.B.
Hartley M.	Holdsworth J.D.	Imray C.H.E.	Johnson B.F.
Harvey C.F.	Holdsworth P.J.	Ingham-Clark C.	Johnson-Nurse C.
Harvey D.R.	Holford C.P.	Ingram N.P.	Johnston A.O.B.
Harvey I.	Holland J.P.	Ingrams D.R.	Johnston S.R.
Harvey J.S.	Holland J.P.	Insall R.	Johri A.
Harvey M.H.	Holland P.A.	Iossifidis A.	Jones B.G.
Harvey R.A.	Holliday H.W.	Iqbal M.J.	Jones D.G.
Hasan A.	Holmes J.T.	Ireland D.	Jones D.J.
Hasan R.I.R.	Holmes S.	Irvin T.T.	Jones D.J.
Hasan S.S.	Holt E.M.	Irvine B.	Jones D.R.
Hashimi H.	Holt G.	Irvine C.D.	Jones D.R.B.
Hastie K.J.	Holt M.	Irwin A.	Jones J.R.
Hatem M.H.M.	Holt S.D.H.	Irwin L.R.	Jones L.S.
Havard T.J.	Homer-Vanniasinkam S.	Irwin P.P.	Jones M.
Haw M.	Hood J.M.	Irwin S.T.	Jones M.W.
Hawthorn I.E.	Hook W.E.	Isbister E.	Jones N.A.G.
Hay D.J.	Hooper T.	Isgar B.	Jones P.A.
Hayes N.	Hope D.T.	Iskander I.S.	Jones R.B.
Haynes S.	Hopkinson B.R.	Ismaiel A.H.	Jones R.N.
Hayward R.	Hopkinson D.N.	Ismail A.M.	Jones S.
Hearn A.R.	Hopkinson-Woolley J.	Ismail T.	Jones W.A.
Heath D.V.	Horgan A.F.	Ismail W.	Joseph J.V.
Heather B.P.	Horgan L.F.	Ivory J.P.	Journeaux S.
Heddle R.M.	Horner J.	Iyer S.V.	Jowett R.L.
Hegab A.I.	Hosie K.B.	Izzidien A.Y.	Joyce A.
Helm R.H.	Hosking S.W.	Jabir M.	Joypaul B.V.
Henderson A.	Houghton A.	Jackaman F.R.	Judd M.
Henderson J.J.	Houghton P.W.J.	Jackson D.	Justin T.
Henderson S.	Housden P.	Jacob S.	Kalifi K.
Hendrickse C.	Howard A.C.	Jacobs P.M.	Kallis P.
Henman P.D.	Howat J.M.T.	Jaffe V.	Kambouroglou G.
Hennessey C.	Hoyle M.	Jaffray B.	Kane V.J.
Henry A.D.	Hudd C.	Jaganathan R.S.	Kanse P.
Hepworth C.	Huddy S.P.J.	Jakeways M.S.	Kapila L.
Hershman M.	Hudson I.	Jameel M.	Karat D.
Hewitt G.R.	Hughes F.	James E.T.R.	Karim M.S.K.
Hickey M.S.J.	Hughes R.	James M.I.	Kashi H.
Hickey N.C.	Hughes R.G.	James P.J.	Kathuria V.
Hicks R.	Hughes S.	James S.E.	Kay P.
Higman D.J.	Huizinga W.K.J.	Jameson J.S.	Kaye J.C.
Hill J.	Hulme A.	Jamieson A.	Kazzazi N.H.
Hill J.T.	Hulton N.R.	Jamison M.H.	Keeling N.
Hill S.	Humphreys W.V.	Jane M.	Keenan D.J.M.
Hilton C.J.	Hunt L.M.	Jarvis A.C.	Keighley M.R.B.
Hind R.	Hunt T.M.	Jayatunga A.P.	Kellerman A.J.
Hindley C.J.	Hunter J.B.	Jefferiss C.D.	Kelly M.J.
Hindmarsh J.R.	Hunter S.	Jeffery P.J.	Kelly S.B.
Hinves B.L.	Hurley P.	Jeffery R.S.	Kemeny A.A.
Hirst P.	Hurlow R.A.	Jellinek D.A.	Kendall S.W.
Hobbiss J.H.	Hurst P.A.	Jenkins A.J.	Kennedy C.L.
Hobbs N.	Huskisson L.J.	Jenkinson L.R.	Kennedy J.A.

Kennedy R.H.
Kenny N.W.
Kenogbon J.I.
Kent S.J.S.
Keogh B.
Kerr G.
Kerr P.
Kerr R.S.C.
Kerr-Wilson R.
Kerrigan D.
Kerry R.M.K.
Kershaw C.J.
Ketzer B.
Keys G.W.
Keys R.
Khaira H.S.
Khalil-Marzouk J.F.
Khan A.
Khan A.H.
Khan I.
Khan M.
Khan O.
Khan S.
Khestigar M.
Khoo C.T.K.
Khoo D.
Khoury G.A.
Khurshid M.
Kiely E.
Kiff R.S.
Kinder R.B.
Kirby R.
Kirby R.M.
Kirk S.
Kirwan P.
Kissin M.W.
Klimach O.
Knight M.J.
Knight S.
Knox A.J.S.
Knox R.
Knudsen C.J.M.
Kohlhardt S.R.
Korsgen S.
Kothari V.M.
Kramer D.G.
Krishna M.
Kulkarni R.P.
Kumar P.K.
Kumar T.M.
Kumar V.
Kurdy N.
Kurer M.H.
Kutiyanawala M.
Ladas G.
Lafferty K.
Lagattolla N.

Lahoti O.
Laidlaw I.
Laing H.
Laing P.W.
Lake D.N.W.
Lake S.P.
Lam F.T.
Lamba M.
Lambert A.W.
Lambert D.
Lambert M.E.
Lambert S.
Lambert W.G.
Lambertz M.M.
Lamerton A.J.
Lang D.
Lansdown M.
Large S.R.
Larvin M.
Latham J.
Latham P.D.
Lattimer C.
Lauffer G.
Lavelle M.A.
Law N.
Lawrence D.
Lawrence R.N.
Lawton F.
Lawton F.G.
Leach R.D.
Lear P.A.
Leather A.
Lee J.O.
Lee M.J.R.
Lee P.W.R.
Lee R.
Lee R.J.
Leeson S.C.
Leicester R.J.
Leinhardt D.
Leitch J.
Lemberger R.J.
Lennox I.A.C.
Lennox J.M.
Leopold P.W.
Levack B.
Leverment J.N.
Leveson S.H.
Levine A.J.
Lewin M.
Lewis G.J.
Lewis J.L.
Lewis K.
Lewis M.H.
Lewis M.P.N.
Lewis P.
Lewis W.

Leyshon R.L.
Li T.C.
Linehan I.P.
Lingham M.K.
Linsell J.C.
Little G.
Livesey S.
Livesley P.J.
Livingstone B.N.
Livingstone J.
Lock M.R.
Locke T.J.
Locker A.
Lodge J.P.A.
Loh A.
London N.
London N.J.
Lonsdale R.J.
Loosemore T.
Lord M.G.
Lotz J.C.
Louette L.
Loughlin V.
Lovell M.
Lowdon I.M.R.
Loxdale P.H.
Loynes R.D.
Lucarotti M.E.
Lucas M.G.
Lyall H.
Lynch M.
Lynch M.C.
Lynch T.
Lyndon P.J.
Lyttle J.A.
Macdonald D.A.
MacDonald R.C.
MacFie J.
MacGowan S.
Mackenney R.P.
Mackenzie M.
Mackie C.R.
Mackie I.G.
Mackinnon J.G.
Mackle E.J.
MacLellan G.E.
MacLennan I.
MacNeill F.A.
Madan M.
Madden N.P.
Madhra K.
Mady S.M.
Magee P.G.
Magnussen P.
Mahendran V.
Mahir M.S.
Mahomed A.

Mair W.S.J.
Maitre D.
Maiwand O.
Majeed A.W.
Majkowski R.S.
Makin C.A.
Malata C.M.
Malcolm G.
Mallucci C.
Mancey-Jones J.B.
Manktelow A.R.J.
Mannas D.
Mansfield A.O.
Manson J.M.
Marchbank A.J.
Mark I.R.
Markandoo P.
Markham N.I.
Marks C.G.
Marks S.M.
Marsh C.H.
Marsh H.T.
Marsh P.J.
Marsh S.
Marshall G.
Marshall J.
Marshall P.D.
Marshall R.E.K.
Marston R.A.
Martin J.L.
Martin L.
Martin R.H.
Martin-Hirsch D.P.
Marzouk D.
Mason M.C.
Mason P.F.
Massey C.I.
Massey J.A.
Masters A.
Masud I.
Mathew G.
Mathews M.G.
Matthews J.G.
Matthews J.G.W.
Mavor A.I.D.
Maxwell H.A.
Maxwell W.A.
May A.R.L.
May P.C.
Maybury N.K.
Mayer A.D.
Maynard N.D.
McAdam J.G.
McCahy P.
McCarthy D.
McClennan I.
McCollum C.N.

McCollum P.T.	Mills C.L.	Murphy P.D.	O'Reilly G.
McConnell R.	Mills S.J.	Murray A.	O'Riordan B.
McCormack M.J.	Minhas T.	Murray J.M.	O'Riordan J.
McCrory D.	Mirza D.	Murray K.H.	Obeid E.M.
McCulloch P.G.	Misra D.	Murty G.	Obeid M.L.
McCullough C.J.	Mitchell I.C.	Muscroft T.	Odom N.J.
McDonald P.	Mitchell I.M.	Nada A.N.	Offori T.
McElroy B.	Modgill V.K.	Nadarajan P.	Ohri S.
McFarland R.J.	Mohammed A.	Naerger H.	Ojo A.
McGee H.	Mohan J.	Naidu V.	Onwudike M.
McGregor A.D.	Mohsen Y.	Naik R.	Ormiston M.C.
McGrouther D.A.	Moir G.C.	Naik S.K.	Ornstein M.H.
McGuigan J.A.	Mok D.W.H.	Nair R.	Orr G.
McIlroy B.S.	Molitor P.J.A.	Nair R.	Osman F.A.
McInerney P.D.	Monk D.	Nair U.	Osman I.S.
McIntosh G.S.	Monro J.L.	Nangalia R.	Ostick D.G.
McIntosh I.H.	Monson J.R.T.	Nanu A.	Oyarzabal M.
McIrvine A.J.	Montgomery A.C.V.	Naqesh-Bandi H.A.	Packer G.
McKie L.	Monypenny I.J.	Narang K.	Padgham N.
McLatchie G.	Moore A.J.	Nash J.R.	Padwick M.
McLoughlin J.	Moore D.	Nashef S.A.M.	Page R.D.
McLoughlin S.J.	Moore P.J.	Nasmyth D.G.	Page R.E.
McMahon M.J.	Moorehead R.J.	Nath F.	Pailthorpe C.A.
McNally J.	Moran B.	Naylor A.R.	Pain J.A.
McNamara M.	Morgan A.R.	Neil-Dwyer G.	Palmer J.G.
McPartlin J.F.	Morgan J.	Nelson I.W.	Palmer J.H.
McSweeney L.	Morgan W.P.	Neoptolemos J.P.	Panayiotopoulos Y.
McVicar I.	Morgans B.T.	Nevelos A.B.	Pancharatnam M.D.
McWhinnie D.L.	Morrell M.T.	Newbegin C.J.R.	Papagrigoriadis S.
Mearns A.J.	Morris B.D.A.	Newey M.L.	Papastefanou S.L.
Mediratta N.K.	Morris G.E.	Newington D.P.	Pardy B.J.
Meehan S.E.	Morris S.	Neyt J.G.V.	Paremain G.
Mehmet V.	Morritt G.N.	Nicholl J.	Parikh D.H.
Meleagros L.M.	Mortensen N.	Nicholls G.	Parker M.C.
Mellor S.	Mortimer C.J.	Nicholls J.C.	Parker P.J.
Mendelow A.D.	Morton M.E.	Nicholls R.J.	Parkinson R.
Mendoza N.	Mosley J.G.	Nicholson R.W.	Parmar J.M.
Menon D.K.	Mosquera D.A.	Nicholson S.	Parnell E.J.
Menon N.	Moss A.L.H.	Niyadurupola T.	Parr N.J.
Menon T.J.	Moss M.C.	Nolan J.F.	Parrott N.R.
Menzies D.	Motson R.W.	Norcott H.C.	Parry A.
Meredith A.D.	Moule I.	Norris J.	Parry G.W.
Metcalfe-Gibson C.	Mowbray M.A.S.	Norris M.G.	Parsons D.C.S.
Mfinanga R.E.	Mubashir A.	North A.D.	Parsons K.F.
Michaels J.A.	Mudawi A.M.	Northover J.M.A.	Partington P.F.
Michaud R.	Muddu B.N.	Nott D.M.	Parvin S.
Michie H.R.	Mufti G.	Novell J.R.	Parys B.T.
Mihaimeed F.M.A.	Mughal M.M.	Nugent K.	Patchava K.M.
Miles A.J.G.	Muir L.	Nwachukwu I.A.	Patel A.
Miles W.F.A.	Munro E.N.	Nyamekye I.	Patel A.D.
Milewski P.J.	Munsch C.M.	O'Brien D.	Patel P.
Miller A.J.	Murali S.	O'Connell J.	Patel R.
Miller G.F.	Murallikuttan K.P.	O'Connor D.	Patel R.L.
Miller G.V.	Murday A.	O'Dowd J.K.	Patel V.
Miller I.M.	Murdoch J.B.	O'Dwyer S.T.	Paterson A.
Miller J.G.	Murphy D.J.	O'Flynn K.	Paterson I.S.
Millner J.	Murphy J.	O'Leary D.	Patterson J.E.

Pattison R.M.	Prasad G.M.	Redfern T.R.	Rooney P.S.
Paul S.	Prescott S.	Redmond E.	Rosenberg B.C.
Payne S.P.K.	Price J.J.	Redwood N.	Rosenberg I.L.
Peace P.K.	Price N.	Reece-Smith H.	Rosin M.D.
Pearse M.F.	Pritchett C.J.	Reed J.	Rosin R.D.
Pearson H.J.	Pryor G.A.	Reed M.W.	Ross A.H.M.
Pearson J.B.	Pugsley W.B	Rees G.M.	Ross E.R.S.
Peart F.	Pullan D.M.	Rees M.	Ross K.R.
Peckham T.	Punjabi P.	Regan M.C.	Ross S.A.
Pegg D.J.	Purkiss S.F.	Regan M.W.	Rossouw D.J.
Pemberton D.	Pusey R.J.	Reid D.	Rothnie N.
Pemberton R.M.	Pye G.	Reilly D.	Rothwell N.
Pengelly A.W.	Pye J.K.	Reinbach D.	Rowe P.H.
Pennie B.	Quarcopoome W.	Reissis N.	Rowlands B.J.
Pentlow B.D.	Quayle A.R.	Rela M.	Rowles J.
Pepper J.R.	Quayle J.B.	Renton S.	Rowley S.
Peracha A.M.	Quick C.R.	Renwick P.	Rowse A.D.
Pereira J.H.	Quiney R.E.	Resouly A.	Roxburgh J.C.
Perkins J.M.T.	Radatz M.W.R.	Rew D.A.	Royle C.
Perry E.P.	Radcliffe A.G.	Reynolds I.S.R.	Royle G.T.
Peters P.	Radcliffe S.	Reynolds J.R.	Roysam G.S.
Peterson D.	Radford P.J.	Rhodes B.	Royston C.M.S.
Petri J.	Radley S.	Ribeiro B.F.	Ruddlesdin C.
Pettersson B.	Rae D.M.	Rice R.	Rundle J.S.H.
Peyton J.W.R.	Raftery A.T.	Richards D.M.	Rushforth G.F.
Pfleiderer A.G.	Raimes S.A.	Richards H.	Russell R.
Pheils P.J.	Raja M.A.	Richards P.	Rutter P.C.
Phillips G.	Rajesh P.B.	Richardson N.G.B.	Ryan P.G.
Phillips M.	Rajkumar V.J.	Richardson P.	Ryan W.G.
Phillips N.	Raju P.G.S.	Richens D.	Sabin H.I.
Phillips R.K.S.	Ralphs D.N.L.	Ricketts D.	Sadler A.G.
Phipps R.S.	Ramani V.	Rickford C.R.K.	Sadler G.
Pickersgill A.	Ramos J.	Ridings P.	Saffar N.
Pierro A.	Ramsden C.	Ridley P.	Sagar P.M.
Pigott T.	Ramsden P.D.	Rigg K.M.	Sagar S.
Pillai R.	Ranaboldo C.	Riley D.	Sagor G.R.
Pillay T.M.	Rand R.J.	Riley T.B.H.	Saharay M.
Pinder I.M.	Rangan A.	Rimington P.D.	Sahu A.
Piper I.H.	Rangecroft L.	Ritchie A.	Saidaiah Y.C.
Pittam M.R.	Rao S.	Ritchie A.W.S.	Sakka S.
Plewes J.L.	Rashed M.D.	Robb P.	Salama F.D.
Plusa S.	Rashid A.	Roberts G.A.	Saleh A.J.
Pobereskin L.H.	Rashid Z.	Roberts J.P.	Salman A.
Pocock R.D.	Rate A.	Roberts P.	Salter M.C.P.
Pollard J.P.	Rather G.	Roberts P.N.	Sambatakakis A.
Pollard R.	Ratliff D.A.	Robertson A.A.	Sampath S.A.C.
Pollard S.G.	Ratnakumar K.	Robertson C.	Samuel A.W.
Poonawala S.S.	Ratnatunga C.P.	Robertson I.J.	Sandeman D.R.
Pople I.	Raut V.	Robinson M.H.	Sanderson C.J.
Port A.	Rawes M.	Robinson V.P.	Sanderson P.L.
Porteous M.J.L.	Rayter Z.	Rochester J.R.	Sandhu D.P.S.
Porter D.P.	Raza S.A.	Roe A.M.	Sandison A.
Poskitt K.R.	Read C.	Rogers C.	Sansom J.R.
Poston G.J.	Reasbeck P.G.	Rogers I.M.	Saran D.
Poulsen J.	Redden J.F.	Rogers M.	Sarin S.
Powell C.S.	Reddy P.	Rogers M.J.	Sarkar S.
Pozzi M.	Redfern R.M.	Rooker G.D.	Sassoon E.

Sauven P.	Shenolikar A.	Somers S.	Sulaiman S.K.
Savage A.P.	Shepherd A.F.I.	Soong C.V.	Sundar M.
Savage R.	Sheppard I.	Souka H.M.	Sundaram S.K.
Saxby P.J.	Sheridan W.G.	Souter R.G.	Super P.
Sayer R.E.	Sherlock D.J.	South L.M.	Suraliwala K.H.
Sayer T.	Sherriff H.M.	Sowinski A.	Suresh G.
Sayers R.	Shetty A.	Sparrow O.C.	Surtees P.
Schilders E.	Shewell P.C.	Speakman C.T.	Sutcliffe J.
Schofield A.D.R.	Shibu M.	Spence R.A.	Sutcliffe M.L.
Scholefield J.H.	Shieff C.L.	Spencer T.S.	Sutton G.
Schranz P.J.	Shipolini A.	Spicer R.D.	Sutton R.
Scott A.D.N.	Shiv Shanker V.	Spitz L.	Swift R.I.
Scott D.J.A.	Shore D.F.	Spooner S.F.	Swinhoe J.R.
Scott G.	Shorthouse A.J.	Springall R.G.	Sykes P.A.
Scott H.J.	Shrivastava M.	Spychal R.T.	Symes J.M.
Scott I.H.K.	Shrivastava R.	Spyt T.	Szypryt E.P.
Scott J.M.	Shute K.	Srinivasan V.	Tacconi L.
Scott M.H.	Siddiqui K.H.	Stanbridge R.D.L.	Tadkjarimi S.
Scott M.M.	Sigurdsson A.	Stanley D.	Taggart D.
Scott N.	Silverman S.H.	Stansby G.P.	Tait W.F.
Scott R.A.P.	Silvester K.C.	Stapleton S.	Talbot D.
Scott W.A.	Simms J.M.	Stebbing J.F.	Talbot R.W.
Scriven M.	Simonis R.B.	Stebbings W.S.L.	Tandon S.K.
Sedman P.	Simpson N.S.	Steger A.C.	Targett J.P.G.
Sells R.A.	Simson J.N.	Stephen I.B.M.	Tarjuman M.
Selvakumar S.	Sinar J.	Stephen J.G.	Tavares S.
Senapati A.	Singh A.B.	Stephenson B.	Taylor A.R.
Sengupta R.P.	Singh C.B.	Stephenson R.N.	Taylor B.A.
Sethia B.	Singh D.	Stevenson I.M.	Taylor G.J.
Sgouros S.	Singh K.	Stewart D.J.	Taylor G.J.S.
Shafighian B.	Singh S.	Stewart H.D.	Taylor G.R.
Shafiq M.	Singh S.	Stewart J.	Taylor H.W.R.
Shaheen M.A.	Sinha A.	Stewart M.	Taylor I.
Shakespeare D.T.	Sinnerton R.	Stewart R.D.	Taylor K.M.
Shami K.	Siriwardena A.	Stewart W.E.	Taylor L.
Shanahan M.D.G.	Sjolin S.U.	Steyn R.	Taylor M.
Shand J.E.G.	Skene A.	Stirling A.	Taylor M.
Shandall A.	Skinner P.	Stirling W.J.I.	Taylor O.M.
Shanker J.	Skinner P.W.	Stirrat A.N.	Taylor P.R.
Shannon M.N.	Skipper D.	Stock S.E.	Taylor S.A.
Shaper N.J.	Slater B.	Stoddard C.J.	Teanby D.N.
Sharara K.	Slater N.	Stonelake P.	Teddy P.J.
Sharif D.	Slater R.N.S.	Stoodley B.J.	Tennant W.
Sharif H.I.	Slibi M.	Stossel C.A.	Terry T.R.
Sharif M.A.	Small P.	Stott M.A.	Tewary A.K.
Sharif U.I.	Smallpiece C.J.	Strachan C.J.L.	Thacker C.R.
Sharma A.K.	Smallwood J.	Strachan R.D.	Theodorou N.
Sharma S.D.	Smedley F.	Stranks G.J.	Thomas A.P.
Sharp D.J.	Smibert J.G.	Strauss P.	Thomas D.
Sharp J.	Smith D.N.	Stringer M.D.	Thomas D.G.T.
Sharpe D.A.	Smith E.E.J.	Stubington S.R.	Thomas D.M.
Sharr M.M.	Smith J.A.R.	Studley J.	Thomas D.R.
Shaw C.J.	Smith R.W.	Sturzaker H.G.	Thomas M.H.
Shaw D.L.	Smith S.R.G.	Sudlow R.A.	Thomas N.
Shea J.G.	Smyth J.V.	Sue-Ling H.M.	Thomas P.A.
Shearman C.P.	Snooks S.J.	Sugarman I.	Thomas P.R.S.
Shennan J.M.	Sobeh M.	Sukumar M.	Thompson J.

Thompson J.F.
Thompson M.H.
Thompson M.R.
Thomson G.J.L.
Thomson H.J.
Thomson W.H.F.
Thorneloe M.H.
Thorpe J.A.C.
Thurston A.
Tillman R.M.
Tilsed J.
Timmons M.J.
Timoney A.
Timperley J.
Tindall S.F.
Tiwari I.B.
Todd B.D.
Todd G.B.
Todd N.V.
Toogood G.J.
Toop K.M.
Townsend E.R.
Trakru S.
Tresadern J.C.
Tricker J.
Trivedi U.H.
Tromans P.M.
Trotter G.
Tsang V.
Tsui S.
Tubbs O.N.
Tucker S.
Tudor J.C.
Tudor R.G.
Tulloch C.J.
Tulwa N.
Turnbull T.J.
Turner A.
Turner A.G.
Turner D.T.L.
Turner R.S.
Turnock R.R.
Tuson K.W.R.
Tweedie J.H.
Tweedle D.E.F.
Twyman R.
Tyagi A.K.
Tyrrell M.R.
Ubhi C.
Ubhi S.
Underwood M.J.
Unsworth-White M.J.
Unwin A.J.
Upsdell S.M.
Vaizey C.J.
Valerio D.
Van Dellen J.

Van Den Bossche M.
Van Hille P.T.
Van Leenhoff J.
Varma J.S.
Varty K.
Vashisht R.
Vaughan R.
Vaughton K.C.
Vellacott K.D.
Venkatesh M.
Venn G.E.
Vennam R.B.
Vetrivel S.M.
Vickers J.
Vickers R.H.
Victoratos G.
Vipond M.
Vishwanath L.
Visvanathan R.
Vloeberghs M.H.
Vohra R.K.
Vowden P.
Vyas J.
Waghorn A.
Wahab K.H.A.
Wake M.
Wake P.N.
Wakeman R.
Walker A.J.
Walker A.P.
Walker C.
Walker D.I.
Walker J.
Walker M.A.
Walker M.G.
Walker R.T.
Wallace D.
Wallace D.M.A.
Wallace I.W.
Wallace R.G.H.
Waller D.A.
Wallis J.
Wallwork J.
Walmsley B.H.
Walsh C.J.
Walsh M.
Walsh W.K.
Walter P.
Wand J.S.
Ward A.S.
Ward M.W.N.
Ward P.J.
Ward R.G.
Warner J.G.
Warnke P.
Warren H.
Warren S.

Warwick A.
Wasserberg J.
Waterworth T.A.
Watkin G.T.
Watkins L.
Watkins R.M.
Watson C.J.E.
Watson D.C.T.
Watson G.M.
Watson J.A.S.
Watson J.S.
Watson R.J.
Watt-Smith S.R.
Way B.G.
Webb P.J.
Webber M.
Webster D.J.T.
Webster K.
Wedgwood K.R.
Weeden D.
Weekes A.R.L.
Wegstapel H.
Weir C.
Weir P.E.
Welbourn R.
Welch M.
Welch N.T.
Wells A.D.
Wells F.C.
Wellwood J.M.
Wemyss-Holden G.
Wenger R.J.J.
Wenham P.W.
West C.G.H.
Wetherall A.P.
Wetherell R.G.
Wetherill M.H.
Wheatley K.E.
Whelan P.
Whiston R.
White A.E
White B.D.
White C.M.
White J.W.
Whitehead S.M.
Whiteley G.S.W.
Whyman M.R.
Wickham M.H.
Wickstead M.
Widdison A.L.
Wilkes R.
Wilkins D.C.
Wilkins J.L.
Wilkinson A.R.
Wilkinson D.
Wilkinson G.A.L.
Wilkinson J.M.

Wilkinson M.
Wilkinson M.J.S.
Willett K.
Williams B.T.
Williams D.H.
Williams G.
Williams G.T.
Williams H.R.
Williams I.M.
Williams J.
Williams J.G.
Williams J.R.
Williams J.T.
Williams M.A.
Williams M.R.
Williams N.
Williams P.
Williams R.J.
Williams R.J.
Williams T.G.
Williams W.
Williamson K.
Williamson R.C.N.
Willis R.G.
Wills M.I.
Willson P.D.
Wilson A.J.
Wilson B.G.
Wilson D.I.
Wilson M.
Wilson N.M.
Wilson P.
Wilson R.G.
Wilson R.Y.
Wilson Y.G.
Wilson-McDonald J.
Windle R.
Winstanley J.H.R.
Wise D.I.
Wise K.S.H.
Wise M.
Wishart G.C.
Withanage A.S.
Witherow R.O.N.
Wolfe J.H.N.
Wolverson R.L.
Womack N.
Wong K.
Wong W.
Wood A.
Wood P.L.
Wood R.F.M.
Woodburn K.R.W.
Woodnut D.J.
Woods D.
Woods W.
Woodyer A.B.

Woolf V.
Woon W.H.
Wright P.D.
Wright T.
Wroblewski B.M.
Wyatt M.G.
Wyman A.
Yardley M.P.J.
Youhana A.Y.
Young A.E.
Young C.P.
Young K.
Young R.A.L.
Young S.K.
Zadeh H.G.
Zafiropoulos G.
Zahir A.G.
Zahn H.
Zaidi A.
Zaman S.A.
Zeiderman M.

.

APPENDIX I

EXCLUSIONS

OPCS Code	Description
A52	Therapeutic lumbar epidural injection
A53	Drainage of spinal canal
A54	Therepeutic spinal puncture
A55	Diagnostic spinal puncture
A70	Neurostimulation of peripheral nerve
A76	Chemical destruction of sympathetic nerve
A77	Cryotherapy to sympathetic nerve
A78	Radiofrequency controlled thermal destruction of sympathetic nerve
A79	Other destruction of sympathetic nerve
A83	Electroconvulsive therapy
A84	Neurophysiological operations
B37	Other operations on breast
C39.5	Radiotherapy to lesion of conjuctiva
C45.5	Radiotherapy to lesion of cornea
C82.3	Radiotherapy to lesion of retina
F14	Orthodontic operations
G21	Other operations on oesophagus
G47	Intubation of stomach
G57	Other operations on duodenum
G67	Other operations on jejunum
G82	Other operations on ileum
H30	Other operations on colon
H46	Other operations on rectum

OPCS Code	Description
K51	Diagnostic transluminal operations on coronary artery
K55	Other open operations on heart
K57	Other therapeutic transluminal operations on heart
K58	Diagnostic transluminal operations on heart
K60	Cardiac pacemaker system introduced through vein
K61	Other cardiac pacemaker system
K63	Contrast radiology of heart
K65	Catheterisation of heart
K66	Other operations on heart
L72	Diagnositic transluminal operations on other artery
L95	Diagnostic transluminal operations on vein
M47	Urethral catheterisation of bladder
N34	Other operations on male genital tract
P06.4	Extirpation of lesion of vulva - Implantation of radioactive substance into vulva
P20.5	Extirpation of lesion of vulva - Implantation of radioactive substance into vagina
Q12	Intrauterine contraception device
Q13	Introduction of gemete into uterine cavity
Q14	Introduction of abortifacient into uterine cavity
Q15	Introduction of other substance into uterine cavity
Q55	Other examination of female genital tract
Q56	Other operations on female genital tract
R01	Therapeutic endoscopic operations on fetus
R02	Diagnostic endoscopic examination of fetus
R03	Selective destruction of fetus
R04	Therapeutic percutaneous operations on fetus
R05	Diagnostic percutaneous examination of fetus
R10	Other operations on amniotic cavity
R12	Operations on gravid uterus.
R14	Surgical induction of labour
R15	Other induction of labour
R17	Elective caesarean delivery
R18	Other caesarean delivery
R19	Breech extraction delivery
R20	Other breech delivery
R21	Forceps cephalic delivery
R22	Vacuum delivery
R23	Cephalic vaginal delivery with abnormal presentation of head at delivery without instrument
R24	Normal delivery
R25	Other methods of delivery
R27	Other operations to facilitate delivery
R28	Instrumental removal of products of conception from delivered uterus
R29	Manual removal of products of conceptions from delivered uterus
R30	Other operations on delivered uterus
R32	Immediate repair of obstetric laceration

OPCS Code	Description
R34	Other obstetric operations
T48	Other operations on peritoneum
T90	Contrast radiology of lymphatic tissue
V48	Denervation of spinal facet joint of vertebra
X17	Separation of conjoined twins
X29	Continuous infusion of therapeutic substance
X30	Injection of therapeutic substance
X31	Injection of radiocontrast material
X32	Exchange blood transfusion
X33	Other blood transfusion
X34	Other intravenous transfusion
X35	Other intravenous injection
X36	Blood withdrawal
X37	Intramuscular injection
X38	Subcutaneous injection
X40	Compensation for renal failure
X41	Placement of ambulatory apparatus for compensation for renal failure
X42	Placement of other apparatus for compensation for renal failure
X45	Donation of organ
X46	Donation of other tissue
X48	Immobilisation using plaster cast
X49	Other immobilisation
X50	External resuscitation
X51	Change of body temperature
X59.9	Unspecified anaesthetic without surgery
Y09	Chemical destruction of organ noc
Y12	Chemical destruction of lesion of organ noc
Y21	Cytology of organ noc
Y33	Puncture of organ noc
Y35	Introduction of removable radioactive material into organ noc
Y36	Introduction of non removable radioactive material into organ noc
Y38	Injection of therapeutic inclusion substance into organ noc
Y39	Injection of other substance into organ noc
Y53	Percutaneous approach to organ under image control
Y90	Other non-operations

APPENDICES

APPENDIX J

CASE STUDIES BY SPECIALTY

APPENDICES

Otorhinolaryngology

Urology

Vascular

APPENDICES